THINK LOGICALLY, LIVE INTUITIVELY

THINK LOGICALLY, LIVE INTUITIVELY

SEEKING THE BALANCE

J. R. MADAUS

HAMPTON ROADS
PUBLISHING COMPANY, INC.

Hampton Roads Publishing Company, Inc.
1125 Stoney Ridge Road
Charlottesville, VA 22902
434-296-2772
fax: 434-296-5096
e-mail: hrpc@hrpub.com
www.hrpub.com

If you are unable to order this book from your local
bookseller, you may order directly from the publisher.
Call 1-800-766-8009, toll-free.

Library of Congress Cataloging-in-Publication Data

Madaus, J. R., 1944-
 Think logically, live intuitively : seeking the balance / J.R. Madaus.
     p. cm.
 Summary: "A memoir of one man's quest to understand the science of
extraordinary phenomena such as out-of-body experiences and
spontaneous healings"--Provided by publisher.
 Includes bibliographical references.
 ISBN 1-57174-426-6 (5-1/2x8-1/2 tp : alk. paper)
 1. Parapsychology. 2. Consciousness. 3. Madaus, J. R., 1944- I.
Title.
 BF1031.M3425 2005
 130--dc22

                                        2005012350

ISBN 1-57174-426-6
10 9 8 7 6 5 4 3 2 1
Printed on acid-free paper in Canada

This book is dedicated to Robert A. Monroe, who went looking for the secrets of the universe, only to realize that we simply have to *allow* ourselves to find them. A portion of the proceeds of the sale of this book goes to his legacy, The Monroe Institute (TMI), for education and research purposes.

And to my wife, best friend, and soul mate, Miss Pamela, for her support and belief in me. True love is beyond the capacity of the human mind to comprehend.

Challenges

To realize that all we know about how the world works might
be false is unthinkable.

When confronted with the unthinkable, we cling to the comfortable and the known and we feel safe.

To jump off a cliff in the darkness of night is madness. Yet
any new breakthrough in understanding is just such a leap.

Balance is that delicate point between safety and madness
from which new realities can be forged.

Seeking such a balance is what this book is all about.

—J. R. Madaus, January 29, 2000, from *Meditation*

The greatest illusion is that man has limitations.

—Robert A. Monroe

Many times,
Many places,
To any who would listen

Contents

Preface xiii

Introduction xv

**Part I. How Can We Get Up to Speed When
We Are Going Too Fast Already?**

1. The "Hurrieder" We Go, the "Behinder" We Get 3

Interlude One: Visionary Insight in the Information Age 6

**Part II. Expanding the Bandwidth of Perception: Beginning to See
What's Not Really There**

2. The Monroe Institute Gateway:
   Activating Expanded Consciousness .11

3. A Step toward Nonphysical Experiences:
   Suspending Disbelief 19

4. An Out-of-Body Experience:
   The Nonphysical Becomes Real 31

5. Pushing the Limits of Belief:
   Testing Our Version of Reality 40

6. Touching Infinity: A Return to Wholeness 46

Interlude Two: Expanding Perspective 53

**Part III. Perception as Reality:
Beginning to Change the Rules**

7. Right Brain, Left Brain, and Whole Brain:
   Perspective and Opportunity 57

8. Accepting What You Only Think You Can See:
Turning the Kaleidoscope 77
9. Keeping Your Head Screwed on Straight
While Expanding Your Awareness 84
10. Can Science Help Us? (or, Don't Confuse Me with the Facts,
I Know What I Want to Believe) 94
11. Moving Past the Limitations of Our Five Senses:
Embracing the Unseen 105
Interlude Three: Changing Perceptions of Reality 111

**Part IV. In the Gap: Exploring the Spaces
between the Physical and the Nonphysical**
12. Other Realms: Fantasizing or
Describing the Indescribable? 115
13. Inner Guidance: Advice from
a Greater Self or Self-Delusion? 134
14. Subtle Energy: The Nonphysical Becomes Physical 149
15. Conscious Beliefs versus Subconscious Realities:
The Complexity of the Perceived World around Us 170
16. Egos Running Amok (or, My Way Is the Only Way) 181
**Interlude Four: Body, Mind, Spirit: The Interplay of
the Physical, the Mental, and the Nonlocal** ...193

**Part V. Embracing the World of Vibration:
The Many Levels of Awareness and Healing**
17. The Miraculous Becomes the Mundane:
The Experience of Healing Touch 199
18. The Interconnected Matrix: Realizing That
What You Think and Feel Affects Others 217
19. Medicine: A Battleground for
Science and the Miraculous 225
20. Influential Consciousness: The Space
between Thought and Physical Matter 235
21. Human Bioenergy: The Dance of the Human
Cell and Vast Unseen Forces 244
22. Viewing Death as Merely a Short-Term Situation:
Taking Consciousness beyond the Physical 254

**Interlude Five: Collaborative Integration of the Physical,
the Nonphysical, and the Spaces in Between** . .266

**Part VI. Interactive Perception: How Can We Keep
Score When We Are All on the Same Team?**
23. Finding What You Are Looking for or Looking
for What You Find? The Formation of Experience 271
24. Oh, Sure, It's All Connected, but to What?
Embracing Multidimensional Possibilities 276
25. Assuming Your True Identity: Becoming
Responsible versus Being in Control 289
26. Transforming Human "Do-ings" into
Human "Be-ings": A Direction for the Future 293
Endnotes 297
Recommended Reading and Other Resources 303
Acknowledgments 307
About the Author 309

Preface

We sat together in her apartment. Caroline, my 26-year-old niece, had treated me to a fine dinner at her favorite restaurant, and for the past four hours, our conversation had focused on my recent extraordinary experiences. I rarely shared the true nature of these events with anyone, but she had asked and I trusted her enough to confide in her. She listened as I told her about how my adventures in expanded states of consciousness challenged my basic belief systems. She did not scoff as I related fantastic events involving psychic phenomena, or psi. She quietly held my hand as I shared my innermost experiences of the profound. She believed me. She not only accepted what had happened to me, she wanted to know more.

"But what advantage is all of this to me?" Caroline asked, her eyes indicating that she really did want an answer. Like many successful young people, when she asks a question, she not only wants an answer, but it had also better be a good one.

I paused in reflection, and a swirl of memories of the previous four years flooded my consciousness. In such a short period of time, I had met so many interesting people from all walks of life including physicians, lawyers, scientific researchers, and business executives. They were all normal in appearance, successful, and well respected in their fields. Yet for fear of ridicule they had steadfastly refused to openly discuss their profound "special" experiences.

"I mean, if I tried any of this stuff you are talking about, how would it be of any benefit to me?" She had permitted me to reflect before responding, but she would not let go of the question. What she didn't realize was that she was probing much deeper issues than she could imagine.

The deepest questions are those we may not even admit to ourselves, much less others. Indeed, we may hide them so well that we don't think about them at all. It's much easier that way. What keeps us from pursuing the most profound insights? Perhaps it is the unspeakable fear that we might find some new truth that shakes our beliefs to their very cores.

Our conversation that night helped me understand that this book had to be written.

Introduction

This book is for the seeker, and I believe we are all seeking in some form or another. Seekers face the uncertainty of the unknown, and the world of our innermost self is an area that is more unknown than many of us are willing to admit. Looking inward knocks on a doorway not just to our selves, but also to broader views of human consciousness.

On one side of the door of consciousness are our logical mind and our normal approach to life. On the other side of the door lie our intuition and dreams. Opening the door to both logic and intuition in states of expanded consciousness can introduce you to your Total Self, a much larger version of you than you ever imagined. Seeking a balance between logic and intuition can be confusing as our head directs us one way and our dreams take us another.

My adventure involves ordinary people having extraordinary experiences. It turns out, however, that extraordinary experiences and expanded consciousness are common to us all in everyday life. We just don't take the time to notice them. It is to be hoped that reading this book will encourage you to begin taking notice.

I think of myself as an ordinary person, who goes to work every day, has too much credit card debt, doesn't exercise enough, watches too much TV, and wonders if I am doing what I "should" be doing with my life. I have been blissfully married to my soul mate and best friend, Pamela, for more than 30 years. I would characterize myself as neither excitable nor lacking in objectivity.

Prior to my efforts to seek more information about consciousness, my formal education gave me the credentials to be a high school teacher in history and mathematics. I combined the technology of instruction with the library world, however, earning, after military service in Vietnam, first a master's degree in library and information science from the University of Texas at Austin in 1970, and then a doctorate. You may observe my librarian background in this book as I strongly encourage you to explore the work of other authors who can expand particular aspects of an area that I only briefly introduce.

Over time, I moved into the emerging field of large-scale online information systems, and I continue in that challenging work today. As a librarian, I have always been a seeker of information both for myself and in helping others find what they need. In my work with large-scale computers, I am constantly seeking answers to issues brought on by the interaction of human consciousness and "machine consciousness." With the writing of this book, seeking information about and a greater understanding of consciousness become my life's work as well.

Logic and intuition are commonly associated with our left and right brains, respectively. Seeking balance requires you to find and learn to use both together. In this book, I will ask you to question yourself in this area, and the first experience comes right now. Turn to chapter 19, read it, and then return to this point. Do you find that suggestion challenging? Under normal circumstances, I certainly would. But humor me, and go ahead and do it anyway. Yes, I mean it. Do not turn the page until you have read chapter 19 and return here. . . .

Welcome back. How did that feel? If you didn't do it, how do you feel as you read this sentence and realize that I *really* did want you to do that? If the thought, or experience, of reading out of sequence causes a twinge of resistance, then you, like me, are skeptical and analytical in nature. You operate primarily out of your left-brain logical self.

On the other hand, those of you who *like* the idea of going out of sequence have probably already read elsewhere in this book before reading the introduction. This may even be the last section you are reading. You are the creative right-brained folks and you have problems with order and structure because they impede your learning and thought processes.

I think we approach life from these two viewpoints in the same manner we approach reading. Neither is right or wrong, but they are different. Each works for the person who likes to read (or live) that way. Further, whichever method works for you, the other will seem challenging and unfamiliar because it is an unknown experience for you. You didn't make a conscious decision to read (or live) from a right- or left-brained approach; it's just the way things are.

Understanding my eventual answer to Caroline's question (see preface) calls for stepping through a doorway that opens to simultaneous use of the logical and intuitive approach. This book follows my personal adventure as I stepped through a doorway of expanded consciousness and found challenges to my basic beliefs in direct personal experience of psi (psychic phenomena such as clairvoyance, out-of-body experiences, precognition, and extrasensory perception [ESP]). The doorway of consciousness also enters a realm being explored by quantum physicists as they find their laboratory research mirroring the world of the mystical. It is a doorway through which you find that esoteric traditions of the past now coincide with frontier scientific inquiry.

As you read, you will find several interlude sections, breaks in the action. Interludes can be viewed as taking time out to rest, or to talk or think about what's going on. Every once in a while, I have felt the need to step outside my style of sequential writing to make a few comments.

What can you believe when all the facts are in, all proven true, and all contradict each other?

—J. R. M.

Part I

How Can We Get Up to Speed
When We Are Going Too Fast Already?

In all affairs, it's a healthy thing now and then to hang a question mark on the things you have long taken for granted.
—Bertrand Russell

1

The "Hurrieder" We Go, the "Behinder" We Get

Caroline and I talked long into the night on the evening this book was born (see preface). Our conversation took several paths. I listened patiently as she expressed her frustration facing an ever-busier lifestyle that she feels increasingly helpless to influence. She is very successful in business, but at a great price. There is not enough time for the things she believes should be important. As Caroline says, "I am so busy all the time, but it doesn't seem that I ever get anything done." She is coming to realize that we live in a culture where the pace of our lives is moving beyond our control.

She listened attentively as I shared my experiences and explained how I had learned that expanded states of consciousness and psi offer tools that can help in dealing with the complications of modern living. I told her how my day had looked just like hers only a short time before. I shared my belief that losing control of our daily activity is more than a time management issue; it is a direct challenge to our freedom to choose our life direction. And life paths are something that should come from deep within us, not be dictated by society.

I told her I had learned that it is no longer good enough to do things right. It is now more important to pick which are the right things to try to do. She needed to understand that when one is faced with nothing but "must-do" items, priority-setting loses clarity as one faces the question of which two of the top ten priorities can be tackled today, or more realistically, in the next hour.

She wanted to know how we can be sure we are right as we make such decisions. In her world, decision-making processes are being squeezed and compacted into unrealistic time frames. Technology and the increasing speed of change are causing the "shelf life" of a decision to be much shorter. In Caroline's world, "long-term" planning may now be viewed as encompassing weeks to a number of months instead of years.

We talked about living in a world where even the speed of the speed of change is speeding up. Today, if a response to an e-mail request for a decision is not made in a matter of minutes, then the decision-maker is considered an obstructionist. Woe be unto those who dare not enter the "connectedness" of mobile e-mail or cell phones and thus are cut off from the business of decision-making and the constant flow of information.

As I thought about these issues later, I realized that there is a great deal of unnecessary anger all around us. It is an obvious by-product of this compaction of time and the mounting pressure to complete an ever-increasing list of tasks that there is seemingly insufficient time to do. Anger, in general, is on the rise in society as we look at the short fuse of many who feel "put upon" to stand in line, wait their turn at the traffic light, or simply be bound by roadway speed limits.

While this may not be the lifestyle of every person now, if current trends continue, it cannot be too far distant. A quick peek at the Internet-capable cell phones carried by teenagers in a shopping mall illustrates that being "connected" has moved far beyond the on-call status of essential workplace personnel of only a short time ago. Even grade school children are intensely focused on their electronic "daily planners" as they are already ensnared by our time-pressured culture.

Facing the issues of a fast-paced world is further complicated by our need to find the right information to make our daily decisions. We are clearly living in an age of information inundation. Facts, figures, and data fuel everything going on around us. From piles of unread books by our bedsides to ever-expanding Internet resources, the predicted "information explosion" may now have even given way to information overload. There is so much information available, yet many times we have difficulty finding just the facts we need. I told Caroline that I believe we are drowning in a sea of data and simultaneously parched for a drink of knowledge, not to mention thirst-quenching wisdom.

If one is lucky enough to find the information one needs, how does one process it and turn it into new ideas? Where are the true sources of inspiration and insight that provide new or breakthrough information and knowledge? And how can we incorporate inspired insight into the fast-paced decisions needed today? Finding the right pieces of information to address difficult questions is also an advantage that Caroline and all of us seek.

Yes, Caroline's world was my world only a short time ago. But that has changed now.

Time is not the rigid equally measured ticks of a second hand.
Time is a perception of the participants in an event.

—J. R. M.

Interlude One

Visionary Insight in the Information Age

Solutions are difficult. I believe that it is solutions that my niece Caroline is seeking when she asks the question "Of what benefit . . . ?"

In this age of technology, searching for coping mechanisms within our time-pressed and stressful lives is the overarching question for many people. Another way of exploring these issues is to ask: What good is all our information and technology with no direction? What about the knowledge and wisdom needed to effectively use abundant information and technology wisely? With all the benefits of modern life, we still seem to be very weak in our basic understanding of why we are here and what direction we should be taking with our lives.

Finding inner direction is the real knowledge I think we are all seeking. Wisdom about our ultimate place in the universe is our real goal of life and the one that counts. Without a perspective on who we are and where we are going, we have little clue as to what information we should be paying attention to. Yet how can we consider something as esoteric as inner wisdom or ultimate life paths amidst the e-mail, cell phone calls, pressing deadlines, and unrealistic expectations of our daily lives?

I mentioned in the introduction that we are all seekers in some form. The limitations of traditional paths do not bind the seeker. This is both fortunate and unfortunate. It is fortunate as new trails are blazed and new worlds explored. It is unfortunate because, on the return trip home, the seeker is faced with a credibility problem. The seeker returns with new knowledge that challenges current concepts of what is true. Natives in tribal cultures who have visited "civilization" are often considered deranged on their return home. Since their families and friends back home have not shared these new experiences firsthand, a balance of traditional constructs of reality and totally new experiences can be difficult to achieve. Just as "seeking" can mean a lot of things to a lot of people, "seeking balance" amidst massive new information can also be very challenging to an individual or a culture.

Caroline's question of "How would expanded consciousness benefit me?" is not easily answered. This book is the result of my efforts to provide an answer. Intertwined with seeking solutions to common problems in our daily lives are much deeper questions. Mystical questions like "Why are we here?" and "How does the universe work?" do not seem like pragmatic avenues of inquiry for solving problems of overscheduled time and too much information. The world of the mystical, however, may contain the very secrets we need to conquer our complex societal problems.

Because of the fear of ridicule, people may be afraid to share the benefits of their journeys into the world of the mystical and unseen. If you are one who is afraid to share your experiences in these areas, you have my sympathy and support. Please understand that you are not alone. Millions have had similar experiences, but because so many are afraid to share them we are unaware of how widespread these phenomena are.

Beginning in the next chapter, I will share with you the experiences I shared with Caroline. Some of this is emotionally and intellectually challenging for me to convey. Every event is true, but I do not share my experiences for the sake of notoriety. Indeed, I struggle mightily to admit some of these occurrences publicly. But I now realize the need to share such activity. I have met many people over the past few years that have been severely ridiculed for sharing similar experiences. Facing the extraordinary impacts you greatly, but not being able to communicate a resulting major insight is extremely frustrating.

In our journey together in this book, we will encounter both personal experience and scientific fact that challenge consensus belief systems. The journey begins with some extraordinary personal experiences in the next few chapters and continues through exploration of related scientific implications in later chapters. The second section of this book is very different from the previous one. The one after that is different from the first two. This is a path with many twists and turns. It is like the collection of different stones that can serve as stepping points to get you across a river. Each adds to a process of eventually arriving at the desired goal.

I hope that traveling the path of this book will not only offer you new approaches for addressing the issues of daily life presented in the last chapter, but will also enable you to realize the existence of greater realms of your consciousness.

Part II

Expanding the Bandwidth of Perception: Beginning to See What's Not Really There

Men stumble over the truth from time to time, but most pick themselves up and hurry off as if nothing happened.
—Winston Churchill

But seek ye first the kingdom of God.
—Matthew 6:33

The kingdom of God is within you.
—Luke 17:20

2

The Monroe Institute Gateway:
Activating Expanded Consciousness

The Monroe Institute, or TMI, is a nonprofit, membership-based, research and education organization nestled in the foothills of the Virginia Blue Ridge Mountains, a 45-minute drive from the Charlottesville regional airport. The main area of the institute is a three-building complex located in a picturesque landscape. TMI performs laboratory research into the physiology and experience of expanded human consciousness, offers "psycho-acoustic" audiocassette products based on more than 30 years of ongoing research and program development, and offers on-site, weeklong residential programs that provide opportunities for participants to easily experience altered states of consciousness.

My initial contact with altered states came through reading books by TMI founder Robert A. Monroe. Bob was an intriguing person who has been overlooked by modern popular culture. He was a Fortune 500 executive, *Who's Who* entry, radio game show producer, and amateur mind scientist whose forays into altered states have become legendary in the field of consciousness research. His biography, *Catapult,* by Bayard Stockton, chronicles Bob's youth, creative and business successes, and consciousness research and program development from Esalen Institute to the fully developed TMI programs of today. Bob's first book, *Journeys Out of the Body,* is a classic on college psychology class reading lists. His lesser known *Far Journeys* offers a novelized perspective drawn from his interpretation of his own out-of-body sojourns; and his pinnacle work, *Ultimate Journey,* charts areas commonly referred to as beyond the limits of our physical world.

Reading *Ultimate Journey* in late 1994 led me to spend a week at Bob Monroe's legacy, The Monroe Institute. I attended the introductory Gateway Voyage program at TMI in April 1995, and the impact of that week continues to this day. Not everyone had the same experience as I. Some had less dramatic experiences, some more. TMI provides people with tools to explore the expansion of consciousness. What you do with those tools is entirely up to you. One attractive element of the TMI experience is that there is no structured belief system to which they are trying to convert people. Yet everyone I have ever met who has attended one of the TMI programs comments that their beliefs have changed as a result of the TMI experience. The following is a description of my experience at that first workshop.

The workshop begins with an introductory session at 7:30 P.M. on a Saturday evening. The group of 24 participants and two trainers settles in for the process of getting acquainted. I am surprised by the composition of the group. It includes a corporate attorney, a surgeon from the Mayo Clinic, a retired nurse from the Netherlands, a practicing midwife, a computer systems engineer, the chief operating officer of a bank, an international executive from Switzerland, a successful psychotherapist, a newly ordained minister, an unemployed aerobics instructor, a publishing house employee, a retired medical lab tech, an unemployed forklift mechanic, a freelance cameraman who had just finished a program for the BBC, a retired federal executive born in Nigeria, a violin maker, a professional photographer recently returned from eight years in the Amazon, a rare book dealer, a psychology student, a recent Peace Corps worker, a medical student in his last residency rotation, a retired accountant, an executive in the Transcendental Meditation organization, and (me) a librarian turned computer nerd. I am taken with the range of occupations, ages (25–74), and international aspects of this group.

These are, for the most part, successful, professional, and hardworking folks. They have all been attracted to TMI by Bob Monroe's unbiased "let's try to figure out what's going on here" attitude of exploration. None admit to having had a previous out-of-body experience (OBE), and most are not sure why they have come, but just "know" that they need to after reading Bob's books. All are deeply saddened and disappointed by his recent passing (three weeks before), but are still very interested in what TMI has to offer yet not certain at this point what that is.

Several comment that, strangely, they already feel more comfortable speaking openly about certain topics since arriving at TMI. Casual conversations have opened new comfort levels to talk with like-minded people about interests and deep personal experiences that were difficult to talk about back home. As a librarian, I note that a significant number comment on having read Bob Monroe's books, those of Deepak Chopra, Edgar Cayce, Carlos Castaneda, and/or Jane Roberts's "Seth" material, whereas others have never heard of these authors. There is a common theme of fear that revealing reading interests or unexplainable experiences will result in being branded as weird or "too far out" in their home or workplace. Many worry that being open about their experiences will bring challenges to the role they play in society. It disturbs me that human communication is so circumscribed by the perceived limitations of a consensus culture.

Though our two workshop leaders are called trainers, they are more like facilitators. Charleene is a practicing psychologist and John is involved in the design of submarines. They explain that this week there will be no televisions, radios, or newspapers, and only one pay phone. Our meals will be prepared for us and our sheets and towels will be taken care of by TMI staff. Our job is to relax and have our individual experiences within the supportive setting of the group. They make a concerted effort to describe the importance of what TMI has defined as "safe space" for the week.

"You must all understand," Charleene says, "that we can each bring our own set of beliefs to this week. Everyone is entitled to whatever they may believe in, or not believe in, and no one is allowed to infringe on what anyone else might believe." She notes that people might have a variety of experiences during this week, and we must all allow each other to have whatever experience unfolds, whether it fits into our own belief system or not. No one will be told that something is "wrong" during this week. We will allow each other the "safe space" for whatever we experienced individually. Group support will be here if needed, but this week is to be about our own explorations into the realms of our own consciousness.

This is to my liking as it reinforces my own style of wanting to find out for myself rather than be directed as to what my experience "should" be.

John and Charleene note that as Bob Monroe began to undergo his out-of-body experiences, he found little reliable information. Most scientific or medical material treated the phenomenon as delusion or fantasy. He also became concerned that the only material in which he could find references to what was happening to him was circumscribed within esoteric or Eastern religions or the occult. This did not fit well with his Western mind, technological approach, or no-nonsense businessman working style.

The things he was experiencing were real to him (and later tested as such in the laboratory) and he did not relish being limited by someone else's religious/cultural beliefs or nomenclature. Not that he felt that others' beliefs were bad in any way, but he wanted to understand what was happening to him independent of any culture or religion.

To talk about his experiences in a standardized way, Monroe created a benign framework within which to operate. Bob developed a descriptive series of "Focus Levels" to denote the plateaus of various experiences within his explorations, assigning each one a number: C-1 (Consciousness-One), then Focus 3, 10, 12, 15, 21, and 27. There were also, as later discovered in the TMI laboratory, relationships of the brain wave patterns within these Focus Levels and the standard physiological stages of sleep.

C-1, or Consciousness-One, is the here and now we call physical reality, the world that we normally consider real. The levels then move up through Focus 3, which is a relaxed state that could be compared to the medically defined "relaxation response" used in stress reduction or calming exercises.

At Focus 10, one enters the first altered state of consciousness, as the mind remains fully alert and awake while the body appears to fall comfortably asleep. This is an altered state, as when the body normally goes to sleep and the mind loses consciousness. "Mind awake, body asleep" is also the state of the practitioner in meditation activities. In this initial altered state, the intuitive mind can provide significant access to the creative spark, and insights of many kinds can occur. It appears that the lines between the physical and the non-physical start to blur a little in this state.

Focus 12 is a state of "expanded consciousness" and the physiological equivalent of REM (rapid eye movement) sleep, yet the mind is still fully alert, awake, and in control, thus at another level of altered state of consciousness. The out-of-body experience, or OBE, can begin to occur in Focus 10 but is more common in this Focus 12 state. (This, of course, perks up a few ears in the audience.) Focus 12 could also be considered a very deep meditative state and is also regularly achieved by advanced meditators, but usually takes some years of practice to accomplish easily. It is also noted that both Focus 10 and 12 states are achievable via drugs and alcohol, but the mind is definitely not totally alert, awake, and in control in these instances; hence any information retrieved might be considered suspect.

As John and Charleene speak, my mind wanders down a path that attempts to bring what they are saying in line with what I know about states of consciousness. The altered states that TMI is calling Focus 10 and 12 are considered by some to be dissociative states. Historically, unsought dissociative states are considered by psychologists to be pathological and are treated with drugs. I begin to wonder if a controlled dissociative state is intuitive in nature and is desirable rather than pathological. I remind myself that many cultures and traditions seek intuition, insight, or guidance by moving into a ritualistic dissociative altered state of consciousness.

Charleene says, "Leaving Focus 12 we can enter Focus 15, and in Focus 15 the concept of time disappears."

I listen intently as the discussion reveals that information accessed in this state is normally available only to one in a coma, in the deepest of meditative states, or in a trance state. Focus 15 sounds very interesting to me, and I wonder if we will actually be able to achieve such a state in less than a week's time.

The discussion moves to Focus 21, physiologically stage IV sleep, or a very deep trance state. In this state, deep inner guidance or an experience like the near-death experience normally occurs. Focus 21 is outlined as the furthest edge of any sort of time-space relationship with the world of physics or the Earth plane as we understand it. This level, too, can be achieved, according to the trainers, with the mind fully awake, alert, aware, and in control. While Focus 10 and 12 could be viewed as dissociative, Focus 15 and 21 could be considered transcendental states. Moving within transcendental states puts one into realms of deep self-exploration, and opens one to exploration of one's spiritual perspective as well.

The idea that such states could be portals to information or pathways to self-exploration makes me desire the lecture to end and us to get on with the program. A mysterious Focus 27 level is also mentioned, an area of graduate studies we will learn about later in the week.

The idea that we might gain the capacity to achieve some of these states by the end of the week is exciting. The experience is to be our own, however, not one already experienced by anyone else—in other words, there are no guarantees you'll have Bob Monroe's experiences, but only your own, whatever they turn out to be. We are cautioned that the best approach for the week is to have no expectations of outcome so as to place no self-imposed limitations on what might happen. This is not to be a week of trying to do something; it is more about allowing some things to occur. The TMI Gateway Voyage program gives us tools to begin to explore altered states of consciousness and possibly experience that we are more than our physical bodies.

Gateway grew out of a program that Monroe had originally been asked to put together for the Esalen Institute in California in 1973. The early days of his research involved the use of sound in the achievement of altered states of consciousness. Gateway changed and grew, but the core of the weeklong program has been in place for years, with only minor changes made in a continuing refinement process. The sound technology, Hemi-Sync, is patented and has become the mainstay of TMI products and research efforts.

Hemi-Sync is the psychoacoustic audio process that made TMI famous in consciousness exploration. An audio tone is sent through one channel of a stereo earphone. A different frequency tone is sent through the other channel. One then hears a pulsing waver in the tone. That waver of sound, however, does not exist on the tape or in the earphones. Your brain internally creates it as the mind puts the two different tones together. The waver of tones is called a "binaural beat," and TMI has performed extensive scientific research on the effects of binaural beat audio technologies.

A person in a relaxed and open state of mind may experience a process that aligns brain wave activity to match the frequency of the waver of the binaural beat. This process is called entrainment. In essence, the brain wave patterns entrain to the binaural beats and the audio products prepared by TMI concentrate on binaural beat frequencies and brain wave signature patterns that assist in the relaxation process and also provide a framework for altered states of consciousness to occur.

A significant by-product of this process is that the right and left hemispheres of the brain synchronize in their brain wave output (hence the name Hemi-Sync); TMI research staff have extensively explored this phenomenon. Other researchers have noted that hemispheric synchronization is a common aspect to altered states of consciousness.

The Focus Levels are considered descriptive tools, and you are free to discard them if you desire. In addition to telling us this, before we leave the orientation, John and Charleene suggest one additional "rule" for the week. Consider two important credos from Bob Monroe's own personal belief system: "You are more than your physical body" and "The only limitations to human potential are belief systems."

3

A Step toward Nonphysical Experiences:
Suspending Disbelief

Our initial session is in the basement of David Francis Hall, the
large meeting and office building of TMI's complex. At the close of
the presentations, we are treated to a wall-sized video projection of
Bob Monroe in which he gives a personal introduction to TMI, perspectives drawn from his experiences, and his views on the nature of
"exploring." From the professional nature of the screen, sound system, and video production, it is clear that Bob came from a successful career in radio and TV. It is also obvious that things had been set
up to continue when he was no longer able to do these presentations
himself.

Bob met with the people in as many residential programs as he
could over the years. How fortunate, I think to myself. Bob is gone,
but his personal introduction to The Monroe Institute experience
can still be shared with every participant for years to come. The
video continued with Bob discussing the need to "suspend disbelief"
and "allow" rather than "try," and emphasizing his perennial credo
of realizing that "you are more than your physical body."

John, the trainer, raises the room lights as the video screen fades.

He comments on how Bob would say at this point that it was up to the participants to go "out there" and come back and "tell me what you find." Invariably, someone would always ask what they should expect to find or what a particular Focus Level was like. There is an obvious anticipation in the room for the response. "Bob would always grin and say, 'I don't know; why don't you go and find out and come back and tell me?'"

It is clear that we are the explorers now. We are instructed to take a short break and reassemble next door at the Nancy Penn Center to meet in the group room in about 15 minutes. We will be introduced to our first tape experience at TMI.

The opening session is over, and we are soon traversing the brick path back to the Nancy Penn Center. The April night air is crisp and the stars appear surreal in this isolated rural area. Most of us are city dwellers, and we find ourselves in reverent silence outside under the sky.

As we gather to receive our initial briefing, Charleene provides us with an overview of the standard format that will be common to all our tape experiences at TMI. Each tape begins with the sound of ocean surf to assist in relaxing. Then, as we continue our relaxation process, we will be guided to place our "baggage" that might interfere with the exercise into an imagined "energy conversion box." The idea is that we are separating from the here and now and beginning to convert our focus to an inner direction.

Then we will "build" a bit of "energy" by doing a round of "resonant tuning," by making a sound similar to the *OM* or *AUM* tones made in many yoga, chi, or other subtle energy exercises. There is then a suggested short affirmation that states our intent to become aware of being "more than our physical body" before we move into the exercise proper. Each guided tape exercise is 30 to 40 minutes in length. After the exercise, we will reassemble in the group room for follow-up discussion and an instructional setup of the next exercise or activity. Our first tape will be a familiarization session, as we need to practice the process. We will not attempt any actual Focus Level work until the next morning.

Instructions completed, we are sent to our rooms by way of the restrooms to ensure a 30-minute tape experience without interruption. This process is to become a hallmark reminder as we enter each exercise. Small lines form near each shared restroom to avoid any distractions from an unwanted "in-the-body" experience.

Each sleeping room contains two desks, two chairs, and two Controlled Holistic Environment Chambers, or CHEC units. This unit serves as our tape-taking location, our bed, and general nest for the week. Entering my assigned CHEC, I am reminded of my bed, or rack, aboard a destroyer at sea 25 years earlier; however, even though fully enclosed, the TMI version feels much more spacious and comfortable.

The CHEC is a Bob Monroe invention and houses a twin bed–sized mattress with a floor-to-ceiling wall around it and a three-foot-square black curtain covering a large crawl-hole entryway. Near your head, one wall contains a convenient panel of knobs and switches to control lighting, speaker and earphone volume, and a small tape recorder for spoken notes. With the curtain drawn over the entryway, you can lie in total darkness or create soft hues with the combined use of the rheostat-controlled red, blue, and gold lights. One toggle switch operates a "ready light," which activates a small red light bulb outside the unit, with a companion outside the door to the room and a third in the central "control room."

This functionally simple but elegant system offers two-way communications throughout the large three-story building. By turning on the ready light, each participant is accounted for both in general readiness to begin and for roll-taking purposes. Or, if a participant encounters technical or personal problems, a simple flashing of the light off and on will alert a trainer that assistance is needed.

Soft music is playing as I settle into my CHEC. I place the studio quality earphones on my head, turn on my ready light, and set my intent to suspend disbelief. I follow the spoken instructions. I relax a bit and begin to voice the TMI resonant tuning sound. My initial sensation is of feeling silly. Here I am, lying in the dark in a closet-sized bedroom, moaning loudly. Thoughts of "what am I doing here?" creep in; however, by the end of the taped instructions, I am becoming refreshed and relaxed. I realize that it is, indeed, an "energy building" experience.

After the tape, we are instructed, via the small speakers in the CHEC unit, to gather for a quick "debriefing" in the group room. Several people offer experiences of feeling silly at first, as I had, but with similar relaxed and refreshed results. There are a few other general comments and a few questions seeking reinforcement that common understanding of the process has been achieved. Then it is popcorn and beverages for the interested, or bed for the travel weary.

My body suggests that bed is the better option in spite of my having no idea what time it is. There are no clocks in the building and our watches were taken from us at the initial briefing session. An awareness of time is not to intrude on our experience. Watches have been declared contraband and placed in the care of the trainers for the week. There is a growing realization of how many times we look at our watches out of habit. This is a week about experience, not about where we are supposed to be or when. We are here to be taken care of, and to be as far from the cares and worries of the outside world as possible. We are to be awakened and guided the rest of the week by gentle bells or soft-spoken words over the speaker system. The trainers will give us our directions to the next event as part of each group session.

Charleene's words echo in my mind as I adjust the lights in my CHEC in preparation for sleep. "We will be taking care of you from this point on, and each event will lead to the next one. Relax and let your experience unfold." I am ready for sleep, and it comes easily.

I am not a morning person. At work, everyone knows that results are much better if I am approached after ten o'clock and considerable coffee. Shortly after laying my head on the pillow, however, the next thing I know I am wide awake and feeling rested and ready to go—a feeling that is not part of my normal awakening process. There is the sound of soft ocean surf all around me and then Bob Monroe's recorded voice comes through the speakers in the CHEC unit: "Good morning, and this is a good morning for you. This is the most important day of your life because it is now. Yesterday was then, tomorrow is when, and this day is now. You can use it and be it, however you so desire."

The traditional first full day of TMI's Gateway Voyage program is beginning.

Stepping out of my CHEC, I am surprised to see the room being illuminated by the early glow of the sun peeking through a light, misty fog. The view is a surreal picture framed by the small window in my room that overlooks the mountain road leading to the institute. I feel like jogging and decide to take action on the unusual thought. I rummage around in the closet for shorts and sneakers and saunter down the hall toward the front door.

I can't believe that I am doing this. I am actually going to jog down a mountain road at sunrise. It is a strange sensation, but also a glorious feeling. The mountain air is crisp and clean, and spectacular panoramic views unfold as the sun begins to burn off the remains of the early-morning fog. I encounter several other group members, either walking or jogging on the road, and each comments on the level of rest achieved and energy found—even after a long travel day.

On my return to the Nancy Penn Center, the aroma of fresh-brewed coffee saturates the air; the institute staff already anticipates our needs. Participants are gathering to partake. I make my way back up to the room, armed with caffeine to begin the morning rituals of shaving and bathing. Ken, my corporate attorney roommate, is mumbling about what time breakfast is served, and at about the same time we both recall that we no longer have watches. We piece together the daily schedule from our notes and the overview of the previous evening. We are to be awakened by the speakers in our CHEC units by music and voice. Then there will be sufficient time for showers, jogging, and so forth, and an optional workout session with TMI's resident trainer, Larry. And then breakfast will be served.

Larry, we had been told, is a local resident and long-time personal friend of Bob Monroe. His morning exercise routine is voluntary all the way around. He is in his seventies and can bend and stretch in ways that both punish and challenge those much younger and supposedly more agile.

Our schedule is unwritten except for our scribbled notes from the evening before, and of course, there are no times noted. The daily routine will include a morning group instructional gathering, followed by several tape sessions to explore our experience in the states of consciousness or Focus Levels. On to lunch and then an extended break, which will be free time for writing, outdoor activity, friendly discussion, or even naps. Then it will be another round of tape sessions beginning in midafternoon, followed by dinner. There will be a formal evening program in the large basement room of David Francis Hall to conclude each day's scheduled program. There will be snacks and optional "bull sessions" each evening, however, for those who are not ready for sleep.

Having put together the schedule we will be facing, Ken and I progress through the essentials of a normal morning. Then off to a pleasant cafeteria-style breakfast and getting acquainted within a newly forming group. Conversations range from discussion of how Larry could possibly move the way he does at his age to where people are from and their family and employment activity.

We hear the first signal chime. There is no question what it is as the powerful melodic tones are emitted from a permanently wall-mounted "energy chime," the kind that is sold in many New Age emporiums. We are reminded of the process of being alerted by the bell for each new session, and instructions are given to reassemble shortly in the group room of the Nancy Penn Center.

We make quick stops in our rooms for writing materials and soon we are all seated on the lush cream-carpeted floor of the group room preparing for our first sojourn toward the magical Focus Levels. We are gently reminded of the no-shoes rule as we enter and find a spot to call ours for the first session. There is a physical sensation of shared anticipation as our first day of activity is beginning. There is discussion of how uncharacteristically rested everyone feels. Several people note the soft sound of ocean surf all through the night that is available through a speaker control on the CHEC unit wall. Charleene and John respond with a short discussion of a "sleep processor," which had been running all night over the speakers in our units.

The sleep processor was one of Bob's inventions that never quite took off, to the chagrin of his entrepreneurial desire. We had been listening to one of the few remaining prototype units. The machine makes use of the years of research into the brain wave state of sleep and what it takes to get you there, which is a hallmark of the original TMI research. Monroe had been pursuing human sleep states that were sensitive to the learning process; such research naturally required exploring sleep states in general.

The sleep processor provides soothing white-noise-type tones in a repetitive 90-minute sleep cycle using embedded Hemi-Sync to provide a "mind asleep, body asleep" experience. A ripple of laughter spreads through the room as we catch the play on words of the standard nomenclature, "mind awake, body asleep," that we had learned was the slightly altered state of consciousness that Bob Monroe had dubbed Focus 10.

"Mind awake, body asleep" is an intriguing concept. Could we achieve it? How will we know when we make it to Focus 10? What should we expect? The questions are immediately voiced by a few people in the group, but echo the sentiments of all.

"No expectations," John notes. "That is the best way to approach our first exercise, and it is a good reminder for the whole week. If we outline what others have experienced in Focus 10, we might limit what you are able to experience. We will talk about it later, after the tape. Remember, as Bob always said, 'The only limitations we have are our belief systems.'"

It is becoming clear that this is not going to be an instructional sequence of statements, expected behavior, and then assessment of our performance. This is going to be about our own self-exploration experiences.

"So let's get started," John continues. A sense of playfulness informs our comments as we gather belongings, seek available restrooms, or grab a last drink of water on the way back to our CHEC units. There is also a slight undercurrent of tension, as we all know that this is the first "real" tape, and there is no way to know what to expect.

In my CHEC, I adjust the curtain to block out the light. Total darkness suddenly seems foreboding, and I adjust the lighting controls until there is a soft golden glow barely visible. This seems calming and I stretch out on my back, lay my head on the pillow, and slip on the earphones. It is a repeat of last night's protocols. There is soft music until all ready lights are on, and then a short introduction by Charleene.

The tape goes according to Charleene's explanation, beginning with the relaxing ocean surf. This is followed by resonant tuning, the proscribed affirmation, and then there is a light hiss of "pink noise." Bob Monroe's voice reminds us to relax and begin counting slowly from one to ten. We are gently encouraged to follow along with a move from C-1 consciousness up to the Focus 10 level. I listen intently to the pink noise and find I can identify a slight, but unmistakable waver, which I decide to identify as the Focus 10 binaural beat pattern. The more intently I listen, the clearer it becomes, but it is very subtle.

I let my intensity subside and begin to relax into the soft sounds. As I do, I find my body beginning to take on an unreal quality that is more a lack of sensation than numbness. With a quick left-brain analysis, I conclude that I am experiencing an extreme relaxation in my physical tissues, but I am in no way sleepy. This is occurring easily and slowly in a dreamlike way, yet I am still mentally awake and alert, and I understand that I can stop the process by simply thinking of stopping it.

I experiment with this idea a few times and prove its efficacy. I can easily stop these sensations by focusing on where I am and what I am doing. Yet I also find that with just a little effort (it is more accurate to say I am "releasing" all effort), I can also reenter the intense sensation of deep relaxation. An "ah-ha" realization hits me that this might be approaching the goal of "mind awake, body asleep."

Suddenly, I am immersed in a pounding sound pulsing in my ears. I realize this is not on the tape. What is that noise? I recoil a bit mentally but not physically, as I want to hold on to the relaxation. It is so loud, and it seems to be everywhere, it's actually as if I am inside it! Then something interesting occurs. I realize that since I had not responded physically to the perception of the noisy interruption there seems to be a new level of awareness in my thought process. I just seem to know the answer to my question. The answer appears and is nothing more than another thought presenting itself in an effortless manner.

I realize the nature of the sound, and I am even more surprised. I am hearing my own heartbeat and blood flow. This is startling. I am amazed at the process of not reacting physically to the initial surprise and frustration of not knowing what is going on. I remain relaxed, mentally aware, but within some new and unknown level of knowing. I am fascinated with this state, the sound itself, and the new levels of sensation.

This is my own heartbeat. I feel it and hear it and the experience of it is intense. I begin wondering how this could be possible, and again the answer simply appears as a deep level of understanding. Apparently, I have achieved a deep enough level of relaxation that my internal mental chatter has quieted. I can now perceive the sound of blood flowing through the structures of my inner ear. This is really cool, I think, simultaneously having the experience and trying to understand and analyze it. The more I try to analyze my thoughts about the experience, however, the more it begins to diminish the effect. I drop trying to figure out what is going on and allow the experience to see what will happen next.

I reenter the flowing nature of the process and feel deeper sensations of my heartbeat. I find an increasing sensation that my body is, in fact, asleep and seeming to "melt away," yet my mind is alert, conscious, and aware. This is an incredible state. A few fleeting scenes appear and my attention drifts away from the heartbeat. Brief images form and then disappear. These visual impressions appear to be snippets of events of the previous five years, but nothing that I can draw inference or meaning from.

Again, that sense of expanded knowing also appears, and I realize that it is not the images that are important, but the process of being able to see them. These are not dreamlike images, nor do they have the mental sense of a memory. These are reexperiences of the events. The sensation and events are brief and the process is like watching (or being within) a movie shown on the back of my eyelids.

As these experiences unfold, the tape abruptly ends with Bob Monroe calling us to "here and now awareness" and focused attention. We then find ourselves counting backward along with Bob's voice as he takes us "down" from Focus 10 back to the normal world of C-1 consciousness. A buzzing alarm clock tone ends the tape. This sound is a beta brain wave audio stimulation signal that aids in the focus of our consciousness even more clearly in an awake and alert level of normal awareness.

My body begins to feel heavy and cumbersome as I again become aware of it upon the return to C-1 consciousness. I open my eyes and suddenly feel confined within the walls of my CHEC. The slight glow of golden light that I had initially created at the outset of the exercise now seems bright and illuminates the CHEC space.

Charleene's voice resumes in our earphones and instructs us that we have a few minutes to jot down notes if we choose, but we should soon assemble in the group room for discussion, or debriefing, as it becomes known. I take off my earphones and make a few hurried notations describing my heartbeat experience, the fleeting imagery toward the end of the tape, and I think of the deep levels of relaxation that had been so quickly attained. Soft music again flows from the speakers in the wall of the unit as I write.

I exit the CHEC and find Ken, my roommate, doing the same. We acknowledge each other but do not feel the need to speak as we join others filling the halls and heading downstairs. An intensity can be felt in the air as I notice that most everyone seems introspective as we shuffle along down the stairway to the group room.

We quietly assemble on the floor again, some taking their previous seats and some choosing new spots. "Anyone have any questions or experiences they would like to share?" John breaks the silence with a query.

No one wants to speak, but his silence creates the space for the participants to talk. After a few more moments, someone notes a deep sense of relaxation. The silence in the room has at last been broken, and almost everyone nods in agreement and many echo the sensation. Almost everyone has achieved some degree of deep relaxation, and many have felt the "numbing" of body sensation in a sleep-like manner but without the normal loss of consciousness. John responds with "That's interesting" and is silent again.

"Well, I didn't feel anything at all. I just went to sleep," blurts Olivia, the newly ordained minister. "It was a nice sleep, but quite frustrating as I hear these interesting experiences everyone else seems to have had."

John notes that this is a very important comment and cautions us that we should not have expectations concerning our experiences. This is to be an individual experience in a group setting, not a uniform or directed group experience with expected similar outcomes. He also warns that one of the worst "diseases" one can catch during TMI's residential program is known as "Focus envy." This is defined as a jealousy of others' experiences or the desire to claim someone else's experience as your own. He reminds us that the best way to open to any experience is to release our expectations or attachment to a particular outcome. This, of course, will be difficult, as our Western culture has been driven along the lines of "keeping up with the Joneses," by getting the same or better of whatever their latest purchase or experience has been.

These comments put the group back into a heavy air of introspective silence, which John breaks with, "Does anyone else have anything they would like to share?"

I volunteer my heartbeat experience. I feel a few eyes peering at me. John again responds with "That's interesting." Again, there is the silence of awaiting input by another participant. After a few moments, others in the group note experiences of relaxation, sleeping, a few visual imagery notations, and one other sound-related phenomenon akin to my own heartbeat experience. John and Charleene acknowledge that each of these are phenomena that people have previously experienced in the Focus 10 state.

"So, what are we supposed to feel like in Focus 10?" Kyle, the elderly psychotherapist, poses this question.

All eyes focus on the trainers, again hoping for an answer to this common question.

Charleene smiles and softly notes, "'Mind awake, body asleep' is about the best we can offer you at this point because to outline anything else might limit your experiences. Have fun, be flexible, and enjoy this new level of awareness." Her eyes twinkle as she adds, "Explore these questions for yourself, and see what you think Focus 10 feels like."

Not many of us are satisfied with that answer, but it is clear we will get nothing more at this point. We move to a discussion about the images that several of us had experienced. It seems that there is a psychologically defined state of consciousness, which is not quite awake, not quite asleep. Called hypnagogia, this level of consciousness is one in which visual imagery can easily form. This naturally occurs during the "twilight sleep" experience as one is dropping off to sleep or in the process of awakening. It is an in-between state of consciousness. Many meditators experience this level, and some people feel that insight and intuition may begin to blossom in this state as well.

Discussion ensues as to whether the Hemi-Sync tones induce this altered state of consciousness. John and Charleene emphasize that it is an entrainment process. An induction process implies that there is some degree of loss of conscious control by the participant. With Hemi-Sync, one is in control of the situation and can choose to ride along with the tones or to counter them with the simplest thought and deter their effects. This idea generates a lively discussion about hypnosis and involuntary induction versus entrainment. The discussion demonstrates, however, that those who felt they had, indeed, reached the Focus 10 level also agree that they were alert, aware, and in control of their actions.

The entrainment scenario is a comfortable one for all concerned, as a state of relaxation is one of the requirements for the tones to assist in entrainment. A simple thought or desire to "not go there" will immediately stop the process of moving into the altered state.

4

An Out-of-Body Experience: The Nonphysical Becomes Real

The echoing tones of the energy chime announce that the break is over. It is time to assemble for the introduction to the second tape of the first full day of the program. The initial tape had generated everything from deep sleep to becoming one with a heartbeat. What could be next? The group of 24 settles into their seats and falls silent in anticipation.

"Is everyone ready to do some more exploring?" Charleene asks through a large and inviting smile. Our nods of positive response are enough for her to continue. "The next tape is called Advanced Focus 10, and it will involve moving into the Focus 10 state and then exploring the energy that can be created there."

"Creating energy there?" Several participants repeat her words with an air of question and skepticism. "We thought you said that these exercises were a movement toward the nonphysical. How can there be energy outside the physical?" The idea is intriguing, but it is also a departure from simply achieving an altered state of consciousness. This exercise is introducing the idea of *doing something* in an altered state, not simply attaining one.

"Remember how you felt with our first experience of resonant tuning last night?" she asks. "I seem to remember you referring to feeling energized by the experience of making the *OM* sound."

"But that was physical," one person says tentatively. "We made physical sounds and felt physical energy."

"Well!" Charleene responds in mock amazement, then offers a challenge. "Perhaps we might want to see what will happen if we explore creating nonphysical energy within the nonphysical."

How one can create or feel energy that is nonphysical is perplexing and sounds almost contradictory. There had to be a physical aspect somewhere to feel energy, didn't there? Charleene reminds us to approach this as an exploration that involves allowing movement beyond what we currently understand. She adds that we should consider imagining a "field of energy" that surrounds the human body and see what happens. The approach on the tape will involve visualizing a ball of energy appearing as light surrounding our physical body. This will be supported by special acoustical sounds on the tape.

What might happen then is unknown and should be approached without expectation. Again, the idea is to explore in a playful manner. Hearing no further questions or comments, she continues. "At TMI, we have adopted Bob Monroe's made-up term REBAL which is short for *R*esonant *E*nergy *BAL*loon to describe this type of light ball energy."

Someone asks if this light ball energy field is what is called an aura. Charleene asks if we could defer that question until after the tape. "Let's not create any expectations or limitations that might grow out of language we have heard or used in the past. Let's simply go exploring and see what happens."

John interjects at this point, "Let's say that we agree that it might be interesting to see if there is a possibility of forming a ball of energy around you and explore that in this exercise." Exploring in this venue clearly does not mean intellectual debate, but the experience of trying things and seeing what happens. John explains that this experience might not only deepen our sensation of Focus 10 through additional practice, but it might allow us to work within a new realm of nonphysical awareness.

As I settle into the CHEC unit, the familiar soft music is already setting the stage. After testing the lighting for various effects, I decide on total darkness. I put on my earphones and settle into the soft pillows. Trainer instructions remind us to turn on our "ready light" if we are in place. I notice that I am one of the "offenders" who has not followed standard procedure, but with a flip of the toggle switch, I am positioned to begin the exercise. The tape follows the previous form, the sounds of calming ocean surf, the "energy conversion box," the drone of the resonant tuning, and finally the affirmation.

We are guided to the Focus 10 state. Once there, we begin to practice forming the "energy ball" around our body. This turns out to be more interesting than I anticipated. The process of forming this Resonant Energy Balloon, or REBAL, is assisted by sound effects on the tape that create a realistic sensation of a three-dimensional ball of energy forming around the body. As we are instructed to visualize the REBAL forming, stimulating sounds of spraying fountains flood our ears.

While I know that this is a generated audio special effect, the overall sensation is one of "energy" magically appearing around various parts of my body. It seems so physical that there is a sensation of being lightly tickled on the skin. This is pleasant and encourages a lightness of my being. It adds to a state of serenity already achieved within Focus 10.

After several practice sequences of forming REBAL energies around our bodies, we are given instructions on the tape to continue exploring on our own. We now have deeper experience within Focus 10, and have additional sensations to play with. Remembering that too much intellectual analysis diminished the effects during the first tape experience, I attempt to "let go" as I begin my unstructured journey. I allow myself to flow along with the pink noise of the tape and its quiet underpinning of binaural beats.

Every so often, however, I take a moment to assess my psychological state. I continue to feel alert and aware, but my body has drifted peacefully asleep as the Focus 10 sound waver is processed in my brain. When I later relived and reflected on this experience, I realized how much of a break in my belief system this state was. Under our normal consensus view of reality, when one is asleep, one cannot also be awake. These terms are mutually exclusive by definition. Yet in a sense, this is exactly what I was experiencing.

As I focus on creating the REBAL, I sense I am floating upward. This is startling in its reality. It is not unpleasant, but it is unexpected. I am aware I am lying in my CHEC unit with my earphones on, yet the physical sensation is of rising upward, as if the mattress had been placed on an elevator. I feel the air moving past my body in breeze-like fashion as the upward motion continues. I open my eyes, or think I do. It is pitch black in the CHEC unit, and difficult to tell whether my physical eyes are open or shut. What follows is challenging to what I consider real and fantasy.

I find myself "seeing" a scene in full color, texture, and detail. I am outside, above the building about 50 feet. This is not like watching a movie; it is a direct experience. While simultaneously experiencing and not believing the experience, my mind races: Is this what an out-of-body experience feels like? The idea that I am having one is not sinking in.

I am looking down on the roof. It is intriguing to realize I am seeing elements of the top of the building that I have not physically observed. I had not yet climbed the circular staircase to the decklike platform on the roof. I note that this is something that can be verified later. I can accept this scene mentally as some sort of dreamlike sequence, but the reality of the physical sensation of it is difficult to comprehend.

This is a very strange situation and places me in an odd intellectual predicament. The reality of the visualization is vivid, but there is no way it could be real (or so one would think), as I am sure that I am still on the mattress of the CHEC unit deep within the walls of the Nancy Penn Center. But I can clearly see the top of the building and its tower at one end. I am not mentally asleep, nor am I dreaming; yet I am "seeing" the roof as if I am suspended from a slow- and low-flying helicopter. I am confused.

These events and internal dialogues take place in an instant of time. Yet in that same moment, I realize I am not alone in this impossible space above the building. I also "see" two other members of the group "floating" together toward the top of the tower. When I say I can see them, it becomes even more difficult to explain. I see a glowing ball of light, or a flickering within the air, but for some reason, I know that it is workshop participants I am seeing. In the same manner that I felt the expanded state of knowing on the previous tape, I suddenly know their names: Kellie, the practicing midwife, and Carol, the chief operating officer of a bank.

I take one of my brief self check-ins and note, in addition to being physically asleep, I am also still aware within Focus 10. I am aware that I am having this experience and simultaneously "stepping aside" and observing it.

The saga continues with an interesting twist as, at this point, I note that it appears that the glowing ball of light I had identified as Kellie begins waving to me as if she, too, has seen me and seeks acknowledgment. I think I am getting creative at weaving a story here, but what the heck, let's see where this goes. Lightheartedly, I wave back to the glowing ball that I have identified as Kellie; this appears to please her and we drift apart slightly. I then find that I can move about or "fly" in a sense, by simply thinking the direction I want to go. This sensation is real and physical in my perception, and yet I "know" that it can't be.

I wonder if others are having this type of experience—dream, fantasy, or whatever it is. Soon, I find myself looking with some sort of X-ray vision into the building. This is interesting. My gaze comes to rest on the sleeping form of another class member in her CHEC unit—Olivia, the newly ordained minister, who had noted her frustration of going to sleep instead of reaching Focus 10. My perception and sensation is not one of intrusion, but of a desire for her inclusion in the experience. I know she would want to join in if only she could wake up.

As I remember her frustration in her report to the group, I attempt to wake her so she might join. Surely she would want to if she could become aware of the pleasurable nature of the sensation of floating and flying. I "yell" at her with great intensity in my thoughts: "Wake up! Don't sleep through this! This is fun!" Then I

35

reach down and try to shake her to wake her up. Throughout this process, I feel that I am actually doing this action, not just thinking or imagining it.

At this point, I realize what I am doing and feel it is past time to rein in my fantasy. Geez, this is going a bit far, I think. My imagination is running away with me! At that moment, Monroe's voice issues in the earphones to end our experience. He tells us to count back down to C-1 and become awake, alert, and aware. As I follow these directions, the altered state of dreamlike but realistic imagery fades and I am back in my CHEC unit and wondering if I also, like Olivia, had gone to sleep during this tape session and simply had a vivid dream.

John's voice in my earphones informs me that we have a few minutes to make notes. The soft music begins in the wall-mounted speakers, and we are further instructed to join the others as soon as possible in the group room for debriefing. As I reflect on the experience and jot down a few notes, I'm not sure what happened. Perhaps I went to sleep, but my mind seemed to be awake and alert during this strange series of events. Could I have had a lucid dream? As I scribble notes, I think, "Well, it was interesting if nothing else." I emerge from the CHEC unit, visit Ken and see that he is still writing, exit my room, and join the group forming in the hallway on the way to the stairs.

By chance, as I get to the end of the hallway, Kellie merges into the line of people directly in front of me. I sense that we are looking at each other as if we each have something to ask but are afraid to. I start to speak and then withdraw. She hesitates too, and then turns to go down the hall toward the stairwell to the group room.

My mind is jumping back and forth between saying something and remaining silent. I have a thousand conflicting conversations with myself with each step: "Why not just ask?" "Nothing ventured nothing gained." "It's probably just a dream anyway, so why not just see if she had any experience at all?" "Geez, what's the big deal?" Finally, the memory of Charleene's speech on "safe space" and being open to experience during this week gets the better of me. I reach forward and tap Kellie on the shoulder just as we reach the stairwell. I can feel my heart racing as she turns in response.

I try to be nonchalant as I ask, "Did you see anything in that last tape?"

"Well," she stops and looks at me intently, her eyes questioning. I hadn't thought of the possibility that she was going through the same level of self-doubt that I was. Then tentatively she says, "This may sound really crazy, but I thought I saw you and someone else up at the top of the tower." She speaks as if she expects either to be viewed with total amazement at the concept or disbelieved entirely. She apparently can perceive by my stunned look that I am going to do neither.

At first I am too shocked to speak. Then words spill out. "This is simply too wild to believe. I thought I saw you and Carol there, quite clearly!" There is a look of astonishment between us as we freeze in that position.

She is quiet for a moment and then becomes pensive. "You know, I think it was Carol that I saw also," Kellie notes almost in a whisper. Silence. As we start down the stairs together in reflective silence, we both eye Carol, who stands alone on the landing. Kellie cannot contain herself and blurts out, "Carol, did you see Richard and me at the tower during that last tape?"

"Well, no," she responds. Our excitement plummets. "But you have to understand," she goes on with a measured tone, "I don't seem to 'see' much visually, I tend to have a 'feeling' of what's around me by sensation alone. But yes, I definitely did go to the top of the tower during that tape. It was a quite real sensation, and I did 'feel' two others 'out there' with me—was that you?"

Kellie and I are speechless. Finally, I speak, "We both think that we saw you at the top of the tower."

"That's where it felt like I was," Carol responds, her voice quivering.

The impact of what we are all saying is beginning to sink in. We continue down the stairs in silence. This is going to take a little thinking about.

I need time to sort all this out. I sit down just outside the group room and notice Olivia talking with trainer John. She is intense, upset about something. In deference, I keep my distance to allow them to complete their discussion. But it is apparently completed and Olivia moves away from John toward the refreshment area.

I need some help sorting all this out and I want John's perspective. I get his attention and move over next to him. I quickly pour out the experience of the mutual "seeing" of Kellie and Carol and my nonphysical attempts at shaking and waking Olivia. John smiles broadly and interrupts me with a call to Olivia to return. She does, but I notice that she still has a look of concern.

"Tell Richard what you were just telling me," John invites Olivia.

She looks at me, apprehensively, again at John, and then speaks. "I was just telling John that I was concerned for my safety because someone was in my CHEC unit and it was very disturbing. I opened my eyes and no one was there, but it was *so* real, I could actually feel someone *shaking* me. It was frightening." She is clearly upset and the experience has been real for her. "Did something like that happen to you too?"

"No," I murmur after a bit of silence and embarrassment. I have no intent of upsetting her. "But I may have been the one that you thought was shaking you."

Her bewildered look quickly moves John to explain my experience to her. With John's assistance, we share the experience from both our perspectives, and it becomes a mind-boggling realization. The implication of what we are saying is a challenge to our belief systems about physical reality.

Before we can reflect even a few moments on the magnitude of this event, the sound of the energy chime announces our need to move to the group room. We all move in that direction and find places to sit. As everyone is settling in, Charleene opens again with "Does anyone have anything they would like to share with the group?"

John interjects, "I think Richard, Kellie, Carol, and Olivia may have had an interesting experience if they would be willing to share it."

Kellie cannot contain herself and announces emphatically that she, Carol, and I had all seen each other above the roof at the tower.

There are quick glances about the room and questions follow. It is interesting to note that there is neither disbelief nor discouraging words in the group. There are many questions about how we felt, what it looked like, and even a couple of comments about how lucky we had been. Indeed, instead of any doubts, it appears that there is more of a sense of appreciation that someone had an experience such as this and been willing to share it.

A few others have a few comments, but our experience has been the highlight of the debriefing session. We have only completed two tapes of the first day of the workshop and already the experiences are almost too much for me. I can easily go home at this point and spend a very long time thinking about these events. The workshop is going to continue, however, and I am snapped back to attentiveness with John's comments: "OK, folks, this next tape is a free-flow tape. You will be going to Focus 10 and exploring on your own. Have fun! Any questions?"

5

Pushing the Limits of Belief:
Testing Our Version of Reality

John's words "Have fun" echo in my ears as we exit the group room and head for the CHEC units. It is becoming a custom to stop by one of the 14 restrooms. "No need to have a call of nature 'in-the-body' interrupt a good 'out-of-body' experience," John reminds us. His instructions are that during this tape we are on our own. We can create our own direction to pursue. In TMI parlance, this is a free-flow tape. Going out to Focus 10, exploring, and having fun are the only directions given.

Just as the group is dispersing to move upstairs, Kellie pulls Carol and me aside. "Let's *try* to do it this time," she teases. She is proposing that we consciously attempt to replicate the earlier experience of meeting in the out-of-body state. Carol and I exchange looks of intrigue and bewilderment. "Could we do it again?" "Did it really happen?" "What if we can't do it again?" We agree that such an attempt would be interesting, but it is clear that Kellie is the most adventurous of the trio.

Again, the thoughts of "Nothing ventured nothing gained" and "Why not, aren't we here for exploration and experience?" ripple in the background of my mind. I admit to a bit of performance anxiety. "What if our mutual tower incident was a fluke and that was all there was?" This question challenges my ego.

We come to an agreement, however, that we will try it. We all want to test the earlier experience. At this point, my Ph.D.-trained left brain asserts itself. "You know, it would be very simple to talk ourselves into believing that we had seen or done similar activities if we just discuss it afterward." I still wonder if Kellie's initial inquiry had inadvertently tipped Carol off to agree that she, too, had shared the same experience. "I think what we need for it to be a valid test is harder evidence—like written record comparison."

They agree, and we establish a test protocol that provides more structure for validating the experience if it does, indeed, occur. We will attempt to meet at the tower, decide where to go, and then travel there together. Nothing else is planned. If we can somehow move as a group in the out-of-body state, then we should have similar experiences to report. At the conclusion of the tape, we will not discuss the experience at all, even as part of the debriefing session. We agree to make as complete a set of written notes as possible, and then set them side by side. If the words on the paper agree that we have shared an experience, then we will have a lot more to think about. If not, then maybe we have been deluding ourselves about the earlier experience.

This makeshift protocol is certainly not at the level of a major scientific laboratory experiment. This time, however, we will attempt to eliminate the possibility that we might talk ourselves into an experience that might not have happened. There is a degree of credibility to this approach that may not only test the experience, but also provide data that could begin to challenge our basic belief systems.

We then join the other participants in the return to the CHECs. The tape session begins with standard TMI structure. Once we have been guided to the Focus 10 state, we are told to explore this realm of consciousness. The following are my notes of this experience:

> I formed my REBAL and "thought" to go to the top of the tower. I met Kellie there. Didn't see Carol. Kellie and I got into a discussion about the fact that we had not decided who was in charge

or how to decide where to go, so I told her to go first. She left, I followed.

I saw a mountain stream with steep wooded hills—very green. Water was wide and peaceful, but flowing.

I said it was my turn to take us somewhere and that water was a clue, so I took us to Palm Beach [Florida] to scuba dive. Big resistance and fear from Kellie as she said no scuba. I said we don't need it anyway and "expanded" the REBAL to be a big glass box. I took us underwater in it. We sat in it looking at turtles and dolphins up close. This was very brief, then we were out and she seemed no longer to be present.

I started hearing a radio show out of my left earphone. I wondered if the technology of all the wires in the building was indeed picking up a radio station. I listened *really* hard and it was a lot of talking and sounded like radio, but I finally realized that it was Carol talking. I couldn't make out what she was saying.

Went to my hometown to show off easily identifiable buildings there. Didn't feel anybody went with me.

Sat back and said OK, where are they? Immediately, I found myself in a big cave. It was like Carlsbad [in California], and Kellie was the guide showing us around.

Briefly encountered cartoon characters and *Star Trek* stuff. Suddenly was alone and had deep feelings of irrelevance.

Felt that Kellie and Carol left me and went somewhere together.

Briefly saw some kind of tent city on the side of a hill.

Saw a traditional Mexican eagle symbol, the one where the eagle has captured a serpent.

Tried to summon Carol and take her to my boyhood home. There was an old man there as a reference point.

Saw big, brown tall building with white slatted trim.

We held hands in a ring at one point.

Came back to the tower to try to link up with Carol and Kellie as Bob Monroe's recorded voice on the tape spoke as a reference point at various times during the exercise.

Went briefly to llama farm (a place near TMI).

I got separated from Carol and Kellie.

Saw all three of us in the snow in Alaska watching the aurora borealis.

Noticed a "hole in the sky." This seemed to be sort of a cave in the clouds going straight up and seemed to have some significance, but I did not go into it. I noted what it felt like, so I could try to return there later.

My anticipation mounts as we follow the normal tape closing process, the trainers instructing us to turn off our ready lights, make notes, and reassemble in the group room. As we move along the hall and down the stairs toward the group room, Kellie, Carol, and I avoid contact to ensure against corrupting our notes. Even though we do not speak, I can tell they, too, are feeling the growing impatience of seeing if we have experienced anything in common. We stick to our agreement to wait, however, until we can lay the pages of notes down side by side for comparison and review. The intensity grows as we keep glancing at one another, and we each grow uncomfortable with remaining attentive to the debriefing session. Charleene notices our tension and asks if there is a problem.

Kellie explains what we attempted to do and that we are eager to compare notes to evaluate how common our experiences might have been. Several classmates encourage us to share right then and there. We decline, as each of us wants to rewrite our notes for clarity and completeness. John suggests that we work through this process during lunch and, if we are agreeable, we might share the results with the rest of the group during our evening session at David Francis Hall. We agree, and the group breaks for lunch and the extended afternoon break period.

Between lunch and our report that evening, we continue doing tapes according to the normal afternoon schedule. We do several tapes, each providing a new level of comfort in the altered state of Focus 10, and each adding small "tools" to accentuate, or ease, the process of becoming comfortable moving into a realm of the nonphysical. As would be expected, there is a full range of experience within the group. A few still have little or nothing to report, while others have rich visual, auditory, or kinesthetic phenomena.

Kellie, Carol, and I stick to our agreed-upon protocol. We do not communicate in any way until we all complete our notes. In summary of our subsequent comparison, we agree that we had experiences that appeared to be related to some degree and some that were unrelated. Here are the experiences we feel we shared:

Kellie and I both recorded meeting at the tower and agreeing to leave together. Kellie saw me, but not Carol. Carol perceived both Kellie and me. This was not considered a major "hit" of shared experience, of course, as it was expected that we meet at the tower to start the exercise. We could have easily imagined this occurrence.

All three of us, however, recorded going to a mountain stream. This we classified as a major "hit" or shared experience. The words "mountain stream" and "river" were written on all three sheets of paper. Carol noted a footbridge over the water and Kellie saw a village off to the side. All three of us made a notation of how green the trees and mountainsides appeared.

Neither Kellie nor Carol made any mention of my attempt to take them scuba diving. On reading my account, however, Kellie volunteered that she has a long-held fear of deep water. Since this was not present in the written notes, we did not count this as a shared experience. I note it here as an intriguing aspect of some sort of communication possibly taking place.

Carol reported that she had a discussion with herself about whether she could do this test experience or not; it was new and challenging to her beliefs. In terms of sequence, this discussion occurred at the time of my experience of the radio show. In this same time period, Kellie recorded being separated from the two of us. Had I somehow overheard Carol's discussion with herself? We thought this had possibilities, but could only grade it as a "maybe" in terms of shared experience.

Kellie had seen Carol take on the look of a wolf. In the sequence, this occurred when I saw the two of them go off together. Kellie's notes said that I was not present during this perception. Carol, it turns out, has a very strong interest in wolves and even collects totemic wolf curios. She also has an abiding interest in dogs. Amazingly, she was doing this tape session under a blanket that had wolves pictured all over it. It is important to note that neither Kellie nor I had seen this blanket at this time. We classified this observation as a highly shared experience.

The experience of snow was common to all three sets of notes. I saw snow in Alaska, Carol saw us together in a snow cave, and Kellie had perceived us in knee-deep snow. This, too, we noted as a "hit" in terms of highly shared experience.

I saw a hole in the sky that we could go through if we wanted to, which seemed almost to match Carol's notes about climbing toward the opening entrance to the snow cave. The hole in the sky seems significant in the sense that it represented an entrance to something.

As promised, we report to the group in the evening program in David Francis Hall. Our classmates receive our discussion with enthusiasm and support, and we are applauded for our efforts and for taking the time to attempt this experiment and to write it all down. There is a growing enthusiasm for the remainder of the week as a result of our sharing. Several members of the group comment privately that they are encouraged by our report in the sense that if we could achieve these things then they might too.

6

Touching Infinity:
A Return to Wholeness

In the previous two chapters, I shared the experiences with Carol and Kellie of our exploratory out-of-body activity. In the second experience, we tested the reality of what was occurring by not discussing the specifics, but writing down our versions, then comparing notes. During that second effort, I noted "a hole in the sky" as part of that Focus 10 tape, and noted it would be an interesting place to revisit. I did return on a later tape, with very significant and what I now know to be life-changing results. Let me now share that experience.

During a free-flow Focus 12 tape, I decide to find that hole in the sky I had seen on the earlier tape. I find it easily by directing my attention and intention back toward the previous experience with the hole in the sky. Almost instantaneously, I am out of my body and floating just below a small hole in the sky with a swirl of clouds slowly drifting around it. It initially resembles a small cave opening. I examine it closer and the interplay of light and shadow reveals a long tunnel-like tube of some kind.

As I hover near it, the hole appears to be just a round, long, dark tunnel of about three or four feet in diameter with no end in sight. I start to drift into it, but hesitate as I realize I have no idea where this might lead or if there might be any danger associated with getting stuck in such a tube in an out-of-body state. I hold this thought briefly, then dismiss it, reasoning that since this is all a nonphysical experience anyway, what could possibly hurt me?

I enter the hole by intending myself to move in that direction. As I drift upward about six feet, darkness is closing in below me. Fear ripples through me. With this hesitation, the darkness seems to become more solid and real. I am getting scared. I feel like I am in a cave of hard rock with sharp crystalline points that could scratch me, and that there is, indeed, an opportunity to get stuck or injured here.

I decide not to fight this fear, but to acknowledge it and seek a sense of playfulness. I emphasize to myself that this is not *physically* happening to me, although it feels like it at this moment. Why can't I just let go and let this happen? With this thought, I look upward in the direction of my drifting and notice a pinhole of light that appears far off. Well, at least I am going *somewhere,* I think.

All of a sudden there is a loud pop, and I am engulfed in a rush of energy and surrounded by bright light. This light seems to replace the air itself if there even is any in this nonphysical state. I have a clarity of thought and perception far beyond the capacity of words to explain. (I preface the remainder of this description with the comment that words are what we communicate with, but they are a very limited and crude mechanism to try to impart even the most elemental aspects of what happened to me next.)

I am within a field of light so bright that there is nothing in the physical world with which to compare it. This field is entwined with a sensation of vastness larger than can be conceived in physical reality. I feel like I am beginning to merge with the vast field of light. I am still myself, and I feel a definition and boundary of self as distinct as in my normal physical body. Yet everything has a crispness and surreal clarity to it. It is frustrating that there are not adequate words to describe these things. I feel I am trivializing the description, but it is the best I can do.

I notice points of light similar to stars but more distinct and clearer than any star. Each point has long lines of light emanating from it, and there are 15 or 20 of these lights floating toward me from my upper right (whatever "upper right" means when there is no space and no time). I realize, or seem to immediately know, that these lights have intelligence. They are *beings* of some sort. I also perceive (or imagine) that there is an instant mutual recognition of some kind. I do not speak; there is no need to—I simply know and can very clearly "hear" anything that "they" communicate.

I realize that this is a form of communication that Bob Monroe dubbed "NVC," for NonVerbal Communication, which he notes in his books about his out-of-body travels. It is a natural and logical communication device since, without a physical body, there are no vocal cords, eardrums, or physics of sound to carry out physical voice-based conversation.

As these light beings approach me, I am overcome with love and beauty. It is a love that is so intense that sexual orgasm is a faint echo of what I am experiencing in this nonphysical realm. I am surrounded with a palpable reality of love in its purest and most unconditional form. There is communication, but I cannot put it into words, except to say that this communication involves multiple levels of meaning, understanding, and experience. This activity is far beyond what humans currently envision as a communication process. Perhaps the best I can do is to record the actual words from my notes written immediately afterward: *I was just "there," but it was a "there" like nothing I can describe in words—I was just there.*

As the experience comes to a close, it is made apparent to me by simple "knowing" that it is time to leave. Suddenly, I am whooshed back into a normal Focus 12 state of consciousness and imagery. Following this "whoosh," I am still "out there" but more or less in a normal Focus 12 state as I "see" my TMI classmates as little "Christmas tree light" spheres of light bobbing up and down. I have an overwhelming feeling of love, peace, and light all rolled into one and I experience a new level of connection to everyone there.

At this point, the taped instruction from Bob Monroe directs us to return to Focus 10. I seem to slide downward very slowly. I feel a numbing sensation in this, yet it is mostly energetic and not quite physical. It just feels like I am getting very heavy the closer I get to Focus 10. Then, as I follow the guided instructions back to C-1 physical consciousness, as my notes say, *". . . my body felt like it was so dense."* I begin to write at a furious pace, attempting to capture the sensation and imagery of the bright light and energy beings. Something important has happened, but, at this point, I am not sure what. It is very important to make notations that will allow me to recapture the moment later. (Little did I know, at that point, that there was so much more to come.)

With a strange sensation of not quite being there, I leave my CHEC unit and go down to the group room for the debriefing session. It seems that everyone is moving at a much slower pace than normal. It is as if time itself has slowed to half speed. The debriefing begins with the standard "Anyone have anything they want to share?" from the trainers.

As the first comments are made, I am overwhelmed with a numbing coldness that permeates every cell in my body. I am not talking about a cool breeze chill, but about getting *really* cold deep in my bones. This comes over me all of a sudden and with no stimulus that I can detect. I begin to shiver uncontrollably, and large goose bumps form on my skin. I better get a blanket. I run upstairs, get two from my CHEC, and return to the group room. I swaddle myself from head to foot. I think I am beginning to look a little stupid, but I am cold and even with two blankets, only a small degree of heat is being retained. I don't understand what is happening, but I shiver uncontrollably every so often.

Then things shift into slow motion. I can see and hear everything that is happening in several views simultaneously, and time is slowing to a molasses state. There is also a new level of understanding, however, as I seem to perceive the feeling behind each word spoken. I am beginning to experience the sensation, emotion, and intent behind the words of each speaker. I think this is strange but interesting, and I focus on the effect. It all seems natural, something to observe.

At this point, an elderly lady, Barbara, speaks. A retired nurse from the Netherlands, Barbara had previously shared her frustration at not being able to achieve things as easily as she felt others did. She begins now to have an emotional release concerning her self-perception of not being able to perform at TMI to her expectations. She is concerned that she is not "getting it," as much as she feels others in the program are getting it. She had done this activity (Focus 12) at home and had done much better there. She feels she is failing (again), as she had done in other attempts at inner exploration and metaphysical inquiry. She begins to weep; as her anger rises, a strong air of emotional support wells up in the group.

As Barbara speaks, tears form in my eyes. Not the type of sympathetic reaction one would expect as a classmate undergoes a cathartic release, but I feel a deep, tearful, and joyous love for this fellow human who carries the divine spark of creation common to each of us. I not only hear her words, but I also experience the impact of the feeling behind them. Sadness wells up within me for Barbara's lack of realization of the value of her own powers and experience. This is a new sensation for me, not only unexpected, but also difficult to comprehend.

Then the insight hits me. My tears for Barbara are a realization. During the previous tape, I had experienced a place of light and love that Barbara might not see until she dies.

As these thoughts play out in my mind, my eyes are awash with tears. I begin to see in a way that I had never imagined before, but have difficulty believing this is actually happening. As the group empathizes with Barbara's outpouring, a stream of golden flecks rise from each person in the room, and all the streams converge to a central point just above Barbara's head and then descend upon her. She is bathed in a stream of golden light of support for the duration of her emotional release. I wonder if others see this. I decide they do not. It is exquisitely beautiful. As she finishes her comments and her emotions quiet, many in the group comfort her with touch.

I, too, want to join in comforting her with my touch, yet I realize it would be awkwardly obvious that I was doing so. I'm not sure why this bothers me. I am self-conscious and still very cold, wrapped mummy-like from head to toe in two blankets. I sit there, wrapped and shivering, with my back against the wall, observing class members saying words of encouragement or comfort. Many sit near her, hug her, and then move on to the short break called by the trainers. Finally, as the group around her is thinning, the person who is seated immediately behind her gets up to leave. I see my chance. I drop my blankets and move behind her where I can be near, yet not conspicuous. I sit cross-legged facing her back and reach out my hand to touch her right shoulder.

What happens next stuns me. With no thought of action or direction, I close my eyes and find myself moving into a Focus 10 altered state. Things begin to happen, definitely not under my control. As my hand touches Barbara's shoulder, I am overwhelmed with sadness. I think I must be connecting with Barbara at a deep level, and the "energy" of her sadness is using me to ground into the Earth.

These are feelings and experiences that I have no background or frame of reference to deal with in any way. It is *too* much for me to bear, and I break down emotionally and leave as quickly as I can release my hand from her shoulder. I discover later from others present that, as I got up, Barbara experienced an almost instantaneous healing from her emotional concerns and became quite calm, peaceful, and accepting of herself. I, on the other hand, become an emotional basket case as I rush outside.

Once outside, my tears flow. No, they do not flow, they gush. My body heaves with the intensity of the sobbing. I realize the sadness of Barbara. I realize the beauty of where I have been, "in the Light." I see for the first time ever the natural wonder of the world. Everything is beautiful and beyond words. I cannot contain the beauty and love. It is *too much* to bear. I weep.

All I can think about is that there is so much beauty, so much love in every direction, in every blade of grass, in the sky, in the ground, in everything alive, the air itself. I hold a tree and cry. I walk. I feel the grass under my feet and I cry. I pick up rocks and I cry. Even the slightest thought of the light beings or Barbara sets me off anew. As I cry, I sob over and over and over, *"Thank you, thank you, thank you."* I offer unconditional praise to the unknowable divinity.

It is instantly clear that our concepts of God are so limited that we *greatly* underestimate the power of creativity. I *know* that everything is as aware of me as I am aware of everything I can see or feel. I cry with joy, and I cry with sadness. And I cry with such uncontrollable intensity that I begin to wonder if I will ever again have any control over my emotions. But I don't care at that point. If I spend the rest of my life sobbing, it will not matter. I *know* that I have experienced the most beautiful thing possible to experience. I believe that we, as human beings, may not yet be "wired" to be able to maintain the experience of joy and unconditional love that is felt during a spiritually transformative event. I am certain, however, that we can evolve into it and that this growing process can be initiated by the experience itself. The initial experience is a level of pleasure, however, that is almost more than one can stand.

Suffice it to say that the expertise needed to deal with such an experience is in place at TMI. Charleene appears at my side and explains that my reaction is a natural one. Emotional control will return and I will be able to return home in a stable state. It will take a few hours to sort though my feelings, however. She directs the class to return to the building and continue with its scheduled tape sessions, John taking charge.

As my emotions begin to stabilize several hours later, I write as much as I can about the experience. I take a shower. I walk several miles. I have more discussions with Charleene. It is decided that I will not immediately share this experience with the class, to allow me time to be with it and not to create a "performance target" for the others. It is much later in the week before I share it at all and then only with a couple of people with whom I had become close.

I learn that something of this nature takes time to process and integrate. In fact, it will be several years before I can share this experience without losing emotional control. Even as I write this today, there are many stops and restarts as the sensations of the peak experience are again touched. I continue trying to understand and integrate this experience.

If we consider this experience to be a *spiritual* one, or minimally an intensely emotional one, it would seem that there is little we can easily and meaningfully share with others. I call for people who have had such experiences to acknowledge them, to share them, and I also encourage our society to accept such experiences with a more open attitude.

Interlude Two

Expanding Perspective

You might be asking yourself: What, if anything, do out-of-body experiences, uncontrollable weeping in bliss, or altered states of consciousness have to do with our social problems of information overload and not enough time to accomplish our daily tasks?

It is going to take a while to answer that question, but there is, indeed, a relationship. We must explore the issue of how we perceive things versus how they might really be. This will involve challenging our beliefs about the world and our role in it. The section just finished is about my experiences in nonordinary states of consciousness. Part of my reason for sharing these things is to provide a background for discussing how much of what we believe may be rooted in other people's perspectives rather than in our own experience.

My time at TMI was intense. The experiences there challenged my beliefs about what is real and what is imaginary. I was faced with a new perspective on both. The experience of these phenomena left me in reflection as I faced more questions than answers. Ordinarily, one would expect a mental roller coaster ride to accompany this level of challenge to the psyche. In retrospect, I was amazed that I constantly found myself in a supportive state of calmness and serenity unlike any I have ever felt before. I attribute this new level of inner peace to the "touching infinity" experience described in the last chapter. That event occurred on April 24, 1995, at TMI. I now understand that this was a life-changing event similar to the ones described by near-death author and researcher P. M. H. Atwater. She calls such activity a "near-death-like experience," or NDLE.

My consciousness moved, or was expanded, to levels of experience that far exceed the capacity of language to communicate. While I have never recaptured this exact sensation again, I do not care. I now believe that the ego can completely surrender or die, from its perspective, only once during a lifetime. I feel lucky and blessed that I did not have to wait until my physical death for this experience. No one does, but it requires openness and vulnerability for such an event to occur.

When we move beyond the five senses, we enter areas that we have long relegated to the philosophers and the world of the esoteric or spiritual. I have read many times that it is estimated that we are using only ten percent of our brains. What if we are using all one hundred percent, but are only aware of the ten percent that we are conscious of through our five senses? Perhaps the movement into the Light, or other such spiritually transformative events, is merely a glimpse of the operation of a much larger consciousness than we realize. What if the 90 percent of the brain that our current instrumentation does not see as active is fully operational but at levels of some type of superconsciousness?

The nonphysical realm traditionally belongs to the world of the seer, mystic, and shaman. Venturing there requires healthy skepticism. A good sense of "bullshit detection" is never a bad thing in life. But let us also be open to the experience of just trying things and seeing what happens. Deciding intellectually that something has no merit without exploring and testing the ideas presented is not skepticism. It is bias.

Having a profound experience in nonphysical realms can be a peak experience in one's life. It can also be the source of permanent frustration because of the limitations of our language to communicate things that exist far beyond the realm of our five senses.

Part III

Perception as Reality: Beginning to Change the Rules

Sit down before a fact as a little child, be prepared to give up every preconceived notion, follow humbly wherever and to whatever abyss nature leads, or you will learn nothing.

—Thomas H. Huxley

7

Right Brain, Left Brain, and Whole Brain: Perspective and Opportunity

Popular culture designates right- and left-brain thinking. It is convenient to generalize the right-brain perspective as artistic, intuitive, or creative in its approach to life. The left-brain viewpoint is more ordered, logical, and structured. There are proponents supporting the integration of right- and left-brain approaches. In simple terms, this "whole-brain" approach represents a synergistic combination of the left and right approaches and might offer a greater level of insight into many things.

For purposes of discussion and illustration, let us return to a few of my experiences during my Gateway Voyage week at TMI to explore right-, left-, and whole-brain explanations of nonordinary experiences. I will provide an example at each Focus Level.

Focus 12

In Focus 12, there is an experience of dissociation from the physical body, yet there is no fear or apprehension about this. I feel buoyant. There is a complex sensation of being energetic and quiet at the same time. I feel serenity and a concentrated sensation of "getting bigger." The impression of freedom is phenomenal. After a formal introduction to Focus 12 and a few practice exercises, we are offered the opportunity for a Focus 12 free-flow experience of our own design. The following is from my notes:

> After achieving the Focus 12 state, I remember that my wife, Pamela, and I had made an agreement about testing TMI experiences. If I felt at any time during the week that I could actually leave my body while at TMI, I would try to visit her at home. Throughout the week, she would be alert to any impression or feeling that I had done so and would note, in writing, the day and time. As I become comfortable in Focus 12 during this tape, I think about her and picture her in my mind with the intent of going to her.
>
> Instantaneously, I find myself standing in our living room and looking at Roger, our pet macaw. I find this to be a realistic and physical scene. As I increase my intensity of focus in this scene, Roger appears to take notice of me. Of course, I have no idea if this is a physical perception or one that might take advantage of some animal level of perception. This could be an interesting discussion in itself. Are animals able to perceive energy formats that we only perceive in altered states? My sense is that Roger is startled by my presence and is reacting to it. I look quickly around for my wife, but do not see her.
>
> I suddenly grow impetuous for no apparent reason. I feel that I cannot take the time to go looking for Pamela, and I become obsessed with the idea that I need to move on and travel some more. This whole event becomes amusing to me. The speed, the freedom, and the lightness of my being provide a surge of positive energy and euphoria.
>
> I realize that on a nonphysical level, my consciousness can be reduced to a single point of light in a vast universe, and I can instantaneously go anywhere I want. This seems to be a brilliant insight and requires immediate action. I must try this out, and I do so. With a simple but focused thought, I successfully become a single point of light and find an immediate rush of power and energy that is

intoxicating. An almost hysterical urge overcomes me. I want to see the entire universe, and *right now!*

I form the thought of the moon and instantly I am there. I can see, feel, and hear the vastness of silence and the huge desert of gray. I have to try as much of this mode of travel as quickly as possible. I begin racing to and fro all around the solar system. I experience planets, galaxies, and stars off in the distance. I know I can return to any of these at any point in the future when I have more time. Right now I just want to see as much as possible as fast as possible.

Abruptly the tape ends. Disappointed, I reluctantly follow Bob Monroe's guided instructions back to the C-1 level and find myself back in my CHEC unit. I scribble notes and return to the group room for the debriefing.

Let's look at this experience from left-brain, right-brain, and whole-brain perspectives. Normally, in Western culture, we utilize the structured approach of a left-brain perspective. Our consensus definitions of what is real come from this perspective; in the case of my experience, we would easily make strong arguments that these sensations of leaving the body are fantasy and exclusively in the realm of imagination.

In this instance, however, there is a situation that challenges this left-brain analysis. When my wife and I compare written records later, her notes reflect that she felt my presence only once during that week. It was the same morning that I had done this Focus 12 tape exercise recording my visit home. About that same time of day, she had been in our bedroom reading, and "felt" me there, noted the time, and also took note that at that same time, our macaw had become very agitated in her cage in the living room for no apparent reason. The left brain assumes that this is "just a coincidence."

From a right-brain perspective, this experience is "the way things are" as accepted by other cultures or within the world of the tribal shaman or skilled Eastern meditator. Some Eastern cultures, for example, have centuries of such explorations that have resulted in highly developed literatures complete with maps and guideposts to what one may find in these states of consciousness. Similarly, in many tribal societies, there are rituals and ceremonies, some with psychotropic trappings, to guide nonphysical sojourners as they seek game in the physical world or battle in the spirit world to protect family and tribe. Even in Western culture, many occultists, mystical thinkers, and New-Agers feel comfortable with this line of thought in terms of "astral travel," in spite of the fact that it is at odds with prevailing science and culture.

Facing hard data presented by documented shared experiences forces us to pause and think about how hard-and-fast we consider the rules of physical reality. This may be the case as one reviews the experimental laboratory research supporting out-of-body phenomena. The late Michael Talbot, author and researcher, provided a stimulating overview of psi experience and frontier quantum physics in his book *The Holographic Universe*:

> OBEs have also been documented in the lab. In one experiment, parapsychologist Charles Tart was able to get a skilled OBEer he identifies only as Miss Z to identify correctly a five-digit number written on a piece of paper that could only be reached if she were floating in an out-of-body state. In a series of experiments conducted at the American Society for Psychical Research in New York, Karliss Osis and psychologist Janet Lee Mitchell found several gifted subjects who were able to "fly in" from various locations around the country and correctly describe a wide range of target images, including an object placed on a table, colored geometric patterns placed on a free floating shelf near the ceiling, and optical illusions that could only be seen when an observer peered through a small window with a special device.[1]

Explaining such phenomena requires a new level of objectivity, one in which neither the right-brain "open" perspective, nor the left-brain "total proof" outlook would predetermine the approach. Whole-brain viewpoints are needed in which nothing is taken for granted. Further, the accepted laws of physical reality would have to be reproven and possibly broadened in light of emerging data about psi and nonlocal phenomena. Acceptance by our culture will require a new openness to discussing personal experiences with such phenomena.

Focus 15

I experience the Focus 15 level as an intensely liberating sensation enshrouded in an all-encompassing gray mist. One of our Focus 15 tapes is a guided experience entitled "Elation Galaxy." The basic construct of this exercise is to envision the energy body, or REBAL, as getting larger and larger. We practice becoming the size of our CHEC unit, the building, the state, the nation, the world, and so on. Eventually, we have self-expanded to the degree that we are larger than the Milky Way, and we are instructed to encircle the galaxy with our arms.

My experience turns out to take this quite a bit further, and with some fascinating side effects. Excerpts from my notes and an expanded narrative of the experience follow:

Reached 10 almost as soon as I closed my eyes. Prep process helped. Good REBAL. Focus 12 was a little shaky, but I finally just decided it was a little lower and closer to 10.

At 15, went over the hills through the mist. Settled in pretty well. Popped out above the tower, but came back as Bob started introductions. Expanded to world by stretching and "opening"— hard to describe. Went to solar system, but didn't stop. I was a giant circle that just kept pushing outward—further and further, faster and further—just kept going forever. Heard Bob talking about clusters and stars, but I was passing through them so fast. I knew that was all physical space, but when you get that large and spread out, the nature of the vibrational distinction starts to become apparent.

When everyone was supposed to be holding the galaxy, I saw many class members doing so. We seemed to attract some attention from "around" us, and then I got the feeling "Oh, it's another one of Bob's classes." This was a big joke and very, very funny.

As soon as the instructions came to return, I started to move fast for a while, then slow, then fast. It seemed that I had to "gather some of me in" as I returned—very airy and light, but I found my physical body still there in the CHEC. It appeared to be very dense.

The return through the Focus Levels felt unusually heavy. 15 felt heavy like 12. 12 felt like 10. I heard the instruction to go to 12 and settled in there pretty well, but then all I heard was the C-1 instruction. My body began jerking and convulsing on its own—pretty heavy at 15, subsided on the way down to 12. Had real trouble getting into C-1. Heard the trainers repeating 1, 1, 1, 1.

It's hard to imagine how dense I feel at this point in the confines of my human form. I feel as if I weigh tons instead of pounds. I find I am so heavy that I cannot seem to lift myself from the mattress in the CHEC unit. I slowly am able to roll onto my side and begin to crawl very slowly out of the CHEC unit. In seemingly extra slow motion, I put on my shorts and a shirt. My slow motion is supported by a sensation of being encased in lead. I have a recurring thought of needing to get outside to "ground."

Grounding is an exercise that we have been taught to apply if we find we have any problem reorienting ourselves after a deep altered-state experience. Specifically, grounding means doing things that bring attention and focus to the physical body. Being outside, perspiring under sunlight, vocalizing primal sounds, physical exercise, being barefoot in the grass, even grabbing rocks, and so on, can help one ground.

Returning to my notes:

I immediately begin to sense a difference as I exit the building and feel cool fresh air around me. My lead-encased body still seems to be exceptionally weak, however, and it is difficult to move. I cannot focus my awareness. It is a very drugged-like sensation. I struggle slowly across the parking lot and sit on the solid rock wall by the parking lot. I feel exhausted. I still know, however, that grounding is the key to recovery. I realize I am sitting on solid rock, so I open my shirt to the sunlight and recline on the wall. This, too, feels good, but I still am not experiencing the expected grounding recovery response.

I decide to try something else. I sit up and take off my shoes, so I can feel the rough gravel against my feet. I do a visualization exercise we have been taught. It involves imagining treelike roots extending down from my spine and growing all the way to the middle of the Earth. Still not much happens. I start to feel a chill, so I button my shirt and lie back down on the rock wall. (Later, in discussion with the trainers, I realized my mistake in all these efforts. I kept shutting my eyes. In so doing, I was immediately drifting back into the very altered states from which I was attempting to escape.)

At this point, Van comes out of the building and spots me lying on the wall. Van is an amiable and jocular unemployed forklift mechanic. He is a lifelong meditator who began the process at age seven in India where his father had been in U.S. government service. This background, combined with his large size, has earned him my nickname of Buddha-Buddha Van. I noted that a few other participants had begun calling him this as well, which he seems to enjoy immensely. Of course, I think Buddha-Buddha Van immensely enjoys almost everything in life.

Buddha-Buddha Van has come out to get one of his beloved Pepsis from his stash in the cooler in his car. He notices me, comes over, smiles heartily, and says "Hello." As he approaches, I struggle, but sit up to talk. Talking counts as grounding, too. He asks if I am OK. I say I am a bit spacey from that last tape and need some grounding, but I am not getting much action.

He kneels down and hugs me around the waist in an attempt to provide a greater connection to the Earth. I feel him touch me, but my sense is that he is simply holding me down, and it keeps me from flying off the planet. I am a bit loopy, and it appears that nothing I can do can get me physically refocused in the here and now. Yet, in all of this, I am very mellow and there is no hint of fear or concern. My perspective is that I am feeling fatigued.

As we sit there, I begin to feel a tingling around my hands. It is as if some sort of energy is building around the area of my fingers and palms. I mention this. Van rises from his kneeling position and sits down. He asks me if I am OK, or if he should get some assistance from the trainers. I respond that my hands are starting to tingle. He takes my hands in his.

"Holy shit!" he exclaims. "Your hands are colder than ice." As he makes the comment, the tingling sensation begins to move rapidly up my arms. It is if there is an electrical energy that now stretches from my hands to my biceps. My arms are *alive* with tingling sensations. This is not numbness but more of an active vibration of some sort of electrical phenomena.

"Van, I think I'm going to need some help," I finally mutter. "But please don't leave me. Please help me inside." Van hoists me up, and I droop over his gargantuan frame. Strangely, I still am not afraid, nor am I in any way disturbed about this strange turn of events. I remain mellow and seem to watch this process as an aloof but interested observer.

About halfway across the parking lot, the electric tingle moves up my arms and starts across my shoulders. In the outer edges of my field of vision appears something akin to "snow" on a television screen. As this black-and-white television snow begins to narrow my field of vision, it is accompanied by popping in my ears. Van somehow gets me inside the building and down the stairs to sit on the couches outside the group room. As he leaves to get assistance, the curtain of flickering snow closes and I can see nothing else. I am so engrossed in watching and listening to this "snow" that I fail to realize that I am no longer able to see anything else. The popping in my ears now surrounds my entire head, and I begin to realize that this is like being *inside* a Fourth-of-July fireworks sparkler.

As I lie on the couch, my mind seems to be simultaneously experiencing and observing what is going on. Some part of my mind recognizes that I should be frightened, but I am not. I am so focused on the strange nature of seemingly being inside an energetic sparkler that the reality of being blind doesn't seem to be much of a big deal. The "electric snow" phenomenon is so interesting that I have no fear or concern. In fact, I am comfortable just wondering what is going to happen next.

"What's the problem?" It is Charleene.

Van has returned from summoning help. I also hear the voices of Carol and Tina, the retired medical technician, who was sitting with Carol and Charleene when Van appeared seeking assistance.

Somehow, I am able to communicate what is happening. The tingling sensation is now giving way to a sense of my body dissolving from physical matter into electrical energy. As soon as Charleene comes near my left arm with her hands, she exclaims, "Oh, yeah, he is *really* charged up. He has brought a *bunch* of energy back with him."

She encourages me to get up and get outside in the grass where she can guide my grounding exercise. I reply that I cannot get up, but that I can possibly slide off the couch and onto the floor if that will help. My state of dual mind is still in play. It seems that I should be scared about what is going on. But no fear develops, only curiosity and fascination. I am experiencing and observing at the same time. It is a strange perspective.

I slide down onto the floor and am surrounded in attempts to "brush away" the excess "energy" that I seem to be experiencing, but with only moderate success. Charleene repeats her plea to get me outside, but my body will not respond. Finally, Buddha-Buddha Van stretches his body across my chest, brings his head very close to my ear and whispers ever so gently, "So, how about it—is this Hemi-Sync stuff a crock of crap? Or what?"

This comment penetrates me to the core, and I laugh hysterically. I lose all control. For some reason, this is the funniest thing that I have ever heard. Charleene asks, "What happened?" as I bend double in guffaws and giggles. Van tells her, and she, too, erupts into a laughing spree. This quickly spreads to Carol and Tina as well.

I laugh so hard my abdomen aches, but with each gasped breath between laughing spells, I realize that the curtains are opening in my vision, and the popping sounds are diminishing. As my eyes clear of TV snow, I see that the group is on the floor, rolling in tearful and obsessive guffaws. It turns out that this type of laughter is about the most grounding thing that can happen.

Although my vision has mostly cleared, I am still weak and need additional attention. Between my giggles, Charleene asks if I think

I might make it outside. I respond that I think I can. I get on my feet with their assistance and we walk outside arm in arm as a group of bonded chucklers, each of us wiping away tears of laughter. Charleene instructs me to lie in the grass and visualize myself as "draining" off energy.

She continues, "You have brought a lot of energy back with you. Mother Earth needs this type of healing energy—give it to her." At this point my hands grab hold of clumps of grass, and I begin a series of abdominal convulsions.

I feel surges of electrical energy pulsing through and around my body. I feel lightning bolts of electricity form deep within my body and discharge into the Earth. I sense the capacity of the Earth to convert these discharges in some manner of healing process. I visualize the planet with me lying on it. I seem so incredibly and insignificantly small, as the scale is so immense. I realize that the convulsive level of electrical lightning bolts that I am experiencing is so small it is unnoticed in the size of the planet. I keep thinking of this, as my body seems to discharge whatever energetic activity is at play here.

As I try to communicate this vision to Charleene, my body drops into deeper convulsive activity. I feel silly as I envision myself flopping about like a fish out of water. I don't know if it actually looks that bad or not. I manage to get out a few words conveying I am not resistant or afraid of this process, whatever it is. I seem to be releasing energy and returning to normal.

The convulsions finally run their course and subside. Charleene asks if I can walk. I sit up and realize all the sparkling, tingling stuff is gone and I can see again, but now with an enhanced, almost surreal, level of clarity. I stand. My legs are stable. Charleene and I walk off arm in arm through the grass.

Almost any comment either of us makes strikes us both as exceptionally humorous and giggles again begin. Charleene keeps our pace brisk and asks if I feel well enough to jog a little with her. I do, and we lope around the area until I am fully functional, tired but strangely calm. When we eventually return inside, the mealtime is over, but the kitchen staff heat up some food for me. Sleep is very deep and good that night.

From a right-brained approach of many New Age proponents, this experience could be termed as an immersion in energy (pick your own name for an otherworldly source) and possibly a transdimensional excursion. Left-brained skeptics could easily dismiss the event as some sort of self-induced hysterical phenomenon or wonder if I should immediately be checked for signs of brain lesions.

But what did happen to me that day? From my own continuing inquiry after my week at TMI, I was fascinated to find that dramatic experiences are common among those who practice meditation and yogic techniques. I found insight in the writing of Fritz Frederick Smith, a medical doctor who later researched Asian medicine. In his thoughtful book *Inner Bridges: A Guide to Energy Movement and Body Structure,* he relates his first exposure to phenomena similar to my TMI convulsive releases. He defines a *kriya* as an involuntary response that happens as powerful subtle energies in the body encounter congestion of some form.

> The first time I encountered a major physical kriya was at a meditative retreat. A man was on the ground, appearing to my medically trained eye to be suffering an epileptic seizure. I rushed over, intending to give first aid, when an experienced meditator came up and calmly touched him on the leg. In a brief moment the seizure began to subside, and the man returned to normal consciousness. To my further surprise, I found, talking with him later, that his experience was not only not a frightening one, but fulfilling and enriching and was followed by a great sense of peace and serenity. Again my medical model was shaken, and I have wondered since how many kriya experiences have been diagnosed as and treated as "epilepsy."[2]

I have given this Focus 15 example primarily as an illustration of heightened sensitivity to subtle forms of energy that are unfamiliar to our normal Western culture, minds, and bodies. I am compelled, however, to share one other aspect of this exercise. What I actually saw as I envisioned myself out among the galaxies did not reach its full impact until four years later. As part of my computer network employment, I was invited to present at the 1999 NASA Partners in Education and Research Conference held in Cocoa Beach, Florida. As part of that conference, participants were treated to a presentation that featured images from the Hubble telescope.

One image not only left me awestruck, but reignited the emotional response of my "Elation Galaxy" experience at TMI, four years before. When the slide of the Hubble Deep Field photo appeared on the screen, I was instantly transported back into my visionary journey and subtle energy experiences. This particular Hubble image contains the deepest view ever of the universe as taken by the Hubble telescope on January 15, 1996. The picture shows hundreds of multicolored galaxies, each far greater in size than the Milky Way. It is such a striking photo that it is sold as a poster entitled *Gallery of Galaxies.*

My immersion in this image was due to the fact that this was the sight I had experienced at TMI. Further, the experience at TMI included the complete scene, not merely the small camera view taken by the Hubble. It was as if one took a snapshot of the Grand Canyon and then was terribly disappointed with the picture because it showed such a small portion of the actual scene. I had not simply seen this scene, however, I had experienced it. As the picture appeared on the screen during the NASA program, the latent emotions from the majesty of my TMI experience overcame me, and I was forced to leave the room to process the interface of these two powerful events.

Trying to share such an experience is like a conversation between two people about Paris. Three different types of communication can occur. If neither person has been to Paris, perception and perspective can only be drawn vicariously—from books, magazines, movies, or television shows. If both have been to Paris, both can talk from a shared experience. In the third type, the most difficult for communication, one has been there, and one has not. This communication option has maximum opportunity for misunderstanding; only partial understanding is possible for each participant. The one who has been to Paris can never again experience it for the first time, and the one who has never been there can only in a limited way understand the emotion, passion, and texture as described by the one who has traveled there.

Human communication is complicated enough when speaking about sense-based data, but trying to describe nonphysical realms in physical terms is fraught with peril. It is akin to an Eastern tradition that outlines an interesting perspective on the process of communication: As a master tries to pass on his experience and knowledge, the limitations of human communication distort it.

An experience exists as a memory and thought for the master. He tries to form words to explain or convey it. He does the best he can. Yet once the words leave the master's mouth, they are no longer the experience of the master, but the interpretations of those words by the student. This is sort of an ultimate level of the old party game "gossip" when each person whispers a saying to the one next to them, and what emerges after going through the whole group usually bears little resemblance to the initial phrase whispered.

Focus 21

Focus 21 is achieved toward the end of the TMI Gateway program. By that point, students feel comfortable with altered states. The tapes still follow the standard format of surf, "energy conversion box," resonant tuning drone, affirmation, REBAL formation, then the taped exercise. In one sense, this is a form of classic conditioning through repetitive process—a standard way to incorporate new skills. The following is an excerpt of my experiences during a tape entitled "Super Flow 21," which is the culmination tape of the week-long Gateway experience.

At the beginning of the exercise, I am tired of the intensity of focused attention, so I decide to just drift along with the pink noise and masked binaural beats of the Hemi-Sync tape. After what feels like 35 to 40 minutes of drifting, but is, in reality, probably only five minutes, I "bump" into something. This causes me to refocus my awareness to perceive better what is going on. I sense that I am at the upper boundary of the Focus 21 state. How can that be? There shouldn't be any boundaries. I don't understand this since we are supposedly in the unlimited realm of the nonphysical. But there is a clear image and sensation that I have bumped into some sort of wall.

This boundary appears as a very thin (only a one-cell thickness) membrane. I know at this point that I can move into the advanced state of Focus 27 (a deeply altered state not covered in this introductory workshop) if I want. That doesn't seem to be the right thing to do, however. I am resting, restoring, and integrating during this tape; I am not in the mood for advanced explorations. A thought forms.

It might be interesting to attempt to prick a hole in the membrane and see what happens. I try this. To my surprise, nothing comes through the pin-sized hole I have made. But then a strong sensation overcomes me and I realize that I am "bubbling" out through the hole that I have seen forming in this membrane.

The imagery and accompanying sensations become more ethereal, lighter, and whiter. All color blurs into a whiter-than-white omnipresence. I continue to drift, with no particular purpose but drifting itself. I realize that I have possibly become pure consciousness. I am formless. There is no longer an energy REBAL. There is no sense of vibration. There is nothing. I am simultaneously "there" and "not there." I am conscious and aware but in a very unusual state of being.

Finally, after what seems to be a week in this state, there is the familiar recorded voice of Bob Monroe, signaling the end of the tape and calling me back. I feel myself start to fall. This turns out to be a falling sensation like nothing I have ever experienced before. It is similar to what a free fall from an airplane must feel like. It is all a *downward* sensation. I have the physical (yet I am very much in the nonphysical) sensation of a very long fall. This is a fall of trillions of miles. I fall for days. I fall for months. I fall for years.

Then comes the feeling, or at least the thought, that I have been "clicking out" in half-sleep and that I will suddenly "wake up" in C-1. Yet this will be difficult, as I am still alert and conscious enough to have this thought. I cannot believe I am falling all this way and am still not out of Focus 21 (or wherever?). All of a sudden, I feel ten or 20 pairs of hands grab me from behind and hold on to me. This is again a physical sensation, yet I am still aware I am within the nonphysical and participating in the tape session. Is this a dream? Words are limited as I attempt to convey these sensations! Finally, after what is an extremely long time, Bob's voice says, "21, 21, you are safe and secure in Focus 21."

I am a little confused but still aware of being conscious through all of this. How far out and where did I go? Then Bob says "21! 21! 21!" As these numbers are spoken, I realize that I am settling in at the "base level" of what I have come to identify as Focus 21 in previous tapes. This experience is beyond the meaning of the words used. I then go quickly from 21 to 15, to 12, and then hesitate there for what seems like several days. I am feeling so light that I am having trouble keeping track of myself. It seems that I am getting lighter as I come down instead of heavier.

From Focus 12 to Focus 10 is a quick trip, but I seem to be getting even lighter still. I think, "Geez, I still feel like I'm at more like Focus 40, if it exists, instead of Focus 10. Why am I so light?"

When I finally arrive at what I think is the C-1 level, I am surprised (but not frightened) to realize that I am looking down (again in the OBE awareness state) on where I am supposed to be lying in the CHEC unit. I find that my physical body is not present in the CHEC unit. My bed is empty. There is a depression there, in the mattress and pillow as if someone is lying there, but no physical form is visible. It finally comes to me that I need to form a body if I ever expect to get back into one. Somehow I manage to create a body by "thinking" one. It *is* me or at least a version of my physical form, but then again it really isn't. Then it seems that there is enough substance there that represents me that it becomes possible to "ooze" into it and create more substance from the inside out.

I am overcome with great joy and humor. I attempt to ground myself into physical reality by verbalizing "C-1, C-1, C-1." The wake-up beta tones go unnoticed about the time I am attempting to ooze into my newly formed body. I keep trying to move my right fingers, but there isn't enough substance to them to have any sensation of physical movement.

I get dense enough that my hand will move, and this allows me to gain more and more physical sensation. Overall, I still feel fairly wispy. With additional effort, I can move a bit physically. I stretch my arms up in front of my face and draw up my legs in a wake-up stretch at the same time. I open my eyes and am surprised to see newborn infant hands instead of my own. I become fascinated with this hallucination.

As I watch, my hands quickly grow to normal size. Concurrently, I realize my body is doing the same thing. I feel the covers slide under my back and legs as my body gets longer and fuller. I realize also that I have a *huge* grin on my face, ear to ear. I feel happier and more alive than I have ever felt.

I roll over on the mattress to make these notes. Surprisingly, there has been no sense of fear during all these strange occurrences, but more a keen interest in being part of them and experiencing them fully. Then I realize that there is a loud knocking at the door.

John, the trainer, is rapping on the door, calling my name repeatedly. He continues to ask if I am OK. Apparently this activity has put me well past all the normal instructions and the participants had already gathered in the group room for debriefing. I have not turned off my "ready light," and there is concern that I may have fallen asleep or may still be in an altered state. I respond that I am fine and have had a wonderful experience. I also say that I am still writing about it, and will be out shortly.

Now for the normal left-brained analysis. I'm sure that many psychologists and psychiatrists could provide a litany of what may be experienced while one is in dissociative, altered states of consciousness. There are probably mounds of research about people seeing and feeling things such as these in drug-induced hallucinatory experiences. Such discourses might even explain away the implications of what might be considered a profound personal experience. But is it all that simple?

On the right-brain side, there can be the interpretations of the mystical, transcendental, and visionary types. Indeed, I have now found that there are voluminous literatures created about this level of transcendental and transformative state. But what does one do with a totally right-brained approach? Other than personal transformation and exploration of philosophical issues, our culture has few outlets for such experiences.

If we pursue whole-brain holistic approaches to such nonordinary experiences, we can broaden the scope of what we allow to be real. If we expand our parameters of experience, investigation, and discussion, we find that great numbers in our society have had experiences either similar to this or as profound. We also find that some people having had such an experience do not feel free to discuss it for fear of being ridiculed.

With a broader view, perhaps we can provide greater insight into claims of experiencing angelic realms, dead relatives, or spirit guides. It is sad that society fails to recognize the value of broadening our horizons to include such experiences as a normal part of human life. Dr. Charles Tart, respected parapsychology researcher, says in his book *Altered States of Consciousness:*

> Within Western culture we have strong negative attitudes toward altered states of consciousness: there is the normal (good) state of consciousness and there are pathological changes in consciousness. Most people make no further distinctions. We have available a great deal of scientific and clinical material on altered states of consciousness associated with psychopathological states such as schizophrenia: by comparison, our scientific knowledge about altered states of consciousness which could be considered "desirable" is extremely limited and generally unknown to science.[3]

Viewing altered states and whole brain approaches as a spiritual activity offers philosophical meaning for our culture. Deepak Chopra comments extensively on this in his *Unconditional Life:*

> The loss of spiritual experience, in both East and West, has shattered the higher aspirations of human life. . . . The intellect's need to explore the world, which began in the remote past and reached its peak in modern times, eventually took us so far into the

diversity of creation that the source of creation—our own awareness—was lost sight of. Inner experiences of bliss and infinite
expansion, of complete freedom and boundless power, became
"mystical." . . . the hard reality of "out there" has become so compelling that spirit is allowed little if any power at all.[4]

We must move our society and ourselves toward a more whole-
brain perspective in discussion, investigation, and acceptance of a
broader view of what is called reality. Such an approach could possibly provide us with new tools for expression of the totality of who
and what we are. Here, too, we may find the secrets needed to
address the compounding problems of a technological society by
expanding the nature of our search for the appropriate tools.

Once having had an experience of a nonphysical or spiritually
transformative nature, it is a natural desire to have another one. The
idea that "I want to feel that good again" or "I want to go back
there" is certainly expected. I suspect that there are those who spend
the rest of their lives trying to do so. If we take the Paris travel communication scenario in a different direction, however, we might find
that a repeat of the original peak experience is impossible.

Rather than Paris this time, let us look at one's first trip to a
beach. The sound and power of the surf, the smell of the salt air, the
feel of the sand can be experienced for the first time only once. Yet
each time one returns to the beach, a wonderful and different experience is possible. This may be the case when one has an intense
experience in expanded consciousness. Once experienced, the base
frame of reference is altered and then can be built on. While we may
not have "the Light" level of experience in its power and profundity
a second time, our worldview may have expanded in such a way that
all of life may be experienced as a "return to the beach" of "the
Light."

While TMI and the technology of Monroe's Hemi-Sync are not
the only path to expanded perception, they have affected a great
many individuals. The noted physician and psychiatrist Dr. Elisabeth
Kübler-Ross was a personal friend of Monroe and visited his home
and laboratory. In one such visit, as a result of a session in Bob's lab-

oratory, she had her own experience with the "Light" and described it in *The Wheel of Life:*

> At this point I realized that I had left my physical body and become energy. Then in front of me, I saw many incredibly beautiful lotus blossoms. These blossoms opened very slowly and became brighter, more colorful and more exquisite, and as time passed they turned into one breathtaking and enormous lotus blossom. From behind the flower, I noticed a light—bright and totally ethereal, the same light that all my patients talked about having seen.
>
> . . . . My vision, which extended for miles and miles, caused me to see everything, from a blade of grass to a wooden door, in its natural molecular structure, its vibrations. I observed, with great awe and respect, that everything had a life, a divinity. All the while, I continued to move slowly through the lotus flower, toward the light. Finally, I was merged with it, one with the warmth, and love. A million everlasting orgasms cannot describe the sensation of the love, warmth, and sense of welcome that I experienced.[5]

Leaving the physical body and returning invites thoughts of conquering death. These are weighty psychological, metaphysical, and religious concepts. Approaching life with a greater knowledge or acceptance of one's view about what one might find there (upon death), however, is certainly a potentially liberating experience. Since my experiences at TMI, I no longer fear death. My view is that I have ever so slightly brushed up against the totality of consciousness that is beyond both birth and death.

That is not to say that I would not fear a group of thugs in a dark alley. Of course I would, but the fear is not from what I might find on the "other side" or whether it even exists. The fear is recognition of possible bodily pain and the awareness of the boundless potential of the options presented in life itself that could be lost. There is so much here to see, do, and experience in this physical life that I value each precious moment of it at a level that was not possible before my experience with "the Light" during the "touching infinity" tape session at TMI.

Indeed, Bob Monroe pondered this in *Ultimate Journey:*

> If I knew with no trace of doubt what I would be and do after I died, it would change me radically. I could live my physical life to the fullest, without a shadow lurking behind every second, the shadow that says *one wrong move and your time is up!* If we knew that each of us had the option to depart when we were certain our physical future held no more light for us, how our lives would be transformed! If we had the assurance that, no matter what happens, we can continue our love bonding beyond the Earth Life System and time-space—if we were certain that when a loved one departs we would know beyond doubt where we can find him or her—what a wonderful freedom we would have![6]

The idea of reaching out and touching more of the totality of who and what we are–the True Self–can be mind-boggling. Reaching out into the unseen, the unfelt, the unheard, the unsmelled, and the untouched can be more than daunting. It can be terrifying. Actually experiencing something in these realms turns the theoretical into the real, and the idea is terrifying that there might be parts of us larger and more powerful than our conscious mind can comprehend, much less control. This would mean that we would be touching far beyond the reach of our egos and it would move us into admitting a totality of self that encompasses the many worlds or dimensions far beyond our limited physical one. Touching this level is an experience, not an intellectual exercise.

8

Accepting What You Only Think You Can See: Turning the Kaleidoscope

I encountered another example of expanded awareness and heightened perception in an experience during the TMI Gateway program. Toward the end of the weeklong program, attendees participate in a no-tape exercise followed by a silent walk. In this exercise, they are encouraged to achieve the altered states represented by the Focus Levels while walking around with eyes open. This is a significant departure from the highly sheltered environment of the CHEC unit supported by psychoacoustic Hemi-Sync technology.

In this no-tape exercise, one experiences all the events that, by this point in the week, have become classically conditioned in a Pavlovian way. One retires to the CHEC unit, puts on the earphones, listens to calming ocean surf, tones, performs the affirmation, forms the REBAL, and moves progressively through the Focus Levels of 10, 12, 15, and 21. Only this time, there is no tape playing. At the beginning of the week, I had felt strange when confronted with the initial tape activity. This feeling subsided as the experiences quickly became both entertaining and challenging.

Faced with the idea of the no-tape exercise, it, too, initially seemed stupid. Lying in your CHEC *pretending* to hear a tape was a bit much for me. Back came the questions of "Why am I doing this?" "This is silly, nothing is going to happen." "You can't achieve an altered state without Hemi-Sync."

In carrying it out, however, I obediently go to my CHEC, place the earphones on my head, and try to figure out how we would know when we are finished the exercise. These questions quickly subside as I begin to hear (or think I do) the sounds of the ocean surf, the resonant tuning tones, and the now-trusted Hemi-Sync. It seems obvious to me that this exercise is a sham—there is indeed a tape playing. I hear the surf, tone along at the appropriate time, say my affirmation, and go right on up through the Focus Levels to have experiences that I will write up in my journal afterward just as before.

Amazingly, we all seem to complete the exercise within just a few minutes of each other, and within the window of the normal tape length. Of course, the trainers assure us during the debriefing that there was no tape playing, but we only partially believe them. My mind "believes" there was a tape, and it was a very real experience.

My left-brain analyzer quickly kicked in. It did seem plausible that after performing this tape routine over and over daily for several days, the mind and body might create a structured set of responses that occur whether the stimulus exists or not. Such conditioning is well known in psychological research. The constant routine enables attendees to move into altered states with greater ease and with increasing speed each day. Of course, the experience of each level of altered states is unique to each individual. Enough commonality was present as we shared our experiences, however, to reinforce the process. This had the effect of both reassuring each individual that other realities may exist and confirming actual experiences of the group in these new environments.

The trainers note a vital point during the debriefing of the no-tape exercise. There was an important lesson to learn. Just as meditators and monastic dwellers have long known, one does not need psychoacoustic assistance to achieve altered states. It is a normal part of who we are, and all we need to do is become more mindful of these states of perception, and possibly suspend the belief that these states are not real and/or are impossible to achieve. It may have been that since many of us "believed" there was a tape playing, our minds filled in the blank spaces of needed physical sound.

The lesson is powerful on two counts. One, that psychoacoustic tape support is not necessary for strong experience and altered states to occur; and two, that the mind can fill in the blank spaces of expected reality to conform to our beliefs about an event.

The silent walk follows the no-tape event. The silent walk is a standard program element that occurs toward the end of the TMI Gateway experience. It is a simple exercise, but one that can challenge the neophyte voyager. Simply stated, one takes an extended walk outside, in silence, avoiding others, and concentrating on achieving the Focus Levels of 10, 12, 15, and 21, which one has experienced during the workshop.

As I move outside to do this exercise, I imagine not much will happen. After all, the experiences so far required a deep state of relaxation, closed eyes, and no distractions. Even the no-tape exercise, which precedes the silent walk, took place in the supportive environment of the undisturbed CHEC unit. As I walk, I review the week and attempt to remember the "feel" of each Focus Level. I think about the events that occurred at Focus 10.

I realize a greater sense of aliveness. I notice that there is more clarity to my vision and hearing than normal. Left-brain thoughts immediately note that, after all, I have been spending most of the week stretched out on a mattress, so maybe I have achieved a deeper state of rest than my normal schedule allows. This would account for a sharpening of the senses in general. I realize that if I rested and took care of myself to the degree that the week had provided, I would probably be a much healthier individual and that this level of vision, hearing, and overall awareness would be my normal state.

What I did not realize until later, and continue to build on even now, is that my mental processes, in collaboration with my consciousness, had risen to a new level of awareness. I was experiencing a level of information input, physical sensitivity, and "being-ness" that was the result of bringing Focus 10 into my normal realm of consciousness and perception. My eyes were open. I was alert, awake, and walking around outdoors. I was also at the end of a week of repeated exercises that constantly shifted my consciousness to the "mind awake, body asleep" level of Focus 10 and beyond. Through these exercises, my mind, body, and consciousness had combined in some new way to broaden and deepen my awareness of the physical world.

In the silent walk, I walk and move into Focus 12. As I relive the experiences of Focus 12 during the past Gateway week, a similar shift in awareness and perception settles in and becomes part of me. I note that not only has my vision and hearing clarified, as in Focus 10, but also the colors of the trees and grass are more intense, more vibrant. They are deeper, richer, with texture I have never experienced. The colors in the sky and the clouds seem three-dimensional, if colors can be described this way. I am aware that the plants around me are living, breathing beings. While we are all probably "aware" of this intellectually, to *experience* this aliveness while walking around is a new way to perceive the world.

Simply being in this expanded state of awareness is pleasurable, but my left brain is operational, taking notes, and remembering the exercise instructions to move through the range of Focus Levels. I stop, close my eyes, and recapture the physical sensation of being in Focus 15. I open my eyes and the world in front of me shifts again. While the colors remain rich and textured, there is a shimmer of energy around almost everything. This is similar to heat rising from hot pavement or the vapors of gasoline as a car is fueled in just the right lighting. I wonder if these are the phenomena referred to by people who "see auras."

I realize I am beginning to see the world around me through a new level of perception. While I might previously have enjoyed a delightful sunset or a moon rising at dusk, I had never before experienced this depth and breadth of vision. I am surprised that it is in no way fleeting. Each shift in Focus Level is a distinct experience, and each seems to broaden the bandwidth of perception in significant ways.

There is not only increased vision and hearing, but also a new level of emotional attachment and feeling connected to what I see. This state of consciousness must be the way that the saints of old felt as they wrote of being *part* of the world in which they lived. This is a profound way of viewing the world and will take some time for me to digest and integrate.

As these realizations sink in, I remember that I still have Focus 21 to do. What will it hold? I take a deep breath and make the move. It is spectacular on multiple levels. The "shimmer" that surrounds things in Focus 15 now blossoms into full-spectrum energetic patterns beyond the capacity of any artist to capture. This expanded vision is physical and real, as if I have suddenly put on a special lens. Every tree, blade of grass, squirrel, bird, and every single thing in the world around me takes on a spectacular new appearance.

In a few moments, my tears flow. The realization of a larger Total Self that is involved in the seeing, hearing, and feeling of all of this emerges. I experience this as sort of a multiple screen show. While my vision and other senses move into new levels of perception of subtle energies, my left-brain, note-taking, and observer self is also at work. I seem to be able to take in this new information and simultaneously watch myself do it. I am still able to make ongoing internal commentary about it. I am emotional and tearful, but also logical, unemotional, and observational. It is like having an experience and watching a movie of it at the same time.

The part of me that is observing and making commentary is also reeling with the possibilities offered by bringing such a level of perception to the ordinary tasks of life. The part of me that is having the emotional experience is moving into a realm of consciousness that I thought was reserved for the mystically gifted. I sit on the grass, one with everything around me. . . .

The bell rings calling us back to normal consciousness and to the debriefing room for a discussion of the experience. It is quiet at the outset; a number of people have clearly undergone deep experiences. I make the initial comment that while I had not experimented with psychedelic drugs in the 1960s, the silent walk enabled visionary perception resembling what I had heard of and read about as being a positive LSD trip. Immediately, a voice from behind me speaks: "That's exactly what it is like, and it brought back memories!" Apparently others in the group had experienced LSD-induced perceptual shifts in their younger years. There is agreement that it is possible to move into the TMI-defined Focus Levels without a tape and while walking around, eyes open, and going about one's business. To me, this realization begins a shift in values about what in the physical world can be taken on face value as presented through the filtering lens of the five physical senses.

I consider myself ordinary. I am not the seventh son of a seventh son with a psychic destiny to fulfill. Nor did I suffer a major life-threatening event and emerge with demonstrable psi talents. No, I had merely been a bit curious. I read a few books and attended a workshop that provided technological support in achieving altered states of consciousness. There are many paths that can lead into altered states. Using one, I had gained a broader view of the world.

I am concerned about an area that many people may overlook. A mistake that many who go to The Monroe Institute make is to believe they are going there to duplicate the out-of-body experiences of Bob Monroe. The mistake is attempting to duplicate the experience of another rather than having your own unique experiences.

Healer, teacher, psychologist, and storyteller Dr. Mitchell May notes the importance of your own experience as part of the process of defining the reality in which you allow yourself to operate. His personal story, chronicled in his audiotape set *Healing, Living and Being,* is a heroic journey during which he recovered from massive injuries received in an automobile accident. His recovery, medically documented, involved significant use of energy healing modalities as part of a psi research effort at the University of California at Los Angeles Medical School.

During this process, Dr. May experienced a spiritual transformation as well as a "medically impossible" physical recovery. As he was presented with standard medical practice and a new approach by a talented hands-on healer, neither appealed to his worldview. He could not face losing his legs to standard medical procedures, nor could he fathom the unfamiliarity of hands-on healing. From this perspective, Dr. May notes:

I wasn't going to accept someone else's reality until it became a direct experience for myself. For me, that would kind of be the difference between having a spiritual experience and a religious experience. A religious experience, to me, is more based upon someone else's experience and what you're supposed to do to get there. A spiritual experience is having one directly for yourself. And that becomes its "own authority" unto your own life.[1]

I agree with Dr. May that direct experience is a key to learning to incorporate in daily life any information gathered from psi and nonlocal phenomena. We disregard the fact that, in using only our five senses, we may overlook large amounts of information that can be perceived only within altered states. We should not limit ourselves in what we can know. Even more important for our society is the need for open discussion of these experiences and letting them become an acceptable part of normal life. If these altered states of consciousness can become part of the normal range of conscious perception, then we may realize that we are on the cusp of an evolutionary leap.

9

Keeping Your Head Screwed on Straight While Expanding Your Awareness

One leaves The Monroe Institute weeklong experience in a highly sensitized state. For a full week you have been without a watch, TV, radio, newspaper, or other connection to the "real" world. You have been in a supportive group of people who accept you for who you are with no pretenses and no trappings of power or hierarchical values. Others prepare food and take care of your daily essentials and your needs. Throughout this week, you have repeatedly experienced a wide range of altered states and shared with others experiences that may have blurred your definitional boundaries.

How long would I maintain my new level of awareness? Would my experiences fade with time? During my plane ride home, I find how easily I can move into a state of deep relaxation. With only the slightest effort, I recapture the emotional and visionary aspects of "merging with the Light," and tears form. How long would such events continue? Such easy moves between altered state and normal perception can become confusing. A picture of shifting to a lifestyle of "dropping out" flashes before me. It can be easy to avoid the issues of everyday life by escaping to the warm comfort of altered states, seeking to rejoin my experience of "the Light." Sensations in blissful states of consciousness easily become seductive. I begin to understand why, historically, people with visionary experiences chose a monastic existence over returning to their pre-experience routines.

I am not a monk, however. I live in modern times and must get up, go to work, and relate with others. Out-of-body states, near-death experiences, and experiences of the ecstatic can easily become avoidance mechanisms, and that concerns me. I realize that separating fact from fantasy can sometimes be difficult in personally intense and emotional events. Shared experiences within a group can also create temporary group bonding at a deep level, and this, too, can confuse aspects of the reality of an experience. Just what occurred?

I review my notes and am struck by the number of times that the events were not simply my own, but had been shared experiences that involved the participation and corroboration of others. I conclude that TMI has provided me a taste of grace, a touch of bliss, or at least a whisper of eternity. Yet, if this is true, how will I ever be able to talk about it with anyone? How will I bring my experiences into some sort of balance with the realities of work and home life?

Fortunately, my return home is to a very supportive environment. My dear wife, Pamela, patiently sits through seven hours of my excited tales of people and events that had impacted my life in one week. She issues no challenge to my sanity. She listens, but also questions and guides me to question myself about aspects of the weeklong trip. I deeply appreciate the island of unconditional acceptance she represents. I wonder about others who return from such an experience to face nonsupportive family or are forced to deal with these experiences alone.

Facing a normal day at the office seems dreamlike after any sojourn to a holiday location. We return from our trip wishing that everyone there could have seen and heard the same things we did. Our mind remains partially within the experiences and sensations of our vacation while we begrudgingly reconnect to office routine. We try to share our experiences with those who did not travel with us, but it is challenging; it was our experience, not theirs. We have photos and stories, but we cannot re-create the sensations or the sights for others at the level we experienced them ourselves. Facing a normal workday after a week at TMI presents an even greater level of challenges than this.

On my return to the office the following Monday morning, I am still highly sensitive and my perceptive abilities sharp. I sense, to some degree, the emotional state of my coworkers and find this uncomfortable. Facing the inevitable questions about my trip, I find myself unable to say much other than it had been a "nice time." I feel awkward, out of place. I cannot bring myself to discuss what happened for fear of ridicule, and also possibly an undermining of my position as the director of a respected organization.

The openness to discuss nonordinary events that had been the hallmark at TMI is absent here. I fear saying something that will brand me as having become strange for no apparent reason. I have undergone a profound experience and now find it impossible to talk about it with anyone. To make matters worse, I apparently have some new level of sensitivity that enables me to sense my coworkers' reactions to my comments. I am not making any effort to move into an altered state, but I easily drift in and out of expanded perception.

Through e-mail contact with fellow TMI participants that day, I find I am not alone. Classmate Laurie, a computer systems engineer, had to leave her office her first day back. She felt stifled and unable to breathe in her high-tech, high-stress work environment. As she sat outside the building collecting herself, she realized she could see the cumulative stress and tension of her workplace as a brown cloud of congestion surrounding her office. Kyle, a psychotherapist, reported that during the first day back at his practice, he was able to sense issues within his clients at insight levels far beyond any he had previously experienced.

The day's schedule of the workplace eventually jars me into the here and now. In my absence, a meeting has been arranged for me with our absentee landlord, Mike. His investment group owns the office park in which our organization is housed, and we need additional space. During my trip, however, there has been an offer by another firm for a large block of space in the park at rates that exceeded what we were currently paying.

My financial staff had met with Mike before my return from Virginia, and he had indicated that he planned to cancel our lease on its upcoming renewal date, only two months away. His decision is to move us out to create more space for the other firm to rent our space at a higher rate. If this occurs, we will have to move our entire operation. This will cause extreme hardship on our office and centralized computer operations and negate our prized extended lease rates that we thought were optioned for years to come.

As I sit down to face Mike, I sense he intends to cancel our lease. I quickly, though unintentionally, slip into the same multiple level of awareness that had been present during the silent walk exercise at TMI. While I do not see auras or subtle energies, I seem to have access to new realms of data. To my surprise, I am able to sense what this man is thinking or feeling. I "know" what he is going to say before he says it. I "see" several possible responses from me play out in my mind, in ultraslow motion, with associated consequences. These scenarios all occur before Mike actually speaks. Yet he still speaks the same sentence I expect him to speak from my new level of seeing.

Strangely, the meeting turns out in our favor: We get a continuation of our contract and we get additional space in the park. My staff is astonished. Their comments center on my actions and demeanor, which are out of character for me. Normally, I would have been excitable, the bargaining position from which Mike expected to be working. I had done the opposite, however, and this had disconcerted him. His ploys were thwarted at every turn, as I quietly sat there and subtly turned every element of the discussion to my favor.

Reflecting on the meeting, I become concerned. Here I am, a solid citizen, a Ph.D., the head of a computer network with major issues and decisions to pursue, and I actually believe that I have just read someone's mind! This is not an easy situation in which to find oneself. I desperately want to maintain a healthy skepticism about my unfolding experiences, yet keep an open mind. This meeting challenged me. I was in unknown territory as to what is real and what a flight of fancy.

In retrospect, there are a number of ways to view the meeting with Mike. I was well rested and alert from my week in Virginia. This could have simply been a case of being relaxed and well prepared physically for what could have been a tense situation. It could also be viewed from the perspective that I was fired up with "nonlocal" perceptive abilities from TMI and that altered states of consciousness were in play that gave me insight from information gathered from outside the normal five senses. I believe it was this.

I did not make a conscious attempt to move into an altered state to meet with Mike. It just happened. I was alert and aware, within a naturally occurring expanded state of perception and heightened awareness. I now believe that this sort of perception is part of our human nature, if we allow it to blossom. This blossoming is a natural and ongoing process that we might attribute to intuition on a superficial level. Couldn't we say that intuitive insight is nothing more than some degree of information taken in from some level of unrealized altered state of consciousness?

I had no idea at what TMI Focus Level I was operating. Indeed, I now believe that once you gain a bit of experience in achieving various degrees of altered states, you simply go to the level at which you need to be working to gain the information necessary. The TMI Focus Levels are mere training wheels for a learning model, and they could also be considered a belief system.

I have become curious about what levels human interaction might move on if we could see beyond our masks and trappings of power and be in the presence of each other in a human, expanded level of communication. If all parties in a meeting were in tune with a broad spectrum of perception of each other, there would be a much greater understanding of each other's position and intent. Deception, deceit, and sly business ploys would not have a place in this scenario, as they would be embarrassingly transparent. Imagine a business meeting in which all the participants are relaxed enough to be open and perceptive to each other at something like the TMI Focus 10 level. A new level of honesty and collaborative opportunity could easily emerge. Further, we might open to the experience of intuitive insight that could offer significant thinking "outside the box" of our existing perspectives.

Over the next several months, I constantly struggle with a strong and healthy skepticism about my experiences at TMI. While at The Monroe Institute, I experienced emotional and significant events. At some level, I know my life is changing. Yet I do not want to be a workshop participant who returns home to quit his job and "find himself." Nor do I plan to announce to everyone that I now know the secrets of the universe.

First, I don't think I know the secrets of the universe. Second, I am suspicious of anyone who says they do. People back home are naturally suspicious of someone who suddenly no longer acts as they did before they left for "vacation." While TMI provided me with some challenging experiences, I don't want to fly off the deep end after only a short exposure to some new way of looking at things.

I find myself battling between seeking the comfort of escape to blissful states and keeping my feet on the ground in response to a lifetime of professional achievement. I have a good job and want to get better at it, not run away and escape with voices from the "astral planes." Yet meditation takes me to levels of such joy and wonder that it's difficult to return. Little by little, I grow comfortable with comments from friends and coworkers concerning my new calm nature and serenity. I have changed my former Type-A personality, in their view, for no apparent reason. In business meetings, I sense the concerns and issues of others, yet this awareness is not something that provides powers of manipulation or superiority. It simply provides understanding of people and the interconnected nature of everything.

I had to learn more about what had happened to me and about the nature of these experiences. I sought books about these phenomena and explored the writings of mystics who had obviously trod these paths before. It was still not possible to discuss these things outside of a small circle of friends, as I was still concerned about being labeled a "weirdo." I devoured volumes of research material and sought solace in the fact that I was not alone in these experiences and that many prestigious universities had researched the field of expanded consciousness and nonlocal phenomena. It was not well accepted by other scientists, nor understood by society at large, but that was of no matter to me.

A snippet of what I found is reflected in the quotes included in this book. Just how exciting and challenging all of this can be is summarized aptly by clinical psychologist and author Dr. Karen Nesbitt Shanor in *The Emerging Mind:*

> These are challenging and thoroughly thrilling times. And when we feel overwhelmed by the latest research, it is important to remember that the finest scientists and mathematicians in the world do, too.[1]

It is said that "All good things must come to an end" and "Time heals all wounds." It is probably true that the most joyous and traumatic experiences grow dull with time. The actions of daily life create emotional content from newer experiences and shove aside our attachment to previous ones. My high sensitivity faded with time, as preexisting patterns of life and work reasserted themselves. The sensitivity did not completely disappear, however, but began to interweave within my conscious awareness in subtle and transformative ways.

The famous psychic Edgar Cayce was quoted many times as saying that he felt he was not doing anything that was not possible for every other human. Could our species be awakening to a new broader level of awareness? It is certainly worthy of consideration.

We must be wary of the obvious hucksterism, however, which seems to collect immediately around any serious consideration of plausible psi events. The tabloids are full of psychic product predators who fleece the uneducated and unwary. This is sad, as it confuses and complicates the serious, objective scientist or layperson who wants to inquire into consciousness exploration. Likewise, we should not allow our imaginations or greed to carry us down a shaded path. One of the worst things that might happen is for us to realize there is more to us than we thought and then approach this realization with the same "give-me-more-so-I-can-have-an-advantage" attitude that we are so famous for in Western culture.

We consider ourselves advanced in our intellectual prowess because we use the vast resources of the Internet and the printed and electronic resources of our libraries. Yet if we found ourselves suddenly transported to a primitive tribal culture in the jungle, we might be considered "uneducated" in reading the "signs" in even simple tasks associated with gathering food and surviving in the environment. We could learn these skills, but we would be unable to "look up the answer" in an intellectual sense. The requisite skills would require analysis and interpretation of very subtle changes in the physical environment. This is a world in which a bent twig, a faint smell, a "sense" that something in the jungle is "different" may represent the combination of many complex interrelationships.

Being adept at primitive survival skills involves experience, training, and apprenticeship. Many tribal cultures that flourish under harsh conditions have belief systems involving the nonphysical that play a strong role in their manner of obtaining food and seeking an appropriate place to locate their camp. There are protocols put into play that may require "visions" sought in altered states of consciousness to perform these tasks. There may even be metaphysical "contractual" agreements with the eventual prey animal to seek its "agreement" to become food to sustain tribal life. In such cases, the role of the altered states can be trivialized by Western scientists and attributed to a mythology of the culture.

It is possible, however, that nonlocal aspects are being brought into play in the tribal activities. The same nonlocal realm that exists in an expanded version of the universe can both accommodate laboratory-supported psi events and assist tribal cultures in the hunt. I believe psi are merely points along a continuum of what is considered real, or not, primarily on the basis of our cultural belief systems. Sadly, our "primitive" kin may more effectively utilize the world of the nonlocal than do those of us who define ourselves as superior due to mere technological differences.

It is my hope that if we can bring the experience of the nonordinary state into the realm of normal consciousness, we can utilize the heightened levels of perception that become available to address more effectively the issues and problems of our daily lives. The potential opened to us through the expansion of our perceptual options is highlighted in the words of Dr. Dawna Markova, pioneering MIT psychologist, in her book *The Open Mind:*

As we open our minds from the conscious state, the front door, to the unconscious, the bedroom, we progress from the most assertive state of mind to the most sensitive, from the most detailed to the most systemic and generative. You may remember that the wider or more expansive the state of mind, the more thinking becomes symbolic—words become songs and sound and hums, letters become visions, actions become gut feelings of ideas of new ways to do something. Most importantly for communication, the person has less and less capacity to filter or screen out stimuli, and so the thinking becomes more and more receptive, intuitive, sacred.[2]

I am not proposing that we cast aside our physical and scientific worldview. That would be folly beyond comprehension. What I am asking is that we soften its edges just a bit to allow a slightly broader worldview to emerge. Softening things a bit is probably a good thing for our society anyway. Culturally, it might be said that we have developed a fear of the subjective, as we tend to avoid anything not scientific or verifiable by physical means. We have become so rigid that we too often think only in the world of black and white, right and wrong, the "single" defining issue, and who should be blamed for *this* particular error.

We should be moving in the direction of seeing how interconnected everything is and how much everything is affected by everything else. There are few issues that can be defined within the limitations of the black or white, yes or no, true or false sort of thinking that computer flow-charting has driven us toward. In truth, there is probably much more that is somewhere on a continuum of shades of gray. I believe that if we were to recognize the reality of the continuum that connects the objective and subjective, we would be much better equipped to deal with the growing complexities of our society.

Recognizing that the expansion of consciousness and altered states can play a role in our information-based society is a delicate yet mandatory area of discussion. The connection is noted well by futurist Peter Russell in *The Global Brain Awakens:*

Rapid as the growth of the information industry is, it may not be the fastest growing area of human activity. There are indications that the movement toward the transformation of consciousness is growing even faster. In terms of sheer numbers the movement may not at present be very significant, but it shows a doubling time of about four years, which makes it one of the steepest growth curves society has ever seen.[3]

Bringing altered states into normal consciousness expands not only what is considered normal, but also our awareness of new elements that could also become part of normalcy at some future time.

—J. R. M.

Can Science Help Us? (or, Don't Confuse Me with the Facts, I Know What I Want to Believe)

Reality is three-dimensional, formed of atoms, and operates under laws that can be reduced to the level of a high school science textbook description. Science itself is built on a process—the scientific method. We are all familiar with the scientific method of proof, which involves well-documented theoretical postulation, experimental testing, replication of results, and then general acceptance of a truth. We scoff at the ignorance of those in earlier times who "knew" that the Earth was flat. Society later moved to the realization that the Earth may indeed be round, but surely the sun revolves around the Earth. Still later, as the realization of a larger solar system became the "new truth," it was assumed that the sun was surely the center of the universe.

Today, the scientific method and modern technology enable us to push our frontiers of awareness and research millions of miles out into the cosmos and deep into the secrets of the atom. Even with the advances that we have made, however, might people in our distant future look back on our smugness in the same way that we now look at the "flat-Earthers"?

We must not forget that it is human beings who perform scientific research. Humans are subject to human nature that sometimes gets in the way of good science. Probably no area of inquiry can so quickly stimulate reactions in some scientists as the word "paranormal." I will not use that word anymore; it is much too emotionally charged and is difficult to define adequately anyway. The word "psi" works much better, and I believe there are some very interesting things that we should pay more attention to in this realm. But with the mention of psi, many scientists quickly and authoritatively pronounce: "There is not one shred of evidence to support the existence of such foolishness!" Such a rigid and predictable reaction is interesting, especially since there is, indeed, a large body of quality scientific research into psi that is well documented and easily available. I will examine here just one area of this research (remote viewing), but at this point it is important to note that an emotional reaction, not an objective response, is a human defensive reaction when one's beliefs are challenged.

This "not one shred of evidence" theme is further complicated as the press many times asks psi-related questions of a scientist whose training is not related in any way to the investigation of psi. Physicists usually do not give opinions on biological issues, and chemists are not usually critical of a new mathematics theory. Each, however, can be an immediate and quotable "expert" on a highly specialized field such as psi research even though this field of inquiry is one in which they are not aware of even the basic research protocols. True, the field of serious scientific research into the psi is small, but it exists and should be given equal footing in the realm of objective science alongside others that properly utilize the scientific method.

When I mention the word "psi," I am *not* referring to the psychic world of séances, fortune-telling, "mumbo-jumbo," and "hocus-pocus." I am referring to a class of events that have been well researched under scientific conditions in major universities such as Princeton, Stanford, and the University of California at Los Angeles. Some of the psi-related phenomena that have been and continue to be investigated include such things as remote viewing, bioenergy fields, and psychokinesis. An emotional "not a shred of evidence" comment by a scientist quoted in the press demonstrates the consensus societal view of the occult rather than the authority of a qualified psi researcher. The scientists making such statements cast aside (or are unaware of) the substantive amount of significant and meaningful research in the field of scientifically anomalous events that are true exceptions to standard science as it is commonly understood.

The cultural nature of this emotional reaction is interesting. In the press, headlined scientists are often supported by stage magicians who seek to prove that an event could be faked through the use of standard (or at least creative) methods of stage magic or illusion. Simply being able to duplicate psi by means of trickery may not, in itself, demonstrate that the original occurrence of the event was actually faked. It simply means that a similar illusion could be manufactured.

More power to the magician who debunks quackery, but where are the doubting scientists or the stage magicians in respect to the mountains of research so painstakingly undertaken in the recommended reading section at the back of this book? Targeting of the obvious sham is a much easier one, of course, and if it protects a reality construct acceptable to the consensus perspective of our current belief system, all the better.

Serious research into psi is more complex and challenging than simply exposing a charlatan. It is difficult enough for science when the phenomenon, species, or event being researched is physical and easily seen and identified. When one moves into the realm of psi, the complications of communication and agreement on even the basic terms and protocols can quickly become complex. Psychologist, author, and psi researcher Dr. Dean Radin, in his book *The Conscious Universe: The Scientific Truth of Psychic Phenomena*, gives an insightful and comprehensive overview of how scientists may fall prey to the pitfalls of being human when faced with the unknown. He notes:

> Science may be defined as a well-accepted body of facts and a method of obtaining these facts. Scientists are quick to disagree,

however, over what "well accepted" means, what "facts" means, what "methods" means, and even sometimes what "and" means.[1]

As with the rest of society, scientists are faced with an ever-increasing abundance of information accompanied by shrinking time to study it. It is logical from the perspective of mainstream science that no priority is given to the scientific anomaly. The anomaly is that exception to the rule, the one thing that doesn't fit, or that one little experiment that doesn't work right all the time. Ironically, focus on the anomaly many times can result in breakthrough science.

Drs. Robert Jahn and Brenda Dunne of the Princeton Engineering Anomalies Research (PEAR) Laboratory push the limits of this area in their research efforts. In their fascinating book *Margins of Reality: The Role of Consciousness in the Physical World*, they write:

> Proper assessment and assimilation of the anomaly, on the other hand, will point to a more penetrating path than that previously followed, along which the science can resume its progress more vigorously than before.[2]

An example of pursuing the anomalous and nontraditional with great benefit is the field of remote viewing, also known as remote sensing, remote perception, and anomalous cognition. Remote viewing involves a subject going into an altered state of consciousness and describing, drawing, or sketching the contents of an unknown (even to the researcher) target site. The target is identified by either geographic coordinates or by a control number established as part of double-blind research protocols. Successful research in this area was conducted over a span of nearly 20 years, in secret, for the intelligence agencies of the United States government at the Stanford Research Institute in California.

The existence of the remote viewing program at Stanford was revealed and declassified in a Government Accounting Office report in 1995, and a wave of press coverage about "psychic spies" resulted immediately. A major portion of the prestigious nightly ABC news show *Nightline,* aired on Tuesday, November 28, 1995, was dedicated to the subject. As one might imagine, the full force of all the issues I have noted involving human nature and scientists followed. I will not go into this topic much here as that research is well documented elsewhere. The interested reader should, however, look at the books listed in the recommended reading at the end of this book.

Of particular importance are the works of scientists Russell Targ, Hal Putoff, Robert Jahn, Dean Radin, remote viewing historian Jim Schnabel, and military intelligence remote viewer Joseph McMoneagle. Reading this compendium of material should easily remove from one's mind the concept that "not one shred of evidence" exists.

What I find interesting is the reaction of our consensus culture to the phenomenal revelations about successful remote viewing. There is major news coverage of the fact that the research has been done and that our government has used it for intelligence-gathering activities. After several weeks of psychic spy headlines, society at large seemed to take little, if any, further notice. Could it be that such a phenomenon pushes us far past our comfort zones? Comfort zones can play a strong role in what we will even consider for inclusion in our belief systems.

Remote viewing is an example of what scientists refer to as non-local phenomena. This means that the phenomena being studied are not subject to influence by their immediate surroundings. In a sense, the phenomena may have their roots outside of the basic three dimensions. While this may be a stretch for many of us, it is a basic element of modern quantum physics theory. In remote viewing, the theoretical construct postulates that a person's mind, or consciousness, can somehow move beyond the "local" environment to sense activity at a remote location. There is much conjecture as to what the physics, biology, psychology, and aspects of consciousness are that explain this, but that is the nature of the current scientific curiosity—to try to figure out this puzzle.

Again, the ability to see psychically, or remotely view, is clearly documented and verified in thousands of replicated laboratory trials as a real phenomenon that exists and can be learned, but no one knows the "how" and "why" of it yet.

Noted quantum physicist and author Dr. Nick Herbert observes:

> Nothing exposes the perplexity at the heart of physics more starkly than certain preposterous-sounding claims a few outspoken physicists are making concerning how the world really works. If we take these claims at face value, the stories physicists tell resemble the tales of mystics and madmen. Physicists are quick to reject such unsavory associations and insist that they speak sober fact. We do not make these claims out of ignorance, they say, like ancient mapmakers filling in terra incognitas with plausible geography. Not ignorance, but the emergence of unexpected knowledge forces on us all new visions of the way things really are.[3]

Aside from the impact of nonlocal phenomena challenging our cultural comfort levels, we must note that the political and cultural aspects of the scientific community cannot be underestimated. Breakthrough science is one of the toughest fields in which to work. Biophysicist Dr. Beverly Rubik in *Life at the Edge of Science* echoes this. Dr. Rubik writes of the frustration of remaining "acceptable" when you have made breakthrough discoveries:

> Perhaps the greatest obstacle that frontier scientists are unprepared for but inevitably face is political—the tendency for human systems to resist change, to resist the impact of new discoveries, especially those that challenge the status quo of the scientific establishment.[4]

Clearly, many scientists face a dilemma: Stay on the beaten path in research and exploration and more easily achieve "acceptance"; or venture forward into areas of the unknown, possibly making discoveries that open locked doors but, in so doing, challenge existing belief systems and cultural values, and risk loss of credibility and alienation from the scientific community.

The brilliant neuroscientist Dr. Candace Pert observes that revolutionary research, no matter how exciting, still works within a tight-knit society of what is considered acceptable. In her book

Molecules of Emotion: Why You Feel the Way You Feel, she relates her feelings about her entry into the "big leagues" of science and compares it to professional sports in the ferocity of competition for notoriety and continued funding:

> While I found the game thrilling to play, I had not been sufficiently conditioned to accept the code of loyalty that it demanded. In a series of events that caused me much heartbreak and earned me much notoriety, I broke the rules and was dealt the cruelest of punishments, alienation from my scientific family.[5]

Part of being human involves reaction to events and our surroundings. Our comfort with what we see around us is based on our belief systems. In Western society, we believe that science, given enough time, will be able to unravel the mechanical aspects behind everything. Mentioning a human experience such as a precognitive dream ("I didn't get on the plane and it crashed") may challenge social belief systems, but the concept of coincidence can smooth it all out or dismiss it as inconsequential. Many of us need to have our belief systems challenged a bit more.

Real challenges to our beliefs happen through things like synchronistic events, near-death experiences, and deep religious or spiritual activities that result in spontaneous remission of diagnosed disease or life-changing personal transformations. Facing these head-on can push us to a level of discomfort that might propel us to pursue their deeper meanings. Of course, it is much easier to discard these events as coincidental and unscientific than to admit that there might be something to them.

Science has gained credibility as it has moved us away from myth and superstition toward objectivity and truth. The continuing knowledge and information explosion is testament, however, to how much there is to learn on so many fronts. In the ever-expanding nature of information, there is also an expansion of the number of items that might be considered breakthrough. How do we find those items? Do we want to? Finding gems of insight may involve challenging what we assume as so basic that we don't consider certain things for review in the first place.

Considering the near-death experience (NDE) as an example of psi presents interesting issues. There are a variety of theoretical medical constructs that attempt to explain the NDE. The commonly expressed sensation of "going into the Light" could be understood via a number of physical approaches. One popular medical perspective is that the NDE is merely a by-product of the sequential process of the brain shutting down. Explanations range from it being the result of oxygen deprivation to the brain to the idea that the death process includes a stage in which the individual may be able to perceive visually the optic nerve itself, which appears as a "point of light." These models all include aspects of bodily functions that are, in some way, becoming visible as part of the normal shutting down of anatomical processes during death.

There are also approaches that attempt to explain the NDE phenomenon by exploring the duplication of it in non-life-threatening situations. An experience that supports the oxygen deprivation model occurs on a regular basis in the training of jet pilots. Training in the centrifuge results in blood drainage from the head during the strong "G" forces. Many pilots experience euphoric states, and some even report seeing "the light." Elsewhere, scientists have pursued an explanation of the NDE through exploring aspects of brain electrical activity and biochemical or biomagnetic interactions.

Neuropsychology researcher Dr. Michael Persinger of Laurentian University in Quebec, Canada, not only has induced out-of-body experiences and NDE states of consciousness, but has even caused the UFO (unidentified flying object) abduction scenario in subjects through the use of phased electromagnetic pulsation in targeted areas of the brain. Others, through ingestion or injection, have called upon various drugs (such as ketamine, LSD, and mescaline) to induce or replicate these sensations.

It is possible to duplicate many of the physical sensations of an out-of-body or near-death experience in the laboratory. One glaring omission I have noted as I have read over countless pages of material, however, is the one key ingredient common to the real NDE: the truly transformative nature of it. Individuals who have undergone the NDE by being in clinical near-death circumstances appear to have undergone life-changing and spiritually transformative shifts in their worldview. This does not seem to be the case for those who have simply undergone similar psycho-physiological sensations under induced or laboratory conditions.

It is almost as if the laboratory experience lacks some key element of the actual event and is therefore diminished in its effects. This appears similar to the difference between the psychological impact of an actual earthquake as compared to the results of an earthquake simulated by the wizards of motion picture special effects. The movie viewer experiences the special effects earthquake and feels short-term fear, excitement, and a rush of adrenaline. While these are the same sensations felt by someone in an actual earthquake, they diminish quickly as the moviegoer leaves the theater. There is no apparent real long-term psychological impact. The actual earthquake victim, however, may suffer long-term traumatic stress or undergo life-changing aftereffects.

To me, there is an important correlation of the nature of the NDE to its long-term effects. The laboratory-induced NDE-like sensations (whether as a result of drugs, pulsed electromagnetic frequencies, or centrifuge jet pilot training) are like the "special effects" version. The true NDE, however, appears to be unsought and has a significant impact on the individual.

It is this transformative aspect of the NDE that I find most interesting. Remarkably, it does not seem to require the danger of being near death to experience it. Many meditators or others adept in some form of altered state have experienced deep, profound, and near-death-like experiential states of consciousness that have resulted in significant life-changing aftereffects. These deep states of consciousness have even been achieved with accompanying near-death-like sensations, imagery, and emotion, which may even include the passage through a tunnel, bright light, feelings of unconditional love, and meetings with benevolent beings of energy and light. Some researchers have begun to utilize the phrase "near-death-like-experiences" (NDLEs) to describe this type of activity.

Whether a person has had an actual NDE from a critical physical condition, or an NDLE from meditation, there are a great number of cases where the NDE/NDLE becomes a major turning point in the one's life. New attitudes of openness, new levels of caring for others, new levels of emotional expression, and, at times, new life directions can be the result of this event. Bookstore and library shelves bear witness to a major increase in books about such experiences, and there is an increasing portion of the population interested not only in these experiences, but also in the state of consciousness that produces them.

The world of science is explored through hypothesis, theory, and facts. Accepting things on faith, of course, is contradictory to the world of science and unacceptable in the application of the scientific method. Touch healer Jane Katra and physicist Russell Targ note an interesting paradox comparing the nature of data accepted by scientists and mystics. They write:

> Science has always had a problem with "faith" in anything but science. But science itself is ever changing. The sixteenth century Italian philosopher Giordano Bruno was burned alive at the stake for declaring that the earth was not the center of the universe, and today it appears from recent astronomical observations that there may indeed be many universes. For a modern physicist, such data come from observing the physical world, and that data changes constantly. Therefore, theories must change. For the mystic, however, the data is his or her experience—and over the past three thousand years the experience of oneness in a quiet mind has been an enduring truth. So it appears that over the course of the millennia, the data of the mystic turns out to be more stable and reliable than the data of the physicist![6]

Mystical experience has never been considered the realm of science. Yet, as noted previously, recent explorations into the physics of nonlocal phenomena begin to sound somewhat more mystical than scientific. These explorations offer new challenges to the limitations created by using only the scientific method. Exploring consciousness itself requires direct human experience that may be subtle but profound. Such explorations may sometimes require the scientific observer to participate in ways not allowed in most scientific proto-cols. Complicating this is the fact that strong nonlocal phenomena may involve experiences that border on spiritual inquiry.

Katra and Targ discuss this situation in the following way:

> Inherent to this universal spiritual philosophy is the idea that human beings are quite capable of not merely knowing about the Divine Ground by inference but of realizing its existence by direct experience or intuition. This direct knowing is outside the realm of reasoning and analysis. It is possible because, as contemporary physics tells us, we live in a nonlocal universe. And ESP research data show that our consciousness is nonlocal.[7]

Embracing broader perspectives that include breakthrough ideas such as psi and nonlocal phenomena might allow us to move into expanded levels of consciousness that support multitasking on a broader scale. These approaches might offer methods of expanding time rather than being subjected to the shrinking of it. Broader perspectives could also enhance our capacities to deal with the information explosion and the stress of modern living. While certainly not a panacea, the opportunities created by moving toward a more direct relationship with the quantum could open doors to new worlds of human endeavor.

> Science is severely limited in what it can explore because it restricts itself to the five senses and observes rather than directly experiences the event being studied.
>
> —J. R. M.

II

Moving Past the Limitations of Our Five Senses: Embracing the Unseen

Scientists involved in serious inquiry into the realm of psi have sometimes been branded "frontier" scientists. Moving beyond accepted constructs of how we believe the physical world operates poses far too many challenges for most of us to consider. Yet this is exactly what is happening in frontier science research in the fields of the quantum universe, consciousness, and nonlocal phenomena.

A striking example can be seen in the work of consciousness researcher Dr. Dean Radin, as outlined in his book *The Conscious Universe: The Scientific Truth of Psychic Phenomena.* Dr. Radin writes:

> In a recent series of experiments in our laboratory at the University of Nevada, Las Vegas, we've explored unconscious nervous system responses to future events. Strictly speaking, such responses are a subset of precognition known as "presentiment," a vague sense or feeling of something about to occur but without any conscious awareness of a particular event.[1]

Radin describes a protocol in which a subject is shown both pleasant and unpleasant photographs while precise measurements are taken of the subject's physiological reactions. Radin's research presents evidence that the human nervous system begins reacting to a stimulus *before* that stimulus is physically presented.

> We saw a clear difference in electrodermal activity before presentation of positive versus negative emotional pictures and essentially no difference after presentation. . . . The findings also suggest—as would be expected if presentiment truly does reflect foreknowledge of future events—that the autonomic nervous system is not just "pre-acting" to a future *shock* to the nervous system, but is pre-acting to the emotional *meaning* of the future event.[2]

This experiment illustrates that the human nervous system registers the emotion that a pleasant versus an unpleasant picture will elicit *just prior to* the subject actually seeing the picture for the first time. This incredible situation occurred when a computer presented the pictures, thus eliminating the potential influence of an investigator unknowingly providing clues. Media coverage of this remarkable research included a televised segment of the Discovery channel series *Impossible Science,* entitled "Invisible Forces." Dr. Radin and Dr. Marilyn Schlitz of the Institute of Noetic Sciences discussed this research effort as part of that television show. This breakthrough scientific evidence has significant implications that challenge the basic underpinnings of three-dimensional reality. Yet has anyone taken much notice?

I find it fascinating that, even with television exposure, there is not broader awareness of either that show or the research itself. A similar situation occurred with the ABC News *Nightline* coverage of remote viewing in November 1995. After short-term and primarily sensational coverage by the news media, there was little, if any, further attention paid to remote viewing by the news media or by society at large. Could it be that we find considering such ideas too uncomfortable to pursue? Could it be that we have no framework into which to put such revolutionary concepts? Do such ideas create fear in us about who might be utilizing remote viewing techniques to snoop into our private lives without our knowledge? Or is this a case of information overload?

With so much information to process, how could we be blamed for not seeing that particular television show or for discarding input that might challenge some of our basic assumptions? There is plenty to worry about without trying to deal with the basic foundations of science, philosophy, and religion. Rather than struggle with such difficult concepts, we may simply say, "Explain it to me when the experts have sorted it all out." This seems to be a standard response when things require large amounts of our already overscheduled time to ponder.

In considering such challenging ideas, we may find solace in a narrowing gap between science and spirituality, as quantum physics findings require a position closer to the realm of the mystic. Religious and philosophical explorations of the esoteric and the mystical have dealt with these issues for centuries. As noted by His Holiness, the 14th Dalai Lama, in his book *Ethics for the New Millennium,* physical reality is an interweaving of almost incomprehensible complexities. He offers insight on the limitations of a reductionist approach to science based only in physical reality and limited by our five senses. He writes:

> In the course of our daily lives, we engage in countless activities and receive huge sensory input from all that we encounter. The problem of misperception, which, of course, varies in degree, usually arises because of our tendency to isolate particular aspects of an event or experience and see them as constituting its totality. This leads to a narrowing of perspective and from there to false expectations. But when we consider reality itself we quickly become aware of its infinite complexity, and we realize that our habitual perception of it is often inadequate.[3]

Ideas of interwoven complexity complicate the scientist's task of creating valid experiments to explore the nonlocal nature of consciousness. Creative approaches to expanding scientific methods to incorporate control mechanisms that will appropriately accommodate nonlocal effects are needed in order to study such effects.

Exploring realms of the nonlocal is a journey into the nonphysical. In Western culture, we have little experience in communicating about such journeys except through poetic and lyrical means. Rapturous, profound, or emotion-based activity can be difficult to explain accurately to others. We communicate through our written and spoken language, and it, too, for all practical purposes, is based in the perceptions formed by our five senses. Our language operates fairly well as we attempt to describe the world of the physical, but moving to the abstract in areas of feeling and emotion, we tend to have problems finding precise descriptions.

In *States of Consciousness*, consciousness researcher Dr. Charles Tart compares the inadequacy of the Western culture-based English language to describe inner explorations as compared to Sanskrit, which arose from the more introspective cultures of the east. He writes:

> Sanskrit, on the other hand, has many presumably precise words for internal events and states that do not translate well into English. There are over 20 words in Sanskrit, for example, which are translated to mean "consciousness" in English, but which carry different shades of meaning in the original.[4]

Even with the broader language skills of the East, the question still exists of how to describe nonphysical activity from the perspective of the physical world in which we live. Dr. Tart asks what is meant when people say they "feel vibrations" in a deep altered state of consciousness. Talented remote viewing research subjects can deliver accurate information about their targets. But it is difficult for them to *describe* adequately the internal and nonphysical processes that allow them to attain such information.

This information is coming from a nonordinary state of consciousness. In these altered states, one not only has moved beyond the world of the physical, but one has also moved into a realm full of information—but information beyond the five senses. Communicating perceptions from within these states may be more individualistic than precise due to the nature and depth of the personal experience involved.

There has been scientific study of specific forms of altered state activity, including research on the life-enhancing aspects of long-term meditation. There has also been research on control of the auto-nomic nervous system exhibited by advanced yoga practitioners, as well as inquiries into near-death experiences, and subjects reporting out-of-body sensations.

A common difficulty in investigations of this type is the inability of the subject to describe what is indescribable. A subject repeatedly saying how beautiful it was during her NDE or how warm and lov-ing it felt does not give data elements meaningful to scientific researchers. This lack of precise language may be one reason that the more subtle realms of consciousness have for so long frustrated science.

Altered states of consciousness have been part of human culture throughout the ages. Seers, sages, vision questers, healers, prophets, and others have all used some degree of intuition, expanded con-sciousness, or trance activity to gain insights into an event or disease, or to gain a prediction. Many of these activities are supported or induced in culturally accepted rituals such as meditation, fasting, or, in some tribal cultures, the use of hallucinogenic drugs. In particu-larly gifted subjects, the degree to which consciousness is altered by design versus it "just happens" may vary.

Edgar Cayce lay on a couch and "slept," then delivered his read-ings. It also appears that attaining such altered states and accessing information from a nonphysical realm requires the capacity to elimi-nate the belief system that such activity is not possible. This move-ment beyond belief systems is noted by Joseph McMoneagle, remote viewer, author, and researcher, in his book *Mind Trek: Exploring Consciousness, Time, and Space through Remote Viewing.* He writes:

> [T]here is a portion of time of the remote viewing experiment which is called the *cool down* period. It is that epoch of time the remote viewer experiences just prior to when s/he is required to

collect information on a target . . . What I didn't realize at the time, but do now, is that I was using this half-hour to create a proper mind set for paranormal functioning. In other words I was preparing myself subconsciously to accept the experience. I was *temporarily suspending my disbelief,* to allow an unusual experience to happen.[5]

Suspending the disbelief that something cannot happen could certainly open one to possibilities that we don't usually consider. If, as nonlocal phenomena research suggests, psi functioning is operating outside the five senses, then there must be other elements of consciousness of which we are not yet cognizant. What an exciting concept, that there are portions of our minds we are not yet fully aware of, not to mention have any mastery over. It is exciting because, as we have seen in the research on remote viewing, it may be possible to learn such mastery, or at least explore it in a consciousness-expanding manner. Realizing that we may encompass so much more might also imply that we have many more perceptual capabilities than we previously imagined.

> Using altered states of consciousness to expand our perception is not something we need to do; it is more about something we need to be able to allow.
>
> —J. R. M.

Changing Perceptions of Reality

A week at The Monroe Institute is probably not for everyone. The same could be said, however, about meditation retreats, religious revivals, monastic life, long-distance running, ritualistic dance/drum-ming, martial arts, inner-derived artistic endeavors, and yoga. Yet any or all of these activities, under the right conditions, can produce altered states of consciousness and expanded mental journeys. Under the right conditions, a sunset, a baby's smile, a church service, look-ing into the eyes of one's love, or a stroll in the park can also produce altered states and even transformative spiritual experiences.

The nonphysical is the home of intuition and inner guidance, yet many ridicule it as the occult or avoid it, fearing it as the unknown. Perhaps we are so smug in our technological society and our self-defined superiority that we do not think we need anything the non-physical might have to offer. Where do we turn for visionary guidance and spiritual leadership? For many, traditional religious institutions fail to provide this, and we no longer have an oracle at Delphi to foresee and divine for us. In this lack of visionary direc-tion, we meander along with the ebb and flow of the entertainment industry or the trends embraced by our peer groups, or we simply allow ourselves to exist in frustration with life.

Aligning our mental, emotional, and spiritual selves should give us direction and a sense of knowing that we are making the right choices on our life path. This involves working with all that we are, both physical and nonphysical. Nonphysical realities may be just as real as our physical one. If they are, then we are long overdue for quality experiences in and education about nonphysical realms. If we do not appropriately integrate the nonphysical and the nonlocal into our everyday lives, we are turning our back on essential parts of who and what we are.

In the Gap: Exploring the Spaces between the Physical and the Nonphysical

The beginning of knowledge is the discovery of something we do not understand.

—Frank Herbert

Our mind is capable of passing beyond the dividing line we have drawn for it.

Beyond the pairs of opposites of which the world consists, other, new insights begin.

—Hermann Hesse

A moment's insight is sometimes worth a life's experience.

—Oliver Wendell Holmes

12

Other Realms: Fantasizing
or Describing the Indescribable?

Transformative events are not easily assimilated into one's life. Following a life-changing occurrence, the rational mind rallies its forces to reassert a former and more familiar world, one in which the intellect is in control. Obviously, my initial trip to The Monroe Institute affected me deeply. After that experience, my intellect struggled with what to believe about my experiences. Simultaneously, I was consumed with an eagerness to explore such experiences further.

I became an information sponge. I took in volumes of information relating to the expansion of consciousness, scientific research in psi, and the growing awareness of the relationship of the mind and body in medicine and healing. It may be that my academic training in librarianship, the seeking and organizing of information, was my salvation from the pressures created by the mind attacking itself. I discovered that many people who have similar transformative experiences go through very difficult times as their intellect suppresses and discounts the reality of their experience altogether.

In *Mind Trek,* remote viewer Joe McMoneagle discusses his

return to work after an extended stay in the hospital recovering from a heart attack and near-death experience:

> So, on the conscious level, everything has smoothed out and your culturally normal philosophy and concepts of reality operate along in a very nonthreatening way and you are able to suppress abnormal input.
>
> On the unconscious level, however, your subconscious aware-ness is screaming out messages and they are going straight into a dead-letter file (cloud) because your conscious mind is ignoring them or, worst yet, egotistically altering the message into something less coherent.[1]

For me, there was great comfort in the fact that a book like *Mind Trek* exists. I benefited from the struggles of others in their attempts to place life-changing events into perspective. Those who had vision-ary experiences in earlier times were challenged by a lack of support-ive literature. The written accounts of transcendental journeys that did exist carried significant cultural or religious trappings along with the description and impact of the experience itself. In 1995, how-ever, I was supported by a growing body of scientific data on psi. Books by amateur "mind scientists" like Bob Monroe also provided the assurance that my experiences were not unique or hallucinatory.

While my mind reeled with the possibilities of psi, I still had to deal with daily life. I battled my doubting intellect by feeding it scien-tific data. I struggled with the seduction of bliss inviting me into altered states. I realized that I had to become anchored in my physi-cal body to avoid spending too much time "out there."

To support a greater sense of my physical body, I began a regi-men of physical exercise and massage. This focus on the physical paid health benefits and planted the seed of an idea. I wondered if it would be possible to integrate the state of transcendence into every-day life. Could daily activity reflect the wondrous by achieving a new level of interconnection of body, mind, and spirit?

While it is personal, I would be remiss if I did not report one area of life that did amplify in intensity. I attribute this new level of experience to new awareness and sensitivity brought about by nonphysical experience. From the outset, my return home from Gateway signaled a significant move into new realms of sexual intimacy for my wife and me. Over our 25 years of marriage, we had continued to grow in our union, both relationally and physically. But now, there seemed to be an expanded and multidimensional physical, mental, and spiritual awakening for both of us during our lovemaking. I did find, after some degree of library research, a few references to the consciousness-expanding nature of Eastern tantric practices, and I postulated that the move into altered states was a key to these ritual explorations of unseen realms.

Sensual experiences aside, my right brain screamed for further exploration into expanded states of consciousness and my left brain desired to determine if the first TMI experiences were unique, or whether these transformative events could be duplicated or continue in some way. I finally made the decision to return to the "scene of the crime." I again enrolled in a program at The Monroe Institute. My explorations would continue in a graduate program called Guidelines.

The TMI literature notes that Guidelines "offers still another step in the development of more complete understanding of self." That sentence caught my attention. I still sought methods to bring together my left- and right-brain perspectives into an integrated approach to life. As I read the literature, it surprised me that most of the issues I was facing daily were addressed in this program.

I wondered if I was being drawn into some cultish attraction to TMI. I rolled this over in my mind, but dismissed it. I was not being recruited by anyone from TMI. My experiences had been my own, as all the other Gateway participants had their unique experiences. We were not being bombarded with literature to return, much less being asked to dress in a funny manner, give away money, or swear allegiance to anyone with some supposed superior power or intellect. We had simply gone deeply into our inner explorations.

I realized how much the experiences of the first TMI trip had far exceeded the program statements of the Gateway brochure. The Guidelines literature states the following:

The theme of Guidelines is to assist you in learning methods in which communication can be established with distinct and different intelligences. Whatever you call such intelligence (e.g., Total Self, Inner Self Helper, Guide, Nonphysical Friend, Universal Consciousness, etc.), it can be any constructive source that has an overview beyond your normal daily physical perception.

In addition, Guidelines encourages the practical application of such communications and states of consciousness. With practice, a person can learn to quickly and directly access whatever information is needed. Our goal is to make such lines of communication as open, direct, and natural as possible, so that during a business meeting, for example, you can calmly and serenely access the communication skills learned and concurrently apply them appropriately within the context of the situation.

Each participant also receives Personal Resources Exploration Program or PREP, a personalized session conducted in a specially designed, secluded cubicle in the lab at the Institute.

While this was clearly the language of an advertisement, to me its contents represented a scintillating set of potential experiences. The thought of a session in the TMI laboratory was, of course, icing on the cake. The chance to be wired up by the same TMI research staff that had worked with Bob Monroe in his explorations was a unique opportunity I could not pass up. My left brain reeled at the possibility of gaining laboratory printouts of data that might quantify my experience of expanded consciousness.

On October 28, 1995, six months after my original visit, I again find myself on the small commuter aircraft touching down at the Charlottesville, Virginia, regional airport. There is the "coming home" aspect of returning to a locale that is the center of meaningful experiences. TMI connections begin, however, even before I make it to Charlottesville. In the hub airport of Cincinnati, I meet three women who are also Guidelines bound. We are not introduced. We have no TMI insignia for the others to recognize. We just "connect" as our eyes meet, and we feel a "bond" of some sort. Almost simultaneously, we each ask if the other is going to TMI.

After we realize we are all heading to TMI, a flight-long discussion ensues. Two of them are traveling together and work in the same state government office in the upper Midwest; the third is a counselor and part-time massage therapist. There is a bonding among us as we share our experiences since Gateway. I realize as we exit the plane how oblivious we have been to the rest of the passengers. We have all bottled up a lot that is spilling out in loud voices in a confined public place. We receive strange looks as we exit the aircraft. We don't care; we are again with people we can talk to and not be misunderstood.

We are met by Mike in the TMI van at the airport, another bit of familiarity and comfort. While the van ride does not have the charged, anticipatory sense of six months ago, there is an air of excitement similar to returning to our favorite summer camp of childhood. How is everyone at the institute? Mike has cut his hair. Why? Does he like it? Has anyone else had this or that sort of experience after Gateway? I feel even more at ease, and a huge sense of relief settles over me as I find that I am not alone in my experiences. Everyone has had similar experiences to some degree and is coming back for further exploration.

Arriving at the institute also has a coming-home feel to it. Instead of the newcomer's tour, we are greeted by a posted list of room and CHEC assignments by the front door—it is up to us to settle in. There are hugs from the staff we know and squeals of delight when Gateway coparticipants reunite. We find out later that six people from one Gateway, who had all promised to return together, actually have done so.

Settling in amounts to meeting people as they arrive, unpacking, grabbing a sandwich from the serve-yourself setup, and going through the intake interview. The interviews are one-on-one sessions with a trainer in which our experiences since our last TMI visit are reviewed, as are our reactions to them and our current state of mind. I feel that I consume far more than my share of time as I relate my past six months to Penny, one of Bob Monroe's stepdaughters and an assistant trainer for this session. A warm and earthy person, she seems genuinely interested in my experiences. She listens intently, is very patient, and assures me that I am not alone in what has happened to me. Further, she helps me feel comfortable with my return to TMI as we talk about areas of trust and self-assurance that might be explored as part of this week's session.

I return to my room to meet Louis, my roommate. He is from Florida and successful in finance and banking. He is one of the group of six who are at Guidelines after sharing a Gateway together. That Gateway had been overpopulated with accountants and fiscal career people as a result of a feature article on the institute in the *Wall Street Journal* on September 20, 1994. He grins broadly as he shares his reason for returning, "I want that Gateway 'high' again."

That Gateway high. I'm not sure I can go through that level of experience again, but I sure want to explore more about what has happened to me. The dinner bell rings and we join others in the dining area to continue meeting our new family for the week. Following dinner, we adjourn to the large group area in David Francis Hall for the formal introductions and beginning of the program.

Joining Penny are our trainers, Karen and Joe. Karen, a transpersonal psychotherapist from California, had been one of Bob Monroe's first trainers hired in the 1970s. Joe, a Ph.D. psychologist from North Carolina, works with autistic children. Joe was also a study subject at the Princeton Engineering Anomalies Research (PEAR) Laboratory of hard science psi exploration fame, and has performed successfully in psychokinesis, or PK, experimentation.

We proceed through the getting-acquainted ritual by learning about our seatmates and then introducing them to the rest of the group. It is a diverse group of 21. Again, as in Gateway, these are not wild-eyed, New Age workshop hoppers. They are successful in their areas of work, and there are even several millionaires (although none ever openly acknowledge this fact) among the group. They have all been to Gateway and now want to explore the deeper realms of who and what they are.

In addition to the three women I had met on the plane and my roommate, Louis, we have an airline pilot, the founder of a major software company, a dean of engineering from a major university (on his seventh trip to TMI), an accountant and hotel chain finance guru, a floor trader from the Chicago Stock Exchange, a construction company and recording studio owner, a salesman, an artist from the Los Angeles entertainment industry, an occupational therapist whose Gateway had made such an impact that she could not return for two and a half years, one unemployed odd-jobber, a Canadian tax accountant, a medical doctor, a self-employed businessman, and a husband and wife team doing their fourth Guidelines. I am surprised to find that my seatmate is Maria, another of Bob Monroe's step-daughters and an artist and interior designer.

There is an introductory overview about the agenda for Guidelines. The time schedule is announced and we are allowed to keep our watches. It proves interesting how many of us had given up wearing them after Gateway. We are in a graduate program now, and the training wheels of the Gateway environment are removed. There is also a short discussion of the process of working with inner guidance and a discussion of our session in the laboratory. There are to be four lab sessions a day beginning at 7:30 A.M. tomorrow. We draw Scrabble tiles from a hat to determine our slot in the lab. I draw a Q–late Wednesday afternoon. Well, at least I will have time to get into the swing of things before I get into the lab.

The trainers remind us that whatever our time slot is, it will turn out to be perfect for us. They say that over the years it has been shown that there is no better, nor worse, time slot. We are instructed not to share anything about our sessions with anyone until Thursday evening, the point at which everyone will have completed their session. This way, no activity by an earlier session will influence or interfere in any way with a later scheduled participant. Each session is to be uninfluenced by all others–again, making it a personal experience within the supportive group setting at TMI.

It is getting late, so we will do only one tape this evening dedicated to resonant tuning (making the *OM* or *AUM* tones). The subtle energy-building aspects of this process can be powerful, and the late-night tape experience is a strong reminder. I cannot help but drift off into Focus 10 for a short exploration. Sensations of separating from my body come easily and I am surprised to experience my body seemingly dissolving in the process. I know I am tired, and my mind can be playing tricks on me, so I just observe this whole process.

I am brought back to physical reality with strong physical tingling sensations throughout a seemingly reforming body and a high-pitched ringing that reverberates in my ears. This is not a tape sound, but something that is being produced in me. Just as the tape closes, I have a visual of automobile headlights on a four-lane highway. What this means, I have no idea.

Only about ten of us show up for the debriefing session, as many are too tired from the day's travel to continue. As the discussion opens, people share their sensations of tingling, goose bumps, or temperature changes. Oddly, four of the ten have also seen headlights on a highway. This *is* going to be another interesting week.

The next morning, my Gateway first-day wake-up repeats itself. I rise at sunup well rested and desire a morning jog. I find others out doing the same, as the cool mountain air of an October morning is most inviting. As I jog along the gravel road, the program overview from the previous evening begins to roll around in my mind. My jog slows to a walk as the pieces begin to fit together in my mind.

Guidelines is to be about getting a stronger and more structured access to the source of my own intuition, conscience, or creative spark. We all have those "ah-ha" moments of inspiration. There is a natural problem, though, in being able to have them when we need them the most. Much later, after the Guidelines experience, I see it aptly put by neurotherapist and brain wave researcher Anna Wise in *The High Performance Mind:*

> When you feel an "ah-ha" experience hit you, it is important not to let it go unnoticed or unheeded. When you identify these types of experiences, it becomes more likely that you will have another one. Sometimes the recognition and acknowledgement of an "ah-ha" experience will cause another one to happen immediately, which may then cause even another, and another.[2]

During my walk, I think about intuitive insights. Besides the "ah-ha" moment, we all have our conscience, that little voice that gives us a tug when we know we are doing something we shouldn't. Would it be possible to bring that to such a level of awareness that we can count on it to be there always and aid our decision-making in our fast-paced lives?

We have all heard of the "spirit guides" with which New Agers constantly seek contact, as well as the familiar guardian angels of many religiously oriented people. Do these represent some form of "out there" guidance that could be incorporated into our lives? If such things exist, do they have to take those anthropomorphic forms, or are they part of an expanded version of the Self?

As these questions rumble through my mind, I envision scenarios of inner guidance as intuition on steroids. That brings a smile. The breakfast bell at the institute rings out across the valley and I jog toward that sound.

Both shower and breakfast are "thinking" times for me. Our trainer, Joe, has outlined the week for us. Guidelines is still a structured TMI program, so I know that we will be taking the concept of "being more than your physical body" to new levels of exploration. Joe has outlined exercises designed to meet or form an "ISH." Always one for making up acronyms, Monroe said ISH is the "Inner Self Helper," an innocuous method of setting up a formal relationship with deeper parts of yourself. The more I think about it, this approach might keep our left-brain analytical mind from getting in the way of our right-brain capacity to delve deeply into the source of intuition and the creative spark.

From another perspective, a whole-brain approach might offer a broader realm of information resources, if not fettered by the normal "filters" of ego programming steeped in experiences of personality. Based on our reactions to such experiences, our ego, as one of its main jobs, sets itself up as the ultimate arbiter of self-protective behaviors that may (or may not) be in our best interest.

We gather in the group room and find that our first tape is to be a reset of Focus 10. TMI's approach is to immerse us immediately in the program and reestablish our familiarity with the Hemi-Sync environment featured in a residential program. We will go through a formal reset of each of the levels through Focus 21. It is comforting to realize that we are once again beginning a week of no cell phones, beepers, e-mail, TV, newspapers, or intrusions of any kind. We are here to explore ourselves.

Settling into the CHEC unit, I wonder if this session will offer any of the drama of the Gateway experience. It doesn't take long to find out. The tape proceeds through the ritual of ocean surf, the energy conversion box, the affirmation, resonant tuning, and we are off on our journey and definitely back in a TMI program structure. My move to Focus 10 comes easily as I relax, begin to lose my body awareness, and settle into the "mind awake, body asleep" state. After sufficient time to allow all participants to reestablish their feelings of Focus 10, Bob's taped instruction takes us through our first exercise.

Each CHEC unit is equipped with a tape recorder, and the trainers activate the master power switch at the precise moment matching Bob's instruction to "reach back into our bodies and make contact with our vocal cords." We are to continue our relaxation to deepen the experience of Focus 10 and simultaneously report on our experience with the tape recorder running. This is disconcerting at first, but eases with additional practice. After this skill-building exercise, Bob instructs us to experience the remainder of the tape as a free-flow activity and "explore the energy and sensation of Focus 10."

I enjoy moving into Focus 10 and feel much more in a "light body" than my physical one. I decide that it might be interesting to attempt to bring this feeling of lightness into physical reality. I succeed in shifting the perception of my body to a new level that I have never experienced before. My visual imagery apparently has an agenda of its own, and I find myself touring the inside of my body with the clarity of an anatomy video. This is odd, but you never know where this stuff might take you. I watch the show as my heart comes into view and I become fascinated with its pumping. It is not as unpleasant as one might imagine; it is unnerving, but also a little exciting.

The more I watch the beating of my heart, the more I think what a wonderful thing one's heart is. This thought becomes stronger as I reflect on the work my heart performs. I think of the millions of times my heart has pumped, that if it stopped, I would die. I had never thought of how vital my heart is. I realize how little I express my appreciation for its life-giving work. I thank my heart for all it has done for me all these years.

At the instant of my expression of gratitude, there is an explosion of white light from my heart that obliterates my heart, me, the CHEC unit, and all of TMI. There is only white light. The light becomes whiter and whiter and eventually turns into a diamond sparkle. At that point, every fragment of my being is consumed with a booming insight/voice/knowing: "The Goddess is in my heart chakra." I am shocked at the intensity and unreality of such an event and immersed in the unconditional love of feminine energy. I become *very* emotional.

Another transcendental event is occurring, and my left brain is screaming for my ego to step in and take charge. As my analytic mind attempts to step in, there is a momentary flicker in the light, and then it expands to overwhelm me with bliss. Tears flow and I lose control. I realize at some level that regardless of what the basis of this energy is, it is washing away a lifetime of hurt, protective behavior, and separation from the emotional aspects of life.

As the tears flow, there is also a strong humming in my ears that I later identify (through exploring various sound frequency technologies) as a 7.8 Hz monotone hum. This sound is the frequency of the Earth called the Schumann resonance, the so-called mystical hum of the Earth that has baffled science since its discovery. Along with this hum, the diamond white light begins to fade, and I am bathed in a surreal green light. My left brain asserts itself again, and I fight through the tears to open my eyes and attempt to examine my surroundings. The green light illuminates the interior of my CHEC unit. It seems I could read by this green light. I can clearly see details of my surroundings. I am experiencing new levels of strange phenomena and the line between reality and unreality is blurring.

Are there strange lights actually appearing in my CHEC? Or am I so deeply separated from physical reality that my mind is creating its own reality, seemingly real but a fantasy? Either way, the event is intense. There is little time to ponder as the green light disappears as if a light switch has been flipped. Then I am stunned as my CHEC unit falls away to reveal a jet-black sky dotted with an infinity of stars. "Just *what* is going on here?" I mutter aloud. If this is a hallucination, it is a vivid one.

As strange as it may sound, I want to stress the seemingly physical nature of all of this. I am there with my eyes open or closed, and my thinking is lucid. I question and I probe mentally with open and closed eyes. The image remains under both conditions, so it must be nonphysical in nature. A figure drifts in front of the star field. It is the most beautiful creature I have ever seen, suspended in the dark space where the end of my CHEC unit used to be. My CHEC is here yet is a portal to this realm. This creature/being appears as a fairy or angel with flowing garments and butterfly-like wings, extending far above the head and below the feet.

Later I make these notes:

> Suspended in blackness is a "light fairy," for want of a better name. She is *beautiful* (oh, to be an artist to capture what I have seen!). She is immense, all transparent light—purple, blue, violet, white overlay upon overlay of light. She is transparent but of many (almost infinite) layers of light at the same time. She has layers and layers of gossamer (I never saw the meaning of that word before now) light hanging as a dress and huge wings that go above her head and below her feet. She is just *there* in front of me in the CHEC unit.
>
> Beautiful beyond words. She smiles at me, and I just stare. Then Bob's recorded voice announces the need to return to C-1. I imagine my C-1 code [a symbol of our own design that we had just learned to form to move easily between Focus Levels] tattooed on my chest. Suddenly, *wham*—I hit my body (or maybe "am consolidated" or "am slammed into" are better words, as I am somewhere in the neighborhood above my body) and enter in through my heart chakra. Feels like I imagine having CPR chest compression would be—a very physical reentry, almost painful. I notice that my physical body has become warm all over.

Go to debrief and try to keep writing notes. Sit near the door, as the opening comments are that this tape seems to them to have something to do with the heart and that the heart is the key to everything. I lose it. I go out on the porch and break into tears. It is Focus 21 emotion all over again. This is early in the week, and already things are getting out of hand.

Took a break. I am a little shaky, but I think I am OK.

This takes some processing, to say the least. I have questions about the event, the imagery, about the reality/unreality of it. As I stand on the porch, my gaze wanders across the serene pastoral area behind the institute and settles on the distant mountains. I need time to think. It is clear from my emotions that I have had a significant experience. The sensations of the light and the accompanying feelings of unconditional love and acceptance are dramatic. I have come to accept my previous deep experiences, but they had no angelic beings. This presents a challenge for me.

Am I enhancing my expanded states of consciousness by adding culturally inspired spiritual imagery? If so, why? If not, is this an actual visitation of some intelligence that exists only in the nonphysical? Have I moved into levels of fantasy that are illustrations of my mind finding new ways to amuse itself? There are plenty of questions, and the obvious, easy answers. But are the easy answers good enough? Something is going on here. What is it—fantasy, religious experience, or something beyond that? How does one decide?

"Richard?" It is Karen, the trainer.

The group debriefing has concluded and a break is under way. I have been allowed my space to explore whatever was troubling me that caused me to leave. Now it is time for the staff to check on me.

"Are you OK? Is there anything I can do for you?" Her questions and concern are genuine. She stands in front of me and looks deep into my eyes. "Is there anything you would like to talk about?"

I am self-conscious about perching on the edge of emotional outburst. I try to respond with a wisecrack about not expecting much in Focus 10. That comment, however, brings the imagery to mind again, and the emotions again overcome me. Karen puts her arm on my shoulder, and we walk down the porch, away from the other participants now emerging with lemonade and snacks.

We stand quietly for a while. I feel the compassion she offers. It is a tangible energetic sensation. Finally, I regain enough composure to relate a skeletal version of the event, but when I attempt to describe the angelic, fairylike creature, I am again a heap of emotional goo. Karen stands there holding my hand and providing the comfort of someone being there for me, a powerful role. As my emotions subside, she places caring hands in a slow dance around various points on my body—my head, my heart, and my lower back. She says nothing, but as her hands move, a cooling and comforting sensation settles in around my body. My emotions begin to stabilize. I wonder what that is all about, but am more than willing at this point to regain composure.

"I'm OK," I say. "I'll be all right. I just need a little more time to think. I want to get something to drink if there is any lemonade left."

She smiles, squeezes my hand, and turns back toward the group of other participants. "I'm available anytime, if you need me, or just want to talk."

There is security in what she says. I still don't know for sure what I think is going on, but at least there is always someone I can talk to about it. I stare at the mountains. I want to be sure that I am again in the driver's seat and that my emotions are stable. Normally, my emotions are held in check. I certainly have emotions; everyone does. Ordinarily, I do not show them in public. TMI experiences, however, are something different from normal ones. I continue to be surprised by the depth of these events, and I have about as much chance of controlling them as pushing back a tidal wave.

The bell rings, signaling the end of the break. I enter the building, gulp down a glass of lemonade, and decide to "get back on the horse." I will move forward in all of this by seeing where it will take me. I enter the group room and sit off to the side. I am ready for the second tape of the day.

We are told that the next tape is, again, familiar territory, a reset of Focus 12. The experience is eventful for me, but I'll share just a few points from my notes of that session:

Go back into 12—instructions to explore—and the light fairy shows up and says, "What are you doing?" I say I am trying to move Focus 12 inside my physical body. She says, "Oh, silly, all you have to do is click," and she clicks her tongue, cheek, and teeth. I try it—click, click—light body/physical body—you can click into each and then click them together—then it goes deeper and up into the center of my skull and sinuses—a click in and a click out at that level—neat. I think of the sound as a Halloween clicker—cosmic joke? It is hilarious.

Then the fairy creature, angel, or whatever, and I have a discussion, and I realize that there is a little girl—or a small fairy and the *big one* that I had seen earlier (either that or she gets bigger and smaller). Anyway, this is the *big one*. She explains that she can live in my heart chakra. This surprises me and my ego wants to take over with a discussion about this all being imagination, but I just flow through that and the angel/fairy smiles. She folds her wings, and then she folds herself, and then slides inside my chest sideways at the left sternum area. I don't see how such an immense being can fit into such a small space. Then, too, I guess this is nonphysical, come to think of it. This thought also strikes me as hilarious. She comes back out, unfolds herself, and says, "I've always been there; you just never let me out before. I live there."

I immediately deny this intellectually, then I *know* this and a great calm comes over me. She folds her wings, goes back in, and Bob says to go to 10. I visualize my reentry code tattooed on my chest again and *zap* I am there. At this point, I start thinking, "Let's not do another compression fracture type heart reentry," so I decide that when Bob says C-1, I will just drift in slowly. I do, and it is very nice. I get everything all lined up and then I wiggle into my body. Very comfortable—even tickled a little bit. Great overall feeling— like I'm putting the pieces together. I seem very tall and straight as I walk downstairs. I feel very "together."

We do a quick debriefing of the reset 12 experiences. I decide not to share anything. One woman relates that she spent the tape watching a donkey pulling a cart full of rocks. Every so often a man would come along and add another rock. She speculates that this might be the way she approaches life. She has gone from crisis to crisis simply adding to her load and never taking the time to look up and see where she is going. She presents all of this material in an amusing way.

We take a quick break so we can do one more tape before lunch.

The next tape is a reset of Focus 15. As I pass through the Focus 10 and 12 levels, I encounter the lovely, gossamer-clad, ethereal creature again, but there is not a lot of interaction. After the taped instructions, I move into Focus 15, that strange area of no time. I find myself in the black void that I first encountered during the Gateway program. A door appears. There is a knock, the door opens, and a traditionally costumed Native American man comes through the door. He looks at me, says "Hi," and then steps off to the side.

That was strange. I make a note to capture this later in my written account. I am given instructions to move between Focus 12 and 15 several times to get a feel for the differences. I wonder what it would be like if one could move the positive sensations of these expanded states into the physical level. The thought strikes me that if one could somehow shift the lightness of being from these states into the physical body itself, it would last a long time.

Again, the debriefing is short. We are glad to be back at TMI, enjoying the reintroduction to the deeper states. With not a lot being shared, we break for lunch.

As we depart the group room, I ask Karen if we can talk over lunch. She agrees, and we take a table to ourselves. I ask her what she was doing with her hands out on the porch when she came over to support and comfort me.

"Oh, I just smoothed out the energy a little," she says, grinning.

"What energy is that? What are you talking about?"

She pauses, as if trying to find the exact words. "There is very great power in simple human touch," she finally says. Then she changes the subject. "But tell me how you are feeling about your experiences this morning."

"Well, I continue to be very surprised by the emotions of it all. And I'm just not sure about this angelic realm sort of thing."

We spend the better part of an hour exploring these issues. There is logical support for a number of explanations. Fantasy is an easy one, but not one that completely fits the experience. The idea of angelic visitation is challenging for me, but I will not rule it out completely. I am fascinated by the connection of expanded states of consciousness and these experiences. I ask Karen repeatedly about others' experiences in this program. Has mine been unique or does this sort of thing go on all the time? She gently brings me back to my experience and encourages me not to compare my experiences with others. After all, isn't mine interesting enough on its own?

As we discuss the possible relationships of an altered state to such an experience, ideas form about how spiritual beliefs and cultural mythology concerning angels, fairies, leprechauns, and the like could have their roots in some type of altered state experience. Could it be that the human psyche interprets sensations in expanded states in a uniform manner and common mythologies are the result?

"What do you believe about your own experience?" Karen asks. Her gaze feels as if it goes into places unknown to me.

"I don't know" is the only response I can muster.

The Guidelines program schedule offers more exercises that afternoon. I again bump into the fairylike creature and the Native American fellow, but nothing of significance happens with them. A question emerges about the implications of expanded states playing a larger role in our normal conscious awareness. During a break, I take a walk to consider the day's events and to process what has been happening. Where is all this headed? What is real and what is symbolic in all this?

After supper, we assemble for the evening program. This night we will do an exercise called Paired Questioning. Karen and Joe, the trainers, demonstrate the exercise and then we are turned loose to try it on our own. We will use our emerging altered-state skills to retrieve information about some of our fellow participants. We are instructed to pair up with someone we have not interacted with much up to this point.

The exercise involves one person asking questions, some silently and some aloud, of the other person, who has entered an altered state. After a series of four or five questions, we will take a short break and then switch roles. It initially appears like "dial-a-psychic" to me, but I am open to anything. Sarah, the female half of the married couple in the group, pairs up with me. The group breaks up as each pair seeks their own area of seclusion and quiet for the exercise.

Sarah and I are lucky to find an excellent secluded area and stake our claim only moments before several other pairs appear, having thought of the same location. We exchange a few pleasantries, but have a few awkward moments. We cannot inquire too much about each other without corrupting the exercise by exploring each other's background. We have selected each other on the basis of little or no interaction to this point in the workshop. We decide to get started, and I take the first turn in the altered state.

I take several moments to go into as deep a Focus 15 state as I can muster and then alert Sarah to my readiness. The silent-question idea intrigues me. Providing answers to questions that you have not even heard is an interesting experiment. What are the odds that your logical mind can come up with anything even remotely related to an unspoken question?

As it turns out, Sarah wants to ask almost all of her questions silently, so the odds for success seem slim. Sarah focuses her intent, silently asks the question, and then tells me she is ready for an answer. I sit in my chair, eyes closed, and report whatever appears in my mind. With my eyes closed, I try to relax into Focus 15. Images of plants of many varieties appear, as if I have entered a greenhouse. There are flowers and potted plants, and I am impressed with how many there are, all healthy and well tended. I report these images. At the end of the exercise, as I return to a normal state of consciousness, I report that the plants seem important to this question, but I can't understand how. I feel that I have blown the exercise.

Sarah sits quietly. Then she tells me in a soft voice that houseplants are her passion. She has more than two hundred in her home, and many of her questions had to do with a possible relocation she and her husband are considering. Moving her plants is a big worry to her, and one of their options is not to relocate at all, but to set her up in a plant business of some type. We both sit quietly for a while. This has been quite an exchange of information. To me, this level of information is not only credible, but also a validation that something is going on here. Where could I have gotten such specific information?

Then we reverse roles. She closes her eyes and begins moving into a relaxed and altered state. She indicates her readiness. I silently form the question: How can I deepen my relationship with my inner self?

Her response: "I see a man and a woman. It is the love from deep in the heart and this is the key. The need to feel emotion is vital."

That, too, from my perspective is a good answer, but both question and answer are vague. Upon later reflection, I find this a profound answer. The continuing journey of inner exploration taken together by my wife and me over the years is, indeed, superbly captured in this simple statement.

I try again silently with "What is my purpose in coming to Guidelines?"

"I'm getting this image of a pair of eyeglasses," she repeats a few times.

Now this, too, is metaphorical, but "seeing better" is an acceptable response. I wonder what the statistical odds in this sort of thing might be. The subjective nature of the questions and responses certainly makes any sort of scientific analysis difficult.

The exercise takes about an hour to complete. The group reassembles and a number of interesting "hits" of very precise information are shared. Sarah and I volunteer the houseplant story. The exercise raises many questions. Where does this information originate? As a culture, we are casual in remarking about being able to "read" someone's mind. Reflecting on my post-Gateway experience with Mike the landlord and the reality of the houseplant insight raises even more questions. How does this all work? The debriefing time has expired, however, the hour is growing late, and another day awaits our exploration.

Deeply seeking answers to the how and why of an experience may raise very interesting new questions about what the experience itself really was.

—J. R. M.

13

Inner Guidance: Advice from a Greater Self or Self-Delusion?

I wake up early on Monday morning, the second full day for Guidelines. Fresh air and a walk help me get the day started. The morning routine moves quickly, and I find myself taking my seat in the group room awaiting instructions for the first tape exercise.

I am excited to hear that our first tape will be of the free-flow type and at the Focus 15 level. I enjoy the open-ended nature of these unstructured experiences. It is but a few moments and we are in our CHECs, easing into the sound of the ocean surf, the opening part of the TMI tape ritual. I follow the preparatory process, then move through the 10 and 12 levels with anticipation. I have a fondness for the Focus 15 level, as it is clearly a transcendental state and seems to open the pathway to deep states of consciousness. Here are excerpts from my notes on this session:

> At the 15 level I am again in the black void. I settle into this state, but *nothing* happens. I feel my ego/intellect step in and comment a bit about the boredom in this. Just a few thoughts like this, and I try to set the mind chatter aside and just *be* in the void and

explore the experience. I realize that I have never really *touched* the void before. I settle into this idea and push deeper into the blackness itself. I relax into the void. Suddenly, I become aware of my breath. The focus on my breath moves to my awareness of my heart activity yesterday. I am much more than simply aware of my breath. I have *become* my breath. I am deeply entwined within each inflow and outflow of the breathing process.

I find myself within a visual image of my lungs. My intellect steps in to make a wisecrack about tuning into the "Surgery Channel." I let this go and try to open to the experience. The realization comes that I am like a speck of consciousness inside my lungs at the cellular level. From this perspective, I cannot visualize my whole body, only the surrounding tissue of the lung cavity. It becomes like an amusement ride at Disney World—I feel the air loudly rushing by me. The air switches directions with each breath. I have to find a piece of lung tissue to grab hold of or I will be swept out with a breath to some unknown outer world. Taking the role of a single cell within lung tissue is intense, but a very interesting experience.

I relax into the experience. I seem to know that this is headed somewhere significant. I become more aware of my breath and this awareness opens into a multilevel experience. As I become one with my breath, I am going into deeper states of consciousness, but I am simultaneously watching, recording, and commenting to myself in the process. My mind reaches for a word. Suddenly, the "ah-ha" hits me. This is the state spoken and written about by Indian culture. This is the essence of pranayama—the yogic definition of the "Breath of Life." I am deep within the breath of the universe, and it is deep within me.

"Wow," I hear myself comment. "This is really neat. Now what do I do?"

"Ride the breath"—the words come in an *awareness*—that strange knowing that just appears at the right moment. I am not sure what "ride the breath" means, so I try to remain where I am in the process. I follow the rise and fall of my breath each second, and each second could be centuries long. There is a staggering timelessness in all of this.

As I ride each inflow and outflow, they merge into one. Simultaneously, a memory appears. I suddenly understand something I read by Deepak Chopra in which he was trying to convey the sense of the quantum. This is the quantum level. I can see why the words do no justice to the reality of the condition. It can only be experienced; it cannot be adequately described. I have ridden my breath into the quantum universe. Then another "ah-ha" hits.

The quantum universe is contained in a single cell in my lungs and is also expansive beyond comprehension at galactic levels of reality. Another realization explodes in my brain. The extremely large size of the physical universe is contained in the smallest cell and vice versa. Everything is within everything.

I drop deeper and deeper into the cellular level of being. The cell gets larger as my perception becomes the nucleus. The nucleus grows in size and disappears, as I become an atom. The atom grows and disappears as I become a proton and I keep going. Then I realize that there is a point at which I can go no smaller. I target that level and find myself at a very thin membrane. On one side is consciousness itself, and as consciousness bubbles up through the membrane, it becomes physical matter in its smallest building block form, whatever that is.

This is incredible. I explore. I observe. I note. I wander off in many directions at once. Is this what is meant in the Bible quotation "In the beginning was the Word"? Is this the essence of thought becoming matter? I push on deeper and find a "vibration" that supports this "membrane" where thought becomes physical reality. I sense the beat of this vibration. I feel it. It is familiar. It is a heartbeat rhythm. Then I realize that this is the vibration of unconditional love. This part of the universe works all by itself, yet is interconnected within our consciousness in ways that we cannot comprehend. Very few people even know that this level of unconditional love exists, much less offer any gratitude for the vital role it plays in the creation of physical reality.

As I am in a near-rapturous state by this point, I am surprised to get another suggestion from that strange level of awareness. I realize that my consciousness is contained in some unimaginably small level within my lungs, yet I still have full access to all my memories, conscious awareness, and reasoning faculties. Can I stay at this level and relive other experiences?

I am led again by the awareness to replay my far-reaching tape event of "Elation Galaxy" from the Gateway program. I am deep within my lungs and also experiencing the far reaches of space only partially seen by the Hubble telescope. Suddenly, the realization also forms that the vastness of the universe has no meaning at this level—large, small, near, far—it is all one.

I return to focus on my breath again. I am interrupted by the taped instructions to return to C-1 as the tape is coming to a close. I do not want to leave this place. But I know that I must. I follow the instructions and move down to Focus 12.

I begin to feel very dense, and everything begins to take on a feeling of heaviness. As I move into Focus 10, there is a reinforcement of the realization of how much the universe is doing at so many levels to support the formation of this physical reality. Accompanying sensations combine into an overwhelming sense of joy, love, and gratitude along with some shame that I have never noticed any of this before. I feel sadness for how much we take all this for granted. Our intellect makes us so arrogant. It takes a bit of time before I can move completely into the conscious awareness of C-1.

After this tape, I scribble notes rapidly. There has been so much information, experience, and emotion that I only hope I can capture even a part of it. The tape took only the normal 35 to 40 minutes, but it was perceptually a much longer experience, something in the neighborhood of days. I keep writing variations of this phrase: "Unconditional love is an underlying component of how the universe works, and you ride your breath to it."

This tape experience seems to have a strong visionary nature to it. The experience is a strong one for me, but I wonder if a psychiatrist might find common themes that are not all that special to someone who works with the human mind on a professional level. It can be easily postulated that this is nothing more than a dramatic visualization of something read in the past about Eastern cultural traditions or the repackaging of a vast array of data by the intricate neural networks of the brain. It was intense, but how uncommon was it?

I have no way of knowing at this point. Conversely, what would be the perspective of practiced meditators or esoteric scholars who might have sought this very sort of experience as validation of their belief system about the relationship of consciousness and physical reality? What is the source of what I am calling "the awareness" that provides answers or opens pathways to explore? I am not sure I am ready to call this a form of "guidance," but it shows up at key points during intense experiences.

Also catching my attention are "vibrations" that seem physical but are in nonphysical realms. I first encountered this sensation during Gateway, but it is appearing during Guidelines as well. The experience of a specific vibration for unconditional love makes this idea intriguing. The level of emotional experience contained in these events adds to my desire to understand what the source of all of this is.

Before exploring these questions further, I will relate one more tape experience that opens the door to additional questions as to what is going on. The tape is entitled "First Contact with ISH" (the Inner Self-Helper). The exercise is to attempt to gain a formal relationship with the source of inspiration, creative spark, conscience, or whatever gives us that sensation of an "ah-ha."

During the tape introduction, the trainers make extra effort to ensure that no one's cultural background or belief system is being challenged by this idea. We are not being directed to create spirit guides, meet guardian angels, or to begin a career in mediumship. It is noted that some people do, indeed, desire these things, and this exercise can be used in that direction. We are free to do that if we desire. But the stated intent is simply one of making contact with a part of the totality of who and what we are. We are being offered an experience of being "more than your physical body." We will be guided to the Focus 21 level, and then challenged to give form to that source point of inspiration, a form comfortable to us.

As I settle into my CHEC, I am apprehensive about this exercise. That surprises me, and I explore the feeling. I find that it centers in both desiring a relationship with some form of inner guidance and fearing being swept up by trendy, New Age spirit-guide imagery. How can I possibly keep my intellect from interfering with inner exploration? Even *these* thoughts are already interfering with the process. This may be tough. The ocean surf is beginning, and I am not anywhere near relaxed.

I try to convince myself to approach this with the naïveté and openness of the Zen "beginner's mind." I want to be as blank and as open to this experience as possible. Analytical thoughts keep being created, however. I am not trying to lobotomize myself. I merely want to be open to an experience without the irritating analytical aspects of prejudgment. How can I put a stop to this mind chatter?

The ocean surf is in full swing, and I am still headed away from relaxation, not toward it. Finally, I attempt a firm and direct conversation with my ego/intellect. I state with focus and intent that it needs to stay put in the here and now with my physical body, as the part of me that is not physical is going on a little trip. And for once, the ego/intellect cannot come along.

I write these session notes afterward:

> As the ocean surf continues, I watch images form. I find this fascinating since I have not yet made any move toward the hypnagogic state. My ego/intellect begins to form into the shape of a small cocker spaniel puppy. It is as if through my commitment to leave it behind on this trip, it has been deeply hurt by my potential neglect and announced separation. This is fascinating. Then I realize that I have confronted a puppy (my ego in physical form) just after it has messed on the floor. It knows that it has done wrong, and is slinking off into the corner, expecting a swat from a rolled newspaper in retribution. The sad eyes of the dog peer back at me in anticipation and regret for the misdeed. I cannot swat the dog. I have not caught it in the act. Nor can I simply say everything is OK and allow it to return to me for petting and comforting, as nothing will have been learned about the misdeed. A conundrum.
>
> Finally I get an idea. I explain to the dog (my ego/intellect) that I have this exercise to do, and if it comes along it will interfere. I

still love the dog, but it cannot accompany me, as that will interfere with what I need to do. As proof that it is not being abandoned, I will send it love and affection at various times during the exercise. The dog makes one final attempt at looking pitiful, but I won't take the bait. Finally the dog seems to accept that it is not going along, and I start to relax into the sound of ocean surf.

At this point, I am startled by the appearance of the costumed Native American fellow who has shown up in the last several tapes. "Hi, my name is Ralph!" he says in a stereotypical Brooklyn accent. "Would you like for me to take care of the dog?"

I am dumbfounded, yet also fascinated. Here I am, seemingly not yet in an altered state, and I am presented with a set of images that seem physical and real, and are *strange*.

"Well, OK," I finally stammer, not knowing what to do.

"You just go on along and do your exercise," he says, with an air of authority. "I'll take care of the dog." With that, he escorts the dog to a kennel that materializes off to one side. They both fade away, as I am finally able to move on to a light Focus 10 level.

I am in sync with the taped instructions now, so I am finally able to deepen my relaxation a bit. We have a couple of minutes to settle into Focus 10, so I take the opportunity to send love and support to the puppy. With this thought, a small aperture appears and I can see the dog and the Native American there together. They acknowledge my attention, and I return to my Focus Level awareness. That accent is just too much. This is getting weird.

The process of attending to the dog repeats itself again at 12, 15, and just before I enter the 21 state. As I settle into Focus 21, I realize that I am going deeper into this state than normal. The sensation is similar to the one experienced during my silent walk at level 21 during Gateway. I feel increasing connection to a much broader and deeper version of myself. Yes, there is a lot more to me than just the physical body!

I hear a taped instruction to "go inside and find that part of yourself" and a few additional directional cues to follow. I try to turn inward. I am blocked—nothing happens. I try this several times. I try to let my mind go, just *let* it happen. "This is not about trying to do something; this is about allowing it to happen," the tape says. I keep trying to encourage myself. "Don't prejudge, don't imagine, just simply allow."

Finally, imagery forms. It is as if there is a transparent blankness that is suddenly being given the power to form itself into matter. A great number of unpleasant things begin to form and swirl about. There are all sorts of gargoyles, demons, and black sorcery graphic displays. These form and reform through morphing. It is like being submerged in a collection of album covers from hard rock musical groups like Megadeath or Metallica.

Get serious, I chide myself. Here I am trying to connect with my innermost self and this is all I can find? This is not who I am. Give me a break! Go away!

I realize that I have reacted rather firmly. I am still within a Focus 21 state, but I need to reconnect to the deeper levels. The movie screen of my mind returns to emptiness, and I detect a voice in the distance. As the volume rises, I realize it is the Brooklyn accent of Ralph, the pet-sitting Native American. The more he talks, the louder he becomes. The louder he becomes, the more pronounced and irritating his accent.

"Whatsamatta? Why don't you like me? Am I not good enough for you? Is all I'm good for is taking care of the dog? Why don't you care about my feelings? Here I am working my butt off trying to get your attention, and you are off playing around with rock group art."

It is a rapid-fire assault and I am the target.

Then it hits me. Ralph is trying to say that he is a representation of my internal guidance. It is clear that Ralph knows the next five thoughts in my mind before they occur, and the peppering attack begins anew.

"Am I not good enough to be your guide?" He hands me a string of epithets about my unwillingness to be open, my stubbornness, then a set of cutting comments about my not appreciating all that is being done for me. "So?" he says firmly as the word-stream finally ceases, "is *this* more what you have in mind?" He snaps his fingers, and immediately I am in a pastoral scene.

New Age music fills the air. There is a formal garden in front of me. I start to walk toward it and see a seated figure in a thronelike setting surrounded by hanging plants and beautiful flowers. The figure rises to greet me. He is a huge man with a long white beard wearing a long white robe. This doesn't feel right. The imagery is beautiful, but something is wrong. I finally utter, "Aw, c'mon, this is a bit schmaltzy, isn't it?" Instantly, I am back with Ralph, and his complaining begins anew about my unwillingness to see what is in front of my face.

"So," I say, "show me who you are and what is going on here."

Ralph gives me a long look, surveying me intently from top to bottom. "You want to see this as it is actually happening?"

"Yes, I do."

Ralph snaps his fingers again, and we become two specks of bright light shining amidst a field of black. That gets my attention. We stay in this image for a few moments and are then back to a physical forms standing across from each other. I am speechless, but my mind is racing.

Ralph gives me another up-one-side, down-the-other sort of look and then says, "Do you *really* want to deal with all of this? Do you really want to find the source of your true guidance?" He knows my answer before I can form it. He reaches behind his back and whirls around, shoving a large mirror in front of my face. "Then *here!*"

Again I am caught off guard and am stunned. I look at my face reflected in a huge mirror. Nothing else exists in the universe. This is intense, real, and physical. I see my face with clarity. Then there is a morphing of my face into Ralph's and an odd feeling envelops me. In the mirror, there is a dance of my face becoming his and his becoming mine. The pace quickens and goes faster and faster until I am both faces at the same time. At this instant, the mirror disappears and a large Native American man stands in front of me.

Now when I say a large fellow, I mean *huge*: he is an NFL lineman type. At the moment he appears, there is a knowingness that consumes me. I *know* he is to be my "guide." He looks startled, but comes closer to me with a big smile. I am filled with his energy and the image of him changing into a huge wolf and back into himself. He morphs again, and a giant gray-white wolf emerges. I hear the words "Gray Wolf" and the wolf changes back into this big man standing in front of me with a huge grin.

Gray Wolf motions for me to follow him. We stand in front of a beautiful, modern log cabin—his home. He says there is a lot of work to be done, but right now I need to settle in and be comfortable, get to know the place. "Want a Coke?" he asks nonchalantly. This shocks me a bit. Just where am I, and what is going on here?

I look around the spacious kitchen. There is a microwave and a refrigerator. I spot a TV set. He notes my scanning looks and says proudly, "Oh, yeah—I got a dish for the TV." This is a little more than I can handle. My intellect kicks in and starts a running commentary. Here I am in an altered state of consciousness, supposedly being greeted by some cosmic level of inner guidance that has taken large-bodied Native American human form. Yet, out here in the depth of transcendence, I am surrounded by modern kitchen appliances? This is bizarre, to say the least!

He takes note of my confusion and says, "Let's take a walk." Instantly, we are in the woods. We walk for several hours, just being together and getting comfortable. During the walk he snaps his fingers, and we again click into specks of light. He does this several times. We become two light beings in a vast empty space. After giving us human form again, he looks at me and says, "Isn't this an easier form for you to understand and work with?"

"Yes."

As we walk back to his house, he laughs and says this form is more fun for him as well. After all, he can't drink Cokes in his light-body form. He opens an opportunity for further discussion. "Any questions?" He asks it with that beaming grin.

I sense that it is impossible for him to be unhappy. He points toward his cabin and says, "Oh, yeah, besides the TV, I also have a computer and really neat technology that I want to show you." He stops abruptly and scratches his head. "Geez, I'm sorry," he drawls, "but I can't show you everything because some of the neater toys haven't been invented yet where you are. Maybe later."

My mind is jumping back and forth between whether this is all fantasy or something insightful is happening and I should pay attention to every detail. I ask him if he was ever alive in our physical reality.

He says, "Sure, lots of times—many as an Indian."

Suddenly, I receive a "rote" of his lives in Indian form. This is a first for me. Bob Monroe talked of "rotes" in his books. They are "thought balls" that contain a huge amount of information that can be passed among people at this level of consciousness. This is an incredible experience as a new form of communication becomes real for me.

Gray Wolf smiles as he watches my excitement about receiving information in this fashion. "We need to speak some more before we run out of time," he says, with a note of seriousness. He talks about how much work we have to do. He mentions the importance of our being in our physical bodies. He mentions that I will also be working with the angelic entity I met earlier.

He mentions that one of my big problems is going to be keeping my ego out of my developmental experiences. I ask about Ralph. Gray Wolf says he had to use that form because I am so *serious* so much of the time. I need to lighten up. He says that we just need to hang out together to bolster an opening of my belief systems.

Then the angelic fairy creature shows up. She introduces herself as Elizabeth. She mentions that she can be any size at any time. Her present size seems very convenient for now. We sit around the kitchen table in the cabin and talk about working on keeping my ego out of this experience. After several hours of discussion, they rise, indicating that it is time for me to go. We exit the cabin together and, arm in arm, they wave to me from the cabin door. The thought hits me: This is all a symbol for the masculine and feminine aspects of guidance. "Nice imagery," I comment to myself.

Bob Monroe's taped voice announces that it is time to return to C-1, and we begin a guided and extended reentry process. We are taken down slowly after this trip. I wonder if this tape over the years has created deep experiences for many people.

I immediately begin to analyze these events and their implications. The perceived event has taken hours, possibly even days, in terms of the activity and information transferred, yet it was contained in the 35- to 40-minute tape window of a standard TMI program. It could easily be described as a mix of actual past events, New Age fantasy, and a small episode of the mythical hero's journey, all thrown into one. For me, however, it has been physical, real, and profound.

The complexity of this event is staggering. Its imagery has a level of reality that could overwhelm the logical mind. What is the nature of its source? What, if anything, is real and useful about this experience? Is it merely a metaphor-filled dreamlike sequence that can be explained away through the exploration of interwoven psychological issues? Or is it a sojourn beyond the limitations of our physical reality or the boundaries of our consensus-based belief systems?

What are we faced with as we explore inner guidance, enlightenment, and visionary experience? Perhaps we should take more time to examine these areas and the role they might play in our lives. This type of experience is, indeed, common among advanced meditators. Further, there are cultures that would see an experience such as this one as a journey of insight. Rather than enter an internal debate about the validity of my experience, I turn to the comments of an expert in the field.

Counselor and certified hypnotherapist Michael Newton, Ph.D., has worked for years gathering data from clients in states of "super-hypnosis," a state that he finds only few clients can achieve. These special clients appear to have access to some level of "pre-birth" and "post-death" consciousness and can provide verbal reports, under a deep hypnotic state, about what they supposedly experience there. Dr. Newton probed this area for years, seeking correlative experience data that he labeled the "between life" experience. After researching and comparing thousands of such accounts, he documented his experience and developed theories in his book *Journey of Souls: Case Studies of Life between Lives*. He comments on the process and phenomena of spiritual guidance from this perspective:

National surveys by psychologists indicate one person in ten admits to hearing voices, which are frequently positive and instructional in nature. It is a relief for many people to learn their inner voices are not the hallucinations associated with the mentally ill. Rather than something to be worried about, an inner voice is like having your own resident counselor on call. . . .

The inner strength, which comes to us in our daily lives, does not arrive as much by a visual picture of actually seeing our guides, as from the feelings and emotions that convince us we are not alone. People who listen and encourage their inner voice through quiet contemplation say they feel a personal connection with an energy beyond themselves which offers support and reassurance. If you prefer to call this internal guidance system inspiration or intuition, that is fine, because the system which aids us is an aspect of ourselves as well as higher powers.[1]

If we heed "higher" guidance, we must also admit that we are not the all-powerful decision-makers, a belief that seems fundamental to psychological health in our culture. I find it paradoxical that, as a technology-based society, we are suspicious of visionary experience, yet sales of books and paraphernalia for shamanism and Earth religions are increasing, and charismatic religious movements are on the rise.

Fortunately for me, later that day at TMI, I am able to spend time with Penny, the assistant trainer of the Guidelines program. We discuss my experience and explore the issue of ego involvement. I express my concern about the physical nature of the "guides" during this tape. I am concerned that this move toward anthropomorphism by giving guidance the forms of Gray Wolf and Elizabeth is a typical New Age approach. A Native American guide and an angel—how much more would it take for me to make the move toward "beads and sandals"?

She grins impishly as she asks, "So, what form of fear is your ego taking with that statement?"

She nails me with that. Here I am, supposedly open to expanding horizons, but I'm defining boundaries based on stereotypes from consensus culture. I have become New Age phobic for no apparent reason. I suppose I feel that concepts drawn from the New Age section in the bookstore will turn me into a "cosmic frou-frou." Perhaps I fear losing my job, not caring, and living as a New Age space cadet, chasing truths from each new guru that comes along. I laugh at this realization.

In graduate school during the 1960s, I watched the 1930s drug education film *Reefer Madness.* The film was a cult hit on campuses. It portrayed straight and narrow young people driven into drug-crazed addictions by a single puff on a marijuana cigarette. Now, here I am, reacting the exact same way to the appearance of "spirit guides," when I had actually initiated an exercise to find some form of connection to inner guidance.

"Remember the background instructions for the tape," Penny offers gently. "You were to seek a form for guidance that you could be comfortable with. Look for what there is in the form taken, Gray Wolf and Elizabeth, that you are finding uncomfortable—there may be something there for you to explore further."

"The ego strikes again." I say, a bit sheepishly. "Boy, this is a really tough area to deal with. It can be so sneaky."

As we talk, the issue of positive versus negative forms of ego activity surfaces. The ego is a survival mechanism. It is a very good thing to have around. It keeps you from doing stupid and dangerous things. That is positive, as the nature of the ego is to want to do good things. It can also, when misguided, lead you to do stupid and dangerous things. That is a negative form of ego activity. This issue is one that has long been explored in Eastern cultures. It involves the attachment of ego to the outcome of an action or event. Negative ego influence results in actions that lead toward some way of being "better than" someone else.

Positive ego influence is centered in realizing that everyone is interconnected at many levels. Attachment to outcome is the ego asserting that you are "better than" and you should prove it. This kind of attachment can lead to "testosterone-based" decision-making to assert your superiority. That, of course, is not conducive to being open to the subtle input of inner guidance, whatever form it takes.

It's not that you shouldn't care how things come out; caring is a good thing, too. Nor is it improper to have passion for what you do. The point is that you shouldn't be attached to the outcome. The subtleties of this become confusing.

Patiently and with gentle wisdom, Penny leads me to understand that our ego is an integral part of being human. It should not, and cannot, be denied. Just as in the metaphor of the puppy dog, she says we must embrace our ego, give it love and support, not deny its right to exist. This, of course, can present numerous challenges, but it is certainly a worthy effort.

This was not the end of my exploration of the relationship of ego and inner guidance. My struggle with this conflict continues to this day. I believe that this issue may be one of the basic human conditions we explore through the process of life itself.

> Finding inner guidance may not be about seeking a new set of rules; it may be much more about letting go of some.
>
> —J. R. M.

14

Subtle Energy: The Nonphysical Becomes Physical

Everyone attending the TMI Guidelines program is a TMI Gateway graduate. Part of the Gateway program includes a tour of the lab and a review of the TMI research activity in multichannel neural brain mapping of lab subjects in expanded states of consciousness. Seeing the isolation booth engenders a desire to be wired up for a session. Here I am, six months from my first TMI program on my way to the lab. To say that one anticipates one's booth sessions at Guidelines with eagerness and anxiety is an understatement. The ever-present ego with its chatter about performance anxiety echoes in my head: What if nothing happens to me in the booth? Maybe everything in the CHEC unit was just my imagination. What if my Focus 21 is only everyone else's Focus 3 level?

These questions run through my mind as I sit in the lab office with Dr. Darlene Miller, the TMI director of programs, as she tapes electrodes to my outstretched hands. It is 3:30 P.M. on November 1, 1995. This is a moment I have desired ever since I saw the booth during my Gateway tour six months earlier. The reality of having a session has my heart pounding. What if I am so nervous I can't relax?

Dar, as Dr. Miller is affectionately known, senses my tension. Her client awareness skills are still sharp from years of practice as a clinical psychologist before she joined Bob Monroe in his programs and research effort.

"Relax," she says, with a twinkle in her blue-gray eyes. "Relax and have fun with this. It's not a test. It should be play!"

Dar takes extra effort to ensure that I have leveled off to a balanced state of relaxation before the session begins. She inquires about my program experiences. She encourages me to talk about the aftereffects of my Gateway program and what has brought me back to TMI. She seems genuinely interested in how my experiences have affected me.

It is time for the session to begin. She accompanies me to the huge soundproof room-within-a-room with its heavy multilayer door. I am shown the proper method to get on the floatation bed. I will be lying on 300 gallons of heavily salted water, but I will be totally dry. It initially feels like a loosely filled waterbed. Once I have settled in, however, the sensation is of support without lying on anything. The water is heated to a constant temperature that assists in the sensation of loss of body boundaries.

The normal PREP (Personal Resources Exploration Program) session lasts about an hour and a half including preparations and post-session debriefing. Part of the process includes monitoring the physiological activity of the person in the booth. The instrumentation measures the GSR (galvanic skin response) to assess the anxiety and/or intellectual arousal, fingertip skin temperature to assess the level of physical relaxation, and skin potential voltage, to monitor skin electrical activity intensity and tracking of the reversal of electrical polarity if it occurs. TMI has documented an interplay of these three factors in such a way that elements of psi can be observed during the session to provide feedback to the researcher.

As my session begins, I have choices of whether to move into Hemi-Sync tones or do the traditional tape format of ocean surf and resonant tuning. For familiarity's sake, I request a little surf and resonant tuning. I might as well do this within a routine framework. The instructions for the next step are given clearly and simply, but apparently (with possible "interference" from inner guidance, I am to find out later) I misunderstand them. What I think I hear Dar say is "I will tell you when you have reached Focus 10, and then we can begin." In reality she said, "Tell me when you feel that you have reached Focus 10, and we will begin."

My documentation of this session later grew beyond my initial session notes. This session turns out to be so personally important that I write an article, "There Are No Mistakes in the Booth," and send it to Dr. Miller. She later tells me that when something seems to become problematic in lab activity, she pulls out my article, has a good laugh, and things seem to turn out all right in the end.

Here is my coverage of the experience:

> I settle in and follow the sounds of surf and resonant tuning. I make my movement toward Focus 10 and feel that I have popped right up to it. I await Dar's voice in my ears confirming that her computer readouts show that I have indeed made it to Focus 10.
>
> Silence.
>
> I wait a bit longer, but there is still no word from Dar. Well, after all, this is the booth, and I *am* probably a little nervous, I think. I take a brief check of my physical state and realize I am breathing heavily. I decide that I can relax more by attempting to move up to levels that I would have defined as Focus 12, or even 15. I do this and then again wait for word from Dar.
>
> Silence.
>
> I'm still not even at Focus 10. I am not quieting down very fast because of nerves. My thoughts continue to flow and I decide that due to my nervous condition, what I have thought was Focus 15 might be only at the real Focus 10 level when supported by lab level instrumentation. My analytical mind steps in and I realize that perhaps relaxing a little more might help. I try to move to my Quantum 15 state (the level of deep intense Focus 15 that I have discovered involves "riding the breath" to a very deep and intense level).
>
> Silence.
>
> There is still no confirmation from Dar that I have even the smallest move to a Focus 10 level. My frustration begins to grow. I

decide to try pushing to my deepest experience level, Focus 21. I settle in a state that "feels" like Focus 21 to me, and I realize that I have little awareness of my body.

I see a full-size human form made of golden energy and flying around the booth. Interesting. I've never seen anything like this before. I wonder if I should say something to Dar about this guy. This would be neat to begin recording on the tape commentary. Then the thought occurs, if I wait just a little longer, Dar will see that I have reached Focus 10 on her computer, tell me, and we can officially begin.

I decide not to say anything. My reasoning is that if I am seeing things like this golden energy entity, then I must assuredly be nearing the Focus 10 level. My left brain directs me to wait a few moments more and surely Dar will tell me I have made it. I can always begin my tape-recorded comments by mentioning this golden energy guy that has joined me in the booth.

I watch the golden energy guy perform lazy figure-eight loops around the top of the booth and then move around in random patterns. I realize that it might be interesting to move around alongside him. I do this easily and without thought. I am floating around the top of the booth with a golden form of energy, but without realizing the implications or reality of what I am doing.

Finally my analytical mind interjects, "Man, I must be really nervous. Surely the computer readouts would show at least Focus 10 level relaxation by this point." My analytical mind is getting restless and has begun to seek new solutions. I ought to concentrate on the Focus 10 level anew. After all, that was the specific instruction. I begin again the whole process by focusing on the Focus 10 protocol. I try to assist this effort with a little quantum breathing.

I feel myself going deeper, but there is still no word from Dar over my earphones. I wonder if I should say something about my frustration, but my pride will not allow it. Suddenly, a physical sensation returns me to a level of body awareness. I begin to feel the heat of the waterbed. Quickly, it becomes very uncomfortable as I feel sweat forming down my back. Again, I think of saying something about what is happening. Again, I decide not to. I will follow the instructions to the letter. I will wait until Dar tells me I have made it to Focus 10.

Silence.

The waterbed begins to get more uncomfortable. It is getting *really* hot. I look for a way to relieve this sensation. Hmm, maybe I ought to try to lift out of my body a little so I won't feel the heat. I accomplish this with a little nudge of the sensation of my body, and I feel my body drop away.

Ah, that's a little better, I sigh. C'mon, Dar, I've got to be relaxing at least a little bit—I'm out of my body, for Pete's sake!

Silence. Again I consider saying something about what I am experiencing, and again I decide not to. I am bound by my understanding of the instructions. Dar will tell me when I achieve Focus 10, so I will wait. I will not say anything, as I am obviously not there yet according to the instruments. My frustration mounts.

My analytical mind again reaches for options and solutions. Maybe I can use some help from those guides. As soon as this thought forms, Gray Wolf materializes to my left, Elizabeth shows up on the right. I ask for some help. Gray Wolf says, "I'm here— you're doing fine." He says something about how he wouldn't miss this for the world.

Now what is that supposed to mean? Elizabeth just stands there and smiles. Fat lot of help they are, shoots through my brain. The gold-energy guy shows up again. I am getting bored; random thoughts roll through my brain.

Silence.

My intellect begins to speculate on possible explanations. I invent scenarios. Maybe tricks are played on every participant in the lab to ensure a good experience. Perhaps a standard practice is to wait 15 to 20 minutes before announcing achievement of Focus 10. This ensures you are totally relaxed. By doing that, participants are guaranteed to reach a deeper Focus 10 than they ever reached in the CHEC unit. As that thought forms, I know I am right. I think, that's why they don't want people to share their experiences before everyone has been in the booth. Well, I can wait them out!

Silence.

I again perform the protocols and move through Focus 10, 12, 15, and 21. I note that I have lost all body awareness. The feeling is liberating. It is as if I don't have a body and never have had one. Bodies are simply not needed. My analytical mind steps in at this point, noting, "Isn't it interesting that I can be so relaxed I cannot even feel my body and still not register at focus 10 in the booth?" With this thought, another follows, "Wow, Focus 21 in the booth must really be *something!*"

My mental processes continue with my concern about not yet hearing from Dar. Clearly, I must go deeper to get to Focus 10. I return my intent to recapture the feeling of Focus 15 breathing again. My resolve is firm as I internalize a dedicated direction: After all this time, I will not be denied. I'm going to get to 10 in this thing, dammit. I decide to ignore Focus Level numbers. They are meaningless training wheels anyway. Then as I feel the flow of breath taking me toward what I consider focus state feeling, I silently chant a new mantra, "Go deeper, go deeper."

There is still no word from Dar. I have still not made it to Focus 10 according to her computer readout.

My intellect moves into speculation mode again. I wonder if she has wandered off, maybe someone caught her attention. I wonder if I should go check on her. At this point, I feel myself get up off the waterbed. Without thought, I walk through the booth door without bothering to open it. I walk around the booth and peek into the control room. I see Dar watching the computer screen. I feel reassured that she is still there. (The fact that this is an out-of-body experience passes me by. I simply needed to check on her and do, without a thought as to how I am doing it.)

Still there is only the silence of pink noise Hemi-Sync in my earphones. No hint of Dar's voice.

OK, so I'm still not showing much relaxation on the readout, "Let's go deeper!" With intensity, I drop further into the quantum breathing processes. I take the time for my left brain to concentrate on my breath rate. I decide that it is about half of what it was the last time I checked. That's cool, we're making progress finally, I comment internally. OK, let's see what my perception of the time might be. I calculate that I must have been in the booth for about 20 minutes. I remember that perceived time is always longer than reality, so it must have actually been 10 minutes or so. My analytical mind is still there for me even though I no longer have a body. A watched clock never moves, even when you don't have one. I chuckle.

Still, nothing from Dar.

In another attempt to try for Focus 10 recognition, I go through the full protocols of Focus 10, 12, 15, and 21. My thoughts are within a timeless realm. Hmmm, no body, no waterbed heat—OK, this is a good sign. I am in nothingness. It must have been at least 15 minutes of time by now. I just know at any second that Dar will be saying "You have reached Focus 10" and we can begin. I need to be patient and go deeper. I check things out and note my breathing rate is continuing to drop. How can I be breathing when I have no body? I think of the breath becoming the body and vice versa.

Silence. Still no Dar.

I continue quantum breathing. I drop into deeper levels of quantum reality, into the vastness of the universe. I am far beyond physical time and space, even beyond the nonphysical levels of Total Self. Wow, OK, I must be getting close to 10—push deeper. I hear a loud snap and catch the beginning of a snore. Well, I must have a body around here somewhere. I laugh.

But my resolve is reasserted with the realization that I have heard a snore. No, we are not going to allow sleep; this is the booth experience. I have waited for years to do this. Sleep is not going to happen—go deeper, I must relax. I am immersed in the pulse of the universe. I realize that there is order to the nonphysical that we may not be able to understand, and there is also an order to the physical. It all begins with unconditional love. The pulse of the universe is the carrier wave of the vibration of unconditional love. I nestle into this sensation and feel the warmth. I am within joy. I become joy itself.

Silence.

After lying in bliss and unconditional love for hours, I decide that maybe I should give up and go to sleep. Then I realize what I have just thought about doing, and reinforce my resolve to reach Focus 10. My left brain will only be satisfied if I have the verification by the instrumentation of the booth. My thoughts roam: how dramatic this will all be when we can actually start at the Focus 10 level. I am solid in my resolve. I know that I will achieve Focus 10 any second, and we will be starting at any moment. I attempt to go even deeper. Faces float by. Unknown symbols and energies surround me. It appears that I am being surrounded by the truly fundamental energy of the universe.

OK, Dar, where are you. I'm *ready!* The thought races through my being.

Silence.

My frustration has reached a point of no return. OK, let's just give up—I am not going to make it to Focus 10 in this damned booth. We'll have to try it again someday.

"Richard."

It's Dar's voice, it's really Dar's voice! Yes! Yes! I scream silently. I've *finally* made it to Focus 10 in the booth!

"Yes," I respond aloud. "I am ready. Is it time to get started?"

My left brain cranks up self-analysis commentary. OK, I have made it to Focus 10 by booth standards. How long did it take? It has to have been at least 30 to 35 minutes. Jeez, I am really slow—why? I really felt deep toward the end. How could I possibly have not started the readouts on the relaxation point by now? Ego—I guess I really was not going as deep as I thought I was—OK—now we're ready!

"How are you doing?" Dar's voice asks in the earphones.

"Fine. Are we ready to start now?"

There is a moment of silent hesitation from Dar. She continues, "10—let's go to 10."

Oh, jeez, that's strange. I thought we just made it to 10. Wait a minute, the tones are going *down*. Hey, I'm going down, too. Jeez, I'm going *way, way, way* down. The sensation of falling is real and physical. It feels like I am falling miles upon miles. I am puzzled and confused.

"10-10-10," comes Dar's voice in the earphones.

"Oh, yeah, I'm there," I say to myself. But I am not at the sensation of a Focus 10 level. I am still way out there somewhere, and I am not sure where. Just what is going on here?

"10-10-let's go to 1."

I am confused. The session is over. Yet apparently just as I got to Focus 10 was the moment the session ended. OK, I didn't even relax enough to get to 10 in the booth . . . bummer.

"Let's count down together. 9-8-7-6-5-4-3-2-1."

Hey, I'm cool. I try to reassure myself as I begin to realize that I still feel like I am about ten feet above my body, but I cannot tell for sure; it is still dark. What a letdown! OK, I'll survive. I'm not sure what is going on, but I'm OK. The light goes on.

"Is the light on?" Dar asks.

"Yes."

"Hmmm," I think, "this is strange." I realize that my body is nowhere near where I think it is. I can see it by looking down on it and I can also feel myself in two places at the same time. I feel I am still separated by about ten feet from my body. Whoa, I am feeling a little dizzy. Am I disoriented!

"Lie still . . . I'll put some music on for you."

"OK."

Soft music begins both in my earphones and from the speakers on the booth wall. I am still struggling to sync up my body sensations with my awareness of where my body should be. This turns out to be more difficult than I thought and requires significant effort. I am also *very* confused and disappointed, as the reality is taking hold that the long-sought booth session is over.

The handle of the large door clicks and Dar enters. She removes the wires and electrodes that have refused to confirm that I had reached Focus 10. "Er . . . what did you mean—is it time to start?"

"I was waiting for you to say that I was at Focus 10."

Dar looks stunned. She recovers quickly and asks, "Just how long do you think you have been in here?"

"Oh, about 30 to 45 minutes," I reply, as I mentally attempt to adjust for nerves, hyper levels of expectation, and time misperception.

"You've been in here nearly two hours. You're not kidding, are you? You don't remember?"

My mind begins to short-circuit with simultaneous thoughts and an inability to think. I recover enough to respond, "Did I speak aloud, and there's all sorts of stuff on tape?" Perhaps I had stepped aside and was unaware of what had happened in the here and now.

"No."

Disappointment and confusion return. We leave the booth and go into the lab office. I probe for understanding. "I've just been try-ing to relax enough to go to a level that would show on your com-puter as Focus 10." I pull myself together enough to parrot my understanding of the instructions I had followed to the letter. "Didn't you say you would tell me when I reached Focus 10 and we could start?" I push my point with my commitment to the instru-mentation, "After all, you were the one with the printouts!"

Dar laughs nervously. "Oh, my—this has never happened to me before. I'm not sure *what* to do." She reflects deeply for a moment or two. Then her decision is made. She begins to put on her coat and says, "Look, I'm really sorry, but I'm late for another appointment, so we'll have to wait and talk tomorrow. I'm so sorry, but I have overstayed my appointment already because I didn't want to interfere with your experience."

"Uh, what experience?" I stammer. "I thought I never even made it to Focus 10."

It is clear that Dar will not discuss my situation any further. She says, "I am really sorry, but I really do have to go. The instructions were for you to *tell me* when you were at 10. You never said any-thing, and you went off in a hurry—I thought you were having great mystical experiences, or something of that nature. My impres-sion was your experiences were so intense that you didn't want to talk about it, so I didn't want to interrupt you."

I know she needs to leave, but I am still confused. I now know I have at least gone "off in a hurry" but what does that mean? "Did your machines at least say I had some sort of Focus Level?"

"Oh, yes," she says, walking over and glancing at the com-puter screen for confirmation. "You were clearly in very deep states.

But we'll have to wait to talk about it tomorrow; I really do have to go. I'll meet you at breakfast. We'll have to wait until then to discuss it again. I really am so sorry."

My booth session is over. I am consumed with the thought that I am a failure. I exit the building and notice that it is now dark outside. Perfect, the dark night can match my mood. I shuffle back to the Nancy Penn Center, where dinner has already begun. As I enter the dining area, the noise of the outside door opening causes everyone to look up. There is a look of "I wonder what happened in *his* session" on faces around the room. If they only knew: nothing happened. Or had it? At least it was an interesting experience.

I pick up the tray of food saved for me. I avoid the questioning eyes that seek an indication of booth session success. I keep my eyes downward at the floor. I want no eye contact. I move to a table in the far corner and sit alone. I am in a funk, but I also wonder what I might learn from this experience. I push my food around and try to explore what has happened. A flush of emotional disappointment fills me. But my left brain never lets me down as it begins its incessant probing. There *has* to be some logic to all of this. There has to be some sort of lesson embedded in this. I have to pry it loose from the catacombs of my brain.

From deep within, I sense a tug of awareness. It is the little sense that an answer is about to appear, and then it bubbles up like a smack up the side of my head. It presents itself as a cosmic joke I have played on myself. My intent for this experience had been to integrate the physical and nonphysical, reality and "out there." I had wanted to make it all into the same thing. Maybe I have accomplished this without even realizing it. I stayed physically aware in the booth, so much so that I had not even realized that I was in an altered state.

Perhaps the lesson is not needing left-brain instrumentation to tell me what I already knew but was too cautious to admit. One part of me feels that this is a stretch toward rationalization just to make me feel better, but something about it feels right. Either way, I will see the data tomorrow.

I am not hungry, so I quit pushing the food around my plate and start to get up just as the bell rings. An announcement of the evening program is due. Most evenings at TMI there is a formal program in David Francis Hall. But as supper comes to a close, the trainers announce that tonight we will do a tape session instead.

We move to the group room and settle in for our pretape instructions. This is to be a discussion with whatever form we have established as our connection to inner guidance. By this point in the week, there have been numerous sessions involving our relationship with guidance ISH, but these sessions have all been guided. This will be the first opportunity for a free-flow dialogue. I might not find out anything further about my experience, but at least the opportunity is there. It is almost too good to be true.

I can go directly to Gray Wolf and Elizabeth and see if they can shed any light on this. I settle into my CHEC and rocket through the process. I skip across the sound of ocean surf. I leap over the drone of resonant tuning. I jump into Focus 21. I picture the cabin where we normally meet and, as so many times before during this week, I find myself physically standing outside it. I am still not sure how all of this works. I just know how real it feels and how visual it is.

Some others in the program have not experienced things visually, but have heard voices, had kinesthetic confirmations, or simply "knew" what was being communicated by their guidance. For them, too, the reality of it has become intense. There is no right or wrong way about all of this. We have each developed a mechanism that works for us.

Here are the session notes from this memorable event:

> I walk into the kitchen of the isolated rural cabin where we always meet. They are both at the kitchen table, coffee cups in front of them. Gray Wolf and Elizabeth have obviously been waiting for me. Their heads are down and they will not look at me.
>
> "Are you mad at us?"
>
> "No."
>
> "Are you sure you are not mad at us?"
>
> "No." I realize they have played some role in the orchestration of the booth session.

"Are you *sure* you are not mad at us?"

It is clear that they are concerned with my disappointment. "No, I am not mad, but I am a little confused. All I want is to understand what happened." I mean that. My initial frustration has subsided. I have created a plausible rationalization. I can live with this. I do want understanding of the event, if there is any.

"Where are you right now?"

I have to reflect on this a minute and then I realize that they want to know the location of my physical body. "I am in a CHEC unit doing a tape."

"And how does it feel?"

"Just like in the booth," the words come out without thought.

Light bulbs go on. No, that is the understatement of all time. The light of understanding explodes in me, as it all becomes clear. Tears flow.

"I don't need a booth. I don't need a CHEC unit. I can do this anywhere, or at any time. This is real and I can learn to use it as a tool."

The next morning I awake at five o'clock, alive with energy. I go down to the group room. No one else is around, and I need to meditate. Understand that I have never been able to stay in any sort of meditation for more than five minutes without my body cramping. Besides this immediate discomfort, my mind also goes off in all sorts of directions—everywhere but in meditation. Well, that is not what happens this time.

According to trainers who passed by (completely unnoticed by me), I sit cross-legged for 45 minutes. No discomfort. I enter deep states that I have previously envisioned as only possible in a CHEC unit or the TMI research lab. How wrong I have been. I am able to relive the entire booth session, moment by moment, sensation by sensation. It is just as real as the previous day. This time, however, I am able to bring new appreciation to the process. I connect with multiple levels of Total Self and experience oneness with the universe.

The TMI Gateway program had sent me far out into the universe.

Guidelines has now taken me deep within the small. Now, sitting here in meditation, I realize that no matter how far out or how far inside you go, you still end up in the same place. You have reached who and what you are.

I meet Dar for breakfast with a big hug and comment that it had been the *greatest* booth session ever. Now it is her turn to be confused. When she had left the evening before, my session had appeared (to me) to be a disaster. She relates that she had even spent an uncomfortable night worrying if she had given the wrong instructions and had ruined my session. I tell the story and she laughs with me. We make so much commotion that others join us and I retell the story with the same results. I realize another joke: I must be the only person ever to spend over an hour in the TMI booth and never "make it" to Focus 10. As the title of my paper to Dar says, "There are no mistakes in the booth."

Let's talk about this a bit. Are there two anthropomorphic, intelligent beings out there in some other dimension named Gray Wolf and Elizabeth? Is there any possibility they can manipulate elements in our physical reality to create such an experience for me? The easy answer is "Of course not, that is ridiculous." Do I believe that Gray Wolf and Elizabeth are figments of my imagination or the results of some potent psychological issue buried deep in my subconscious? No. I am not ready to jump down that path either.

Before I continue, let me step back before that last paragraph and restate it to make sure you don't misunderstand me, or think I am crazy, or both. Do I believe there are two people that live in some other dimension who are manipulating my existence in this one? No, I do not.

Are there such things as spirit guides who control our destiny? No, I do not believe that either.

OK, just what am I trying to say then? I propose that there may be more involved than we consider in our usual approach to such things. But before we move into discussions that lead to how all of this relates to facing the complex issues that I described as part of my niece Caroline's world, I want to share two additional events at TMI.

My tape experience with Gray Wolf and Elizabeth that Wednesday night after the booth session did not end with the realization that these altered states and their expanded perceptions are available any time any place. The tape continued with a lecture concerning the interplay between the mind, body, and spirit in these activities. From my notes:

Gray Wolf speaks in a serious tone. He says: "The idea and concept of forging mind, body, and spirit in a triangular and interconnected way is a good one. The reality, however, is a validation of the experiences you've been having to this point in time. Because you have now realized that being in the CHEC unit and the booth are no different, you can have the experiences anywhere. You can have the booth experience outdoors. The chart tomorrow [the physiological printout from the booth] will show a very strong experience, but you must understand that this level of experience is not limited to the booth. It can be experienced anywhere. There is love involved in all of this, too. You *must* also give love."

"I understand that now," I comment.

Gray Wolf flashes a big beaming "I'm so proud of you" smile and says, "Go on—go back to your tape exercise, and don't forget to have a good time."

Elizabeth is beaming, too, as I turn to leave the cabin. I thank them both and send them my love and gratitude as I go out the kitchen door.

I drop down to Focus 15 and approach a version of the TMI building that exists "there." This "TMI-there" image has been a target in earlier exercises, and I find Guidelines participants assembled in the group room.

I join the group, and we begin spiraling upward to some unknown destination "out there." There is a transition from physical forms into light forms. We rise upward into a golden glow above us. As we approach this golden glow, there is sensation of great warmth and love.

I am suspended in the moment. Suddenly, and from nowhere in particular, there is a brilliant flash of diamond light. Now when I say that there is a flash of light, I am not talking about anything small here. I am talking about a mega-experience of light so bright and sparkling that it cannot be described, only experienced. This experience lives vividly within you for the rest of your life.

It is as if there is a planet-sized diamond that reflects a thousand layers of light, and they all emanate from a single tiny point above me. All I can see is a brilliance of diamond-like light streaming outward from this point. There is nothing else to see—everything is obliterated or consumed within this light. There is also an infinity of time for the experience to take place. It may be seconds or centuries. In the instant that all of this happens, I am filled with an impression of "the Goddess." This occurs as a *knowing* and *being* at the same time. There is the same love and warmth I experienced during my first tape session of Guidelines.

In the next moment (or the next millennium—it is the same to me), two things happen. First, tears flow; I am consumed in joy, bliss, love, whatever words one can find meaning in for such an event. Second, I am picked up as a physical force grabs me, as if a giant hand grabs my heart and picks up my body by the chest. My face contorts in terror and bliss. I am skeptical of levitation, but this is what it feels like. Oh, for a video camera in my CHEC this night.

I remain in this awkward position for some time. My chest is contorted upward, as if some giant hand shakes me slowly up and down. All the while, I feel fear and bliss as if held between heaven and hell and knowing that both are merely stop-off points on a greater journey. Finally, I am released and I fall to the mattress in a heap. It seems to be about a three-foot fall.

I am weak and cannot move under my own power. My roommate, Louis, has a habit of bailing out of the CHEC as soon as the instructions are given to return to C-1. Then he runs downstairs to scribble notes before anyone else arrives in the group room. I manage to shift my weak body enough to move my hand to pull back the heavy black curtain. I notice that this time, thankfully, Louis is still in his CHEC. I lie there in a strange position, my arm extends far outside, until the tape ends and he pulls back his curtain. I tell him I need help. I am so weak I cannot stand without assistance. I remember my previous energy-zapping experiences, and I know that I need to be grounded. I need to get outdoors.

Louis helps me from my CHEC and half-carries me down the hall past others now emerging from their rooms. Elaine, one of the other participants, has had training in working with the subtle energies of the body. She asks what is going on and responds to my request for assistance in grounding. Louis steps aside, and Elaine helps me to the parking lot.

As soon as we hit the gravel area, the "electrical" discharges begin. My body contorts and convulses as I attempt to remain upright. These energetic discharges make my initial experiences at Gateway following the "Elation Galaxy" tape seem tame. I am not going blind this time, but the effects are dramatic. I convulse standing up, as powerful energy reams me out.

Penny, the trainer, comes out to ask what is going on. At this point, I am down on all fours being zapped several feet off the ground in successive discharges, yet I feel no fear. I seem to be more of an interested observer than a frightened participant.

Elaine asks Penny if she knows what is happening. As I noted earlier, Penny and I had talked about her studies at an esoteric school of "energy mastery," and this seems to be right down that alley. She says nothing, but assumes a wide-stance pose in front of me as I stand up, shaking uncontrollably. She holds her arms in a semicircle around me. I perceive green energy form a tube around me, as if a giant green glass test tube has been put down around my body. The shaking begins to subside. I ask what she is doing.

"Just holding some space for you."

After a few minutes, she confers with Elaine as to what is going on and what she is doing, but I cannot hear the conversation. Within ten minutes, it is all over, and I want an explanation.

"Well," Penny pauses, searching for words. "Some would say that you just had a little excess energy to burn off, while others would say that you just had an initiation."

"What kind of initiation?"

There is no response. Penny smiles and comments, "Sometimes it's best to just have the experience and move on." She turns to go back inside the building, and then adds, "Don't let your left brain get in there and mess up your experience."

I'm not sure what this means, and I am in no way satisfied. But apparently, it is all the explanation I will be getting at this point.

Neither Penny nor Elaine shares any of the parking lot episode with anyone. To those who inquire about my being carried out, they just say I needed grounding, and they have helped me. I want further explanations from Penny, but she will offer only that it would not make sense to me until there is more time to process the event. While this frustrates me, I realize how exhausted this experience has left me. I surrender to the need for rest and retire for the evening. I sleep very well.

I have one more experience to relate to bring this chapter and my TMI activity to a close. The following morning is the last full day of the program. By this point in a TMI program, one is saturated with experience and ready to return home, yet lamenting the fact that another inner exploration is about to end. As we assemble in the group room for the first tape instruction, I sense the anticipation of the final day.

Our first tape is a free-flow at the Focus 21 level. We have explored many new skills during this week. We have learned to report without losing contact with our altered state. We have learned to vibrationally "phase" our nonphysical bodies into nonphysical realms beyond Focus 21. We have established contact and formed a relationship with some part of our inner selves we have identified as our guidance. This tape will give us the opportunity to explore any of these areas we desire.

What happens after this tape session is most important. We reassemble in the group room for the debriefing. Keith, the airline pilot, sits next to me as the session begins. He speaks first. His speech is slow and deliberate. It is clear that he has just gone through some deep level of personal experience. His eyes water as he speaks, but he does not lose emotional control. He speaks of experiencing the far reaches of the universe. As his version of the tape event unfolds, it sounds like he has been through something similar to my "Elation Galaxy" journey through the cosmos.

He speaks of star fields and unity with the core of the universe. His language is a mix of the technical and the emotional as he tells of the universe of stars that he has experienced. As he finishes, I look deeply and supportively into his eyes with the intent of saying "I understand, I've been there, too." I give him a hug. A tear runs down his face.

As we separate from this embrace, his eyes lock with mine and I sense his understanding of our shared experience. He tells me later, however, that at the point when he locked eyes with me something strange happened. He experienced the same star field as in the tape, but emerging from my eyes.

What I see in his eyes is a merely a very peculiar look, as if he is asking a question, but communicating only with his eyes. This is a look that I would expect to be exchanged between people about to experience sex for the first time. Something akin to "Are we actually going to do this?" With this look, a series of events begins that, according to the others who witness it, takes only seconds, but to me seems about 15 minutes of slow-motion action.

As Keith pulls away from me, my right hand slides down to his sacrum. At that same moment, my left hand forcefully comes up of its own accord and attaches itself to his heart area, and I sternly say, "Keith, it's OK, let it go!" He falls over backward with a loud cry. He lies on the floor. Where my actions and words came from, I do not know, but it happens quickly and then the events unfold as if they are on their own track.

Keith lets out an animal cry and convulses like I did. A combination of all of my experiences at TMI comes into play. My hands tingle as they had when I had gone blind with the energetic overload of the "Elation Galaxy" tape. I feel surges between my hands and flowing up my right arm and back down my spine into the Earth. I have no clue what to do.

I look to Penny, my energetic crucible from the night before, and somehow calmly say, "I think I need a little help here."

She rises from her place at the front of the room and places a cushion under Keith's head to provide padding as Keith continues to jerk and move about. He is in no apparent pain, but some sort of emotional or energetic cleansing is going on in the area of his heart, accompanied by deep vocalization.

A sound rises in my throat. It is the *AUM* of resonant tuning. Within a moment of my own *AUM* vocalization, the group chimes in and a chorus of interwoven tones fills the room. Penny simply sits there, apparently "holding space." The vibration continues in my hands and Keith continues to writhe and jerk about, oblivious to everything that is happening.

In what seems like a half-hour to me (later confirmed by others to be only two minutes), it is over. Keith opens his eyes with joy and fear. I know what has to be done. He needs to be grounded. It is my own Gateway experience all over again, but this time I am the one guiding the process. It is as if my prior experience has been some sort of apprenticeship, and this is the final exam. Little do I know at this point that this experience is only the beginning of a much greater one that will extend over the next few years. I ask Keith if he can stand. He can, and we go outside for grounding exercises followed by a short jog together. Most of the others follow us outside to continue observing.

Just what is going on here? I am not a psychologist, but it appears to me that, in one sense, Keith experienced an intense cathartic release of some trauma or issue unresolved until that moment. New Age followers or subtle energy healers might say that he had a "clearing" of his heart chakra. From a medical perspective, I was drawn into a long discussion with Fred, the medical doctor attending Guidelines. He said that he did not know what had happened, but he was intensely curious about it.

We discussed and explored this event as a group later that day. Some of the most interesting things to me were the varying perceptions of the time elapsed from the time Keith went to the floor until it was all over. The estimates ranged from less than a minute to 15 minutes or more. Of even greater interest was the revelation that five other people in the group had intense co-experiences involving emotional or psychological releases having to do with their relationships with others or themselves and centered in the area of the physical heart.

It was as if some powerful field of energy had manifested between my hands providing a catalyst for multiple cathartic releases in people physically close to Keith and me. This was fascinating. But what did it mean? What was its source? How could anything more be learned about this type of energy being released during this experience, if indeed energy is what it was?

What happens to me if I suddenly discover there is a whole lot more to me than I could ever have imagined? Perhaps that may be the beginning of true wisdom and a whole new level of humility.

—J. R. M.

15

Conscious Beliefs versus Subconscious Realities: The Complexity of the Perceived World around Us

Science provides us with a strong and stable basis for understanding our physical reality and making judgments as to what might be considered real. Religion and philosophy have provided us with moral and ethical codes as well as guidelines for appropriate human interaction. We shape our view of how the world should operate with some degree of both scientific and religious perspectives to assist us. Examination of the operational aspects of both the scientific and the religious paradigms reveal how they differ and how they might actually be more similar that we imagine.

The scientific method, with its concentration on objectivity, is one of the underpinnings of Western culture. For something to be considered real, according to science, it must prove itself over and over again under standardized conditions. That is, something is not considered true unless the supportive experimentation can be replicated, not just once, but repeatedly and with predictable results. With this emphasis on replication, the viewpoint or experience of an individual event loses its importance. To develop an acceptable framework of reality, it is not important what your individual experience is. It is only important that it is similar to others being tested. The goal is the statistical norm, not the anomaly of uniqueness in a single trial.

But what happens if the most important issue to pursue is embedded within that unique experience of an individual? What might be learned in many scientific inquiries if more time were spent pursuing the cause of the anomaly rather than discounting it in the search for the statistical norm?

Probably nowhere is this more graphically illustrated than in research on psi. Even the very gifted psi subject cannot perform one hundred percent of the time. In the worst-case experiment, it may even be possible that only a single but powerful phenomenon is observed. For example, in a well-constructed psychokinesis experiment, a subject is able to move the mercury in a barometer within a bell jar two millimeters by concentration alone.

This is well observed and well documented, but, unfortunately, the phenomenon cannot be reproduced, except by another individual and perhaps years later. It is anomalous; this anomaly is unnerving for the scientist, and the phenomenon is considered irrelevant for scientific purposes. The impossible actually happened, yet it cannot be easily replicated for further study. Over time, scientists may observe multiple occurrences of such events, but the events themselves appear anomalous within the greater collection of data. New insight may occur if the anomalous subset is studied as holding potential for an understanding that may impact the paradigm of causality.

Explorations into the world of the nonphysical encounter a similar situation with the unique individual experience. This is a major element that creates complications in trying to construct objective experimentation in this field. It is difficult to be externally objective about another individual's personal experience. For example, let someone say that God has personally appeared to him, and the immediate questions arise as to what is his proof of the visitation. A person appears to have had a profound experience, yet only his word is offered as proof. Even if the experience has demonstrable life-changing by-products, the issue of proof of an action in the realm of the nonphysical is particularly perplexing to Western culture.

In other cultures, a profound individual experience may be highly respected as an indication that this person is a visionary or teacher of some sort. In many primitive cultures, a spiritual experience may even qualify one for a leadership position. But that is the situation of the primitive society, and we, in our modern society, are considered more culturally and technologically advanced. Of what use are profound personal experiences in addressing the issues of everyday life in a modern sophisticated culture, one whose technology has taken Man to the moon and invented the Internet?

In one sense, we are revealing a lack of balance in our human nature by such a one-sided focus on physical reality, and our long-term development as a species will suffer for it. If we continue to deny the nonphysical elements that also play a significant role in who we are, we may eventually erode our capacity to dream or be visionary in any way. That would be a significant loss. Smugly, we imagine that our current beliefs about how the world works are correct and will never change. But wasn't that the belief system of almost every culture in history during their heyday?

It is easy to see why such personal experiences are defined as outside the world of science and relegated to the realm of the religious and philosophical. Yet it is equally important to determine some way to explore such profound experiences in the pursuit of truth.

How we approach such issues in one sense partially defines our culture. How comfortable are we in embracing the unknown? I am speaking here of the type of unknown that challenges scientific and religious levels of reality. Take, for example, a UFO, complete with ambassadorial staff, landing on the lawn of the White House and inviting the United Nations to join the "United Planets." That would be a belief-challenging concept! But just for the sake of discussion, let's take this idea seriously. What would be the impact on our belief systems?

The mere mention of UFOs and flying saucers usually brings up a powerful response, as it seems to engender emotional reactions immediately. Why is that? From my perspective, one reason is this issue strikes at the core of our belief systems. That is, too much of what we believe in and consider real is challenged by even the potential for such a phenomenon to be true.

In a report for NASA, prepared by the prestigious Brookings Institution, the need to explore such implications is noted. The document, "Proposed Studies on the Implications of Peaceful Space Activities for Human Affairs," is a cherished document of UFO enthusiasts who theorize that the government has long withheld information about the reality of extraterrestrial life due to the potential impact on worldwide culture. I must admit that this is an interesting claim in itself, but my curiosity here is for the concept of challenges to our basic belief systems.

A flying saucer, complete with alien ambassadorial staff, landing on the White House lawn would certainly offer complications to our perspective of what we think we know about things. How would the leaders of religions be able to incorporate nonhuman life into their belief systems? How might we view alien religious beliefs and reconcile them with our own? What happens to our own values and concept of self-worth when we are presented with such evidence of being a second-rate culture in the field of space technology?

Since we didn't land on their planet's White House lawn before they came here, we must be inferior. That is a scary thought. There are, of course, the opportunists that would speak of the potential for business, trade, and intellectual cross-fertilization. There would also be the paranoid, however, who would be consumed by how easily such technology could be used to conquer our planet. What are these aliens up to anyway?

While this is an extreme example, it illustrates a dilemma. As a society, we are not well equipped to deal with things that don't fit our previously existing models. I believe that this is the case as we face the exploration of consciousness itself. As we are presented with hard evidence that challenges our core belief systems, we tend to want to cling to our comfort zones.

Needing to stay within comfort zone boundaries may be one of the reasons that we have not made more progress in the exploration of age-old mysteries pertaining to the relationship of mind, the brain, and the "I." These areas present problems to the strict boundaries required by the scientific method and to the acceptability of individual experience in the philosophical realm. With advanced degrees in psychology and physiology, pioneering consciousness researcher Dr. Valerie Hunt, of the University of California at Los Angeles, has spent a lifetime studying core issues of mind, brain, and consciousness. In *Infinite Mind*, she writes:

> When a problem has remained unsolved for so many centuries, the approach and some of the fundamental tenets are probably incorrect. Our long-held premises about the mind are probably wrong because the linear, frontal attack has not answered many questions about the mind and human experience. New approaches loom where the mind is explored through extended realities, different types of awareness, thought, and spiritual experiences.[1]

We probably don't realize the degree to which we operate from within our belief systems. We think we operate from the perspective of how things actually are. People in the Middle Ages didn't realize they were ignorant of the scientific method and had significant misinformation as to the movements of the solar system and even the rotation of the Earth. They thought they understood exactly how things worked and believed it deeply enough to shape their society around it.

Religious trends and movements may even reflect the current worldview. When there were vast open spaces in the world and very little population, there was a sense that God had provided the resources of the world for Man to utilize. The abundance of the world was unlimited. Man had the God-given right to conquer and dominate nature; it was there to serve him. The exploitation of nature, manifest destiny, and colonialism could then all be supported by the religious tenets of the time.

As a population grows and there is a realization of finite resources and a "shrinking planet," there should be an accompanying move toward inner exploration, conservation of resources, and the adoption of a worldview of interconnection. Even though science and religion split with the rise of the scientific method, there is still a significant connection between them in terms of consensus-based cultural ideas of what is acceptable and what is not.

Objectively investigating the world of consciousness and the implications of psi requires us to be open to the idea that psi may operate in the background of our universe whether we believe in it or not. This idea, taken as fact, presents us with challenges to our belief systems that many of us would rather not consider. This is the type of challenge currently being presented by quantum physics as research challenges basic tenets of the scientific method. This concept is well summarized by Russell Targ, noted physicist and psi researcher, in his book *Miracles of Mind.* He writes:

> The quantum physicist's view is that we live in a "nonlocal" reality, which is to say that we can be affected by events that are distant from our ordinary awareness. This is a very alarming idea for an experimental physicist, because it means that laboratory experiments set up on an isolated table are subject to outside influences that may be beyond the scientist's control. In fact, the data from precognition research strongly suggests that an experiment could, in principle, be affected by a signal sent from the future![2]

The experimental physicist noted by Dr. Targ must be able to accept that what may appear as anomalous in the physicist's results actually has more validity than previously considered. Nonlocal influences are not dramatic or confrontational. The influence of the nonlocal works in the background. The world of the quantum and the nonlocal is very subtle, like the dripping of a water faucet. No notice is taken of it until gallons of water are seen to have disappeared. How can we incorporate quantum physics into our worldview and open ourselves to a broader spectrum of consciousness? Any such effort will require a much broader and multidimensional viewpoint.

How might we explore new approaches to consciousness and belief systems? First, what can we learn about quantum theory? I am not a quantum physicist, nor is it my place to outline the theory here. I recommend the excellent and easily readable works of two authors that have made the world of the quantum and consciousness more understandable. Dr. Dean Radin's *The Conscious Universe: The Scientific Truth of Psychic Phenomena* provides a masterful outline of the nonlocal nature of consciousness and the interplay of mind and matter. Michael Talbot summarized vast amounts of breakthrough research from a variety of fields and created an easy-to-read classic, *The Holographic Universe.*

These two authors offer new understanding of our evolving consciousness. Their perspectives give weight to the validity of the individual experience. Their model to explain psi activity is akin to the nature of the psychology of Carl Jung and his model of a universal consciousness. Both Radin and Talbot offer vast amounts of scientific research that not only support such a model, but also connect it with the recent theories of quantum physics.

Do any of these approaches explain the sort of experiences I had at TMI? I believe they do. My experiences at TMI might represent the opening of a doorway to a greater understanding of the universe from a scientific and spiritual perspective. Daily, people around the world undergo experiences similar to mine with little or no background to interpret them. As we approach these experiences, it is important to understand that there are explanations and scientific theories that reinforce such experiences. Such experiences are natural and embody models of the universe that go far beyond consensus belief.

Scientists are also seeking new ways to understand the building blocks of the universe and the relationships that intertwine matter, energy, and consciousness. Dr. Amit Goswami, professor of physics at the University of Oregon, describes the relationship of consciousness and matter in *The Self-Aware Universe:*

> What we call the mind consists of objects that are akin to objects of submicroscopic matter and that obey rules similar to those of quantum mechanics.
>
> Let me put this revolutionary idea differently. Just as ordinary matter consists ultimately of submicroscopic quantum objects that can be called the archetypes of matter, let us assume that the mind

consists ultimately of the archetypes of mental objects (very much like what Plato called ideas). I further suggest that they are made of the same basic substance that material archetypes are made of and that they also obey quantum mechanics. Thus quantum measurement considerations apply to them as well.[3]

When we consider consciousness and physical matter to be more related than is taught in high school physics, we are moving into territory unknown to most people. This is the opportune time to spend a few moments discussing what happens when the mind encounters something unfamiliar. We try to classify it, name it, make it familiar, and only then possibly explore what lies beyond.

Since the nonlocal and associated nonordinary states of consciousness lie outside the five senses, they are difficult to describe. In the face of this, we make up words or we try to describe the event in terms that make sense to our five-sense understanding. During many of my experiences at TMI, I referred to "vibrations" within the nonphysical. This is a good example as, conceptually, vibration needs a physical medium to vibrate within. There should be no vibrations possible within the nonphysical; however, I could only describe the sensation as like a "vibration."

I am not playing word games here, but attempting to convey the difficulty in reporting phenomena beyond our five senses' capacity to interpret. Such activity calls for a new language and communication process. Since many of the experiences are individualistic in nature, this further complicates the issue.

In regard to my initial booth session during the Guidelines program, I spoke at length during a later TMI trip with F. Holmes "Skip" Atwater, the director of research at TMI. My issue was the sensation of scalding heat generated by the flotation waterbed during my session. Skip noted that the small five-watt heater element could not quickly do much heating of three hundred gallons of heavily salted water. So what caused this real sensation?

Skip postulated that I might have become consciously aware at a level normally experienced only when unconscious. That is, my brain was presented with data it didn't know how to process. As I entered deeper states, I became more aware of subtle energies, and my rational mind had no experience with such forms of invisible energy. Had I been unconscious, there would have been no problem, as no conscious interpretation would be required; being unconscious is the state in which the brain has existing protocols, such as dreaming, for dealing with such energies. Being conscious and facing phenomena normally dealt with only in unconscious states, however, forces the issue of data resolution.

Faced with input about unknown subtle energies and not being able to identify them, my brain searched its database of experience for something familiar that could be inserted as an identity for these new unclassified sensations. The only thing remotely similar was the idea of "being roasted on a barbecue pit." Not that this is the reality of the subtle energy sensation, but that was the best my brain could do from its database, so that sensation was plugged in for me to experience.

After discussion with Skip about this issue, my conscious mind held new interpretive information that could resolve any future data input concerning subtle energies. I did not have the "being barbecued" sensation again, but I found myself more capable of identifying subtle energetic movements as I moved into deep states of consciousness.

Just as the "being barbecued" scenario proved to be a lesson in learning the language of sensation in deeper altered states, perhaps the entire experience of inner guidance might be similar. The highly structured experiences of the TMI Guidelines program offer a way to approach elements of the deeper self in a measured manner. Similar approaches can be found in wisdom traditions around the world. People seek totemic animal and nature spirit support in tribal cultures. In modern culture, those of spiritual and New Age inclinations seek spiritual guides and helpers in many forms.

Almost every religion includes some form of prayer or ritualistic application for support and guidance from a higher power. Many of these approaches include elements of focused or altered states, whether they are identified as such or not. There are associated cultural belief systems that surround all such activity, and I challenge none of these. I do not want to judge the belief systems of others, and hope they do the same for me. What I do wish is that people will regularly examine their belief systems and constantly ensure that their belief systems serve their needs. This is an important undertaking.

Faced with such challenging ideas, we can each make choices as to how we will deal with their implications for our belief systems. We can remain comfortable in our current state, and much of our society does this regularly. We can blindly accept the experience of others and their interpretation of it. Many cults and numerous religious sects have been born from this approach. Or we can seek our own experiences and challenge our belief systems in ways that will either expand them or justify them via testing and personal experience. To explore fully the realms of our totality requires not that we believe we are something greater than our physical selves, but that we momentarily suspend the disbelief that we are not.

I am not saying that one should disregard skepticism or critical thinking. Individual experience is vital to the exploration of consciousness. Psychology has long shown, however, that individual perception is not to be blindly trusted. Our perceptive abilities can be easily influenced, and we are quick to misinterpret physical events. The simplest optical illusions easily demonstrate this fact.

Numerous psychology experiments show we will perceive familiar patterns whether that is the actual physical reality presented or not. We face challenges in any effort to broaden our powers of perception. Our belief systems and our habits of perceiving only through the limitations of our five senses may represent obstacles to our growth. Moving beyond these limitations can open the door to a greater view of the self and provide access to the source of our imagination.

The role of creativity and inspiration as part of how we learn is the subject of speculation by many authors and researchers. One expert in the field of consciousness research, Mona Lisa Schulz, M.D., Ph.D., a neuropsychiatrist and neuroscientist, writes:

> Whether we call them hunches, gut feelings, senses, or dreams, they're all the same thing—intuition, speaking to us, giving us insight and knowledge to help us make sound decisions about any

number of actions we take. Intuition occurs when we directly perceive facts outside the range of the usual five senses and independently of the reasoning process.[4]

Whether through religion, self-inquiry, the rigors of science, or psychoacoustic supported journeys into altered states, taking the path to a broader perspective of self and human potential is important. How far can we go if we can suspend disbelief and remove our limiting belief systems?

I cannot answer that. It is to be hoped that no one can, as an answer would be a limiting belief in itself. Perhaps it is best said by Caroline Myss and physician C. Norman Shealy in their book *The Creation of Health:*

> When ordinary thinking can no longer accommodate the demands of the times, new paradigms of conceptual thinking must be sought in relation to the nature and spectrum of the crises. We clearly need to grasp the fact that all crises are now global in proportion and no longer limited to national boundaries. Thus, we must create a paradigm of conceptual thinking that is inclusive of the whole globe rather than just selective nations.
>
> . . . These insights have enough potency to transform the way we live and the manner in which we understand reality. They are so powerful, in fact, that one must consider why these perceptions are now simultaneously penetrating into every level of life. Like a foundation being laid to house an entirely new species, we must ask, "Who is the architect of this design and for what purpose is this happening? Is it possible that we are being directed by Divine Guidance to enter into a process of transformation in order to ensure the survival of life on this planet?"[5]

Defining yourself totally from a physical perspective may allow you to be perceived as less eccentric, but cut you off from the most important part of who you really are.

—J. R. M.

16

Egos Running Amok
(or, My Way Is the Only Way)

There are no easy answers to age-old attempts to better understand the complexities of the human mind. Deep questions remain as to whether the center of consciousness is physical or nonphysical in nature. In the West, we often become confused on this issue, as our egos and analytical minds are hard at work in the attempt to convince us that their function forms our nature. Are we merely the sum of our life experiences as we react to stimuli? Is our mind merely operating software in some physical brain-based "computer"? Or is there validity to the traditional religious concept of the soul? Science, philosophy, and religion continue to dance around these questions about the physical versus nonphysical underpinnings of consciousness.

Because of the technological orientation of Western culture, we focus on five-sense-based science and tend to avoid self-definition issues. In Eastern cultures, there is a long tradition of reflection and inner exploration. Each approach has its benefits. The late Claire Myers Owens, psychologist, researcher, and Zen author, summarized Eastern and Western approaches as follows:

Neither the rational man of the West nor the intuitive man of the East has been able *alone* to solve the problems of the world. The West has contributed reason, science, technology, and wealth, but suffered spiritually. The East has contributed intuitive wisdom, the religious life, and spiritual art, but suffered from poverty, disease, and illiteracy. Nations and cultures as well as individual man may be moving in the direction of wholeness. The West is in need especially of training in self-realization.[1]

In our Western worldview, we may be unsure what is meant by self-realization. With the mere mention of the words, we may conjure imagery of isolated ascetics in contemplation. Our analytical mind questions the pragmatism of such efforts. Let us view self-realization as being open to the idea that there is a "you" that exists independent of ego-supervised response mechanisms. Self-realization efforts involve activities to make contact with this greater "you," and also to think and pre-consider your actions from this level rather than from only the ego-directed perspective. I propose that nonlocal phenomena are an indication of the existence of this greater self and that establishing a relationship with this level of self may result in a range of natural psi activity that we now consider anomalous.

Breakthrough science has now postulated that consciousness may be nonlocal in nature. While numerous theories define consciousness and the mind existing as a fieldlike phenomenon, there is also recognition of the physical realities represented by brain anatomy and function. Deepak Chopra, M.D., emphasizes the importance of the physical (the brain) and nonphysical (the field of consciousness). In his book *How to Know God,* Dr. Chopra writes:

As soon as one uses the term *field*, a step has been taken into the realm of quantum reality. The brain is a thing with material structures like a cortex and a limbic system. A field is not a thing. The magnetic field of the earth exerts a pull over every iron particle, causing it to move this way or that, yet nothing visible or tangible is doing the moving. In the same way the mind causes the brain to move this way or that.[2]

For illustration purposes, let us use an example of an iceberg and say that an entire iceberg could be a representation of the field of consciousness. With this model, we can then make several comments about the role and formation of the ego and analytical mind.

The tip of the iceberg that we see floating on top of the ocean represents our conscious awareness in the physical world. This is a world that is supervised perceptually by the ego and well documented by modern psychology. From the perspective of the ego, the operating principles of physical reality are all in that portion of the iceberg floating above the water. The wind and wave action that shape that portion of the iceberg could represent the life experience that has provided a frame of reference for the ego and analytical mind. Is this all there is to us? No, of course not.

From our perspective looking at the iceberg from afar, we know that there is much more. From the perspective of the ego iceberg tip, however, all that exists is known to be that portion above the water. Philosopher Eckhart Tolle masterfully explains the falseness of this view. In his book *The Power of Now,* he writes:

> As you grow up, you form a mental image of who you are, based on your personal and cultural conditioning. We may call this phantom self the ego. It consists of mind activity and can only be kept going through constant thinking. The term ego means different things to different people, but when I use it here it means a false self, created by unconscious identification with the mind.[3]

Staying with our iceberg example, the ego and analytical mind are kept busy perceiving the world and interpreting it from the perspective of the iceberg tip. The integrity of the iceberg tip is determined by its ability to maintain itself while subjected to the life experiences of wind, rain, and wave actions. As these challenges are presented, the ego and analytical mind attempt to hold to a previous self-image by trying not to melt, not to have chunks fall off, and not to be eroded by the wind.

In our human form, this mental perspective is noted by psychologist, yoga teacher, and author Stephen Cope in his best-selling book *Yoga and the Quest for the True Self.* He writes:

To some extent, most of us are unconsciously driven by our ego ideal. The ego ideal is simply a set of ideas in the mind about how we should show up, how we should look, feel, behave, think. This collection of ideas and mental images is created out of fragments of highly charged experiences with important love objects in our lives, and out of the messages we receive in our interactions with the world as we grow. It remains largely out of our awareness. The blueprint for the ego ideal is first laid down by our parental injunctions about how to be, or how not to be. These highly charged messages are taken in whole. They become our scripts for life.[4]

Clearly, our ego has an arsenal of scripts from life experience that combine into a worldview and attempt to outline the proper actions within it. In this example, the tip of the iceberg has no conscious awareness of the vast amount of subconscious or nonphysical ice that holds it above the water, much less the ocean in which it is floating. In this situation, ignorance is a form of bliss, as there is much less to consider when all that can be perceived is above the waterline. This, in one sense, is the way we normally experience our lives within physical reality.

But what path is open to the ego and analytical mind if an event occurs that defies the view shaped by consensus constructs of reality? What happens if there is a realization of the totality of the iceberg, above and below the waterline, not to mention the ocean on which it floats? This challenges the status quo beliefs about the nature of physical reality and who is in charge. The ego is stunned by the possibility that there is more to the iceberg than imagined from the above-the-waterline perspective.

The ego must now assert itself even more strongly as protection from being part of something larger that it cannot control. The base belief systems of the above-the-waterline world must be reestablished. Any direct challenge to these belief systems is a direct assault on the role of the ego to interpret reality. The ego exerts all effort possible to bring the experience of this world into alignment with its analysis of what is in our best interests.

I now believe that this is the situation I faced during my initial experiences at The Monroe Institute. My initial reactions were those of anyone faced with belief-challenging events. These reactions are the primary way that our ego-based defense systems remain in control of our perception and perspective. The following is my version of the normal sequence of events.

First, the ego summons the analytical mind. In the midst of some subtle energy manifestation or the sense that some level of information might be available from the broader field of consciousness, the analytical mind jumps in and interferes. It starts spouting all the reasons that such a thing cannot be happening. Issues of doubt mushroom with comments like, "This is not possible!" The intellect becomes active and overcomes the experience through overanalysis of what might or might not be happening.

Second, the ego summons forces to challenge one's mental stability. Internal commentary rages: "Get a grip on reality." "You must surely be losing your mind by even considering such a thing." Questions are presented, like "What would your friends think if they saw you acting in this manner?"

Third, every possible resource in one's background and belief systems is energized against the possibility of the experience and the wisdom of letting it continue. Here is where religious taboos as well as societal sanctions will challenge any movement toward a recognition of and relationship with a powerful and greater form of self. Issues related to "losing control" quickly arise to frighten the seeker.

Fourth, given any moment of inactivity or solitude, the analytical mind asserts boredom and seeks ways to amuse itself. This is a very effective tool for keeping the conscious mind from discovery of some sense of greater self. We must not forget that actual experience of a larger self automatically relegates the analytical mind to a second-class status. Keeping your intellect occupied is an excellent way to keep your conscious mind steered away from any sort of contact with your greater self.

To prove this, simply close this book and attempt to think of nothing for several minutes. You will find that it is extremely difficult to do. Thoughts simply appear, and the more you attempt to seek a state of no-thoughts the more intense the thought formation becomes. Attempting this exercise gives you instant appreciation for the practiced meditator who has some degree of success in such an activity.

We face a number of challenges in trying to become aware of the physical and nonphysical parts of ourselves. These challenges must be met if we are to achieve the goal of gaining conscious access to all that we are. We must remember that our ego/intellect will work overtime to convince us that we have already achieved magic contact with our inner direction. The ego-directed path to this feeling is accepting the false idea that we are already *better* than someone else. Thinking that one has the answer to enlightenment or the true path to inner direction is a self-defeating activity.

For example, it is a self-serving idea that I'm going to Heaven because of my belief system and that you are not because you don't believe the same way I do. Such a belief system is significantly influenced by the ego and can easily lead to the attitude that I am better than you in the current reality of the here and now because of my beliefs.

The idea of absolute truth, from a religious or philosophical orientation, arises here, and I do not want to lose the focus of my comment. My focus is to note that the ego and analytical mind work in ways that seek to create "better thans" in order to retain their grasp on the steering wheel of perception and perspective. I am very suspicious of any belief system that provides *me* some sort of merit badge that *you* don't have because *you* don't believe the same way *I* do. Clearly, this is ego centered.

Another way of looking at all of this is from the perspective of judgment. Judgment is a powerful tool and a potential instrument of bigotry. Used properly, it can be a healthy discrimination mechanism as to what is a positive experience or situation to be pursued versus an experience better avoided. Used improperly, judgment can determine ways of being "better than" others in a vast array of situations. In the "better than" scenario, judgment is merely a filter for already decided questions. Since one already knows the answer—mine is the true belief system and all others are wrong—then judgment is merely the process we use to apply this belief system. Conversely, in an open discussion or analysis, judgment can assist you in piecing together your perspective on complex issues, taking all possible input and treating it objectively.

Sadly, many of us can get caught up in the concept of being "better than" in some area as an important element of how we define ourselves. This can take many forms in a materialistic and competitive culture such as ours. Because much of our Western culture has incorporated elements of competition in our formative and working lives, we can easily be intoxicated with the strong need to be "better than" as a basis of self-worth. We may need a bigger car than our neighbors in order to feel psychologically complete. We may need a certain salary level, a specific label on our clothes, or membership in a particular group or club to help define our self-worth. We may not even be aware of these drives as they are subtle and are quietly manipulated by the ego in an attempt to make us feel better about ourselves.

Eckhart Tolle notes this approach to life as he continues his commentary on the primary materialistic activity of the false self-based ego:

> Since the ego is a derived sense of self, it needs to identify with external things. It needs to be both defended and fed constantly. The most common ego identifications have to do with possessions, the work you do, social status and recognition, knowledge and education, physical appearance, special abilities, relationships, personal and family history, belief systems, and often also political, nationalistic, racial, religious, and other collective identifications. None of these things is you.[5]

So what is "you"? How can you have a conscious relationship with the "real you"? Apparently, we are all asking this question with greater frequency. In the most consumer-oriented country in the world, bookshelves are filled with self-help material about defining oneself through inner rather than outer means. The popularity of such material is indicative of our cultural hunger for increased inner awareness. Many people are beginning to seek meaning beyond technology and creature comforts. Apparently, there is a growing response to Claire Myers Owens's statement, cited previously, about the need in the West for greater efforts at self-realization.

Perhaps one sure way to challenge the ego's strong control on reality is to expand conscious awareness through altered states of consciousness. Nonordinary awareness may provide a doorway to the realization of the totality of the iceberg, including that portion below the sea. Journeys into expanded states can provide deep, intense, and even profound levels of experience. These activities offer actual experience of a greater totality of self.

It is my opinion that such a situation occurs when we begin to experience expanded states of consciousness, whether through a TMI program, meditative practice, religious ritual, or even a near-death experience. Drugs can also induce altered states of perception, but offer little of positive value. Artificially induced shifts of perception are flights of fantasy rather than the direct experience of expanded consciousness. Drug-based altered states involve a surrender to external physical forces (chemicals) that inhibit rather than open pathways to contacting greater selfhood.

I offer seekers a word of caution in the attempt to experience expanded states of consciousness. The wily ego and adept analytical mind will constantly try to reassert their control. The caution is: Be wary of their influence in realms of the nonphysical where they have no authority.

It is easy to understand why such things as immersion in bliss and contact with one's inner guidance challenge the ego. Significant pressures may be placed on those portions of our selves that, under ordinary conditions, assume major roles in discriminating the real from the unreal, determine our decision-making processes in general, and provide the basis of our perspective on self-worth. Even under less challenging conditions, our egos are under extreme pressure to balance huge levels of decision-making about who we think we are, where we fit in, and what an appropriate response to some stimulus might be.

An ego, or the analytical mind, can easily be overloaded when confronted with some form of greater self and a universe beyond the normal physical sphere. Such a vista is all right for the ego to consider intellectually, as the analytical mind loves intellectual games. *Experience* of a greater self, however, is another thing entirely.

Clearly, the analytical mind can interfere with attempts to access and explore aspects of a greater self. If you can make peace with your ego and intellect during such an event, however, a greater problem awaits you after the experience. In Western culture, we have little to prepare us for experiences of expanded states of consciousness. Actually experiencing a greater self, making contact with guidance, or being immersed in unconditional love is intense, intellectually and emotionally. The ego can easily step in at this point and declare that you have touched God and that you are the one to save the world. Emotions are easily overloaded in blissful states, and we must never forget that we actually live within the physical and must be able to continue to operate effectively there.

Please note here that I am not saying simply surrender your analytical intellect in this circumstance. On the contrary, when faced with a greater selfhood, I strongly encourage you to keep your intellect at a peak function. Skepticism and the analytical mind should step in at this point. Faced with the profound, however, you might not be able to stop and consider it.

Our language and view of the world are based in how our five senses perceive. Movement into nonphysical realms goes far beyond the five senses, yet the experience must be interpreted through intellectual activity of language, imagery, and feeling. You should not, however, let your intellect get in the way of the experience of an expanded state of consciousness that may lead to a realization of a greater selfhood. Allow the experience first. Immerse yourself in it, and then examine it from every angle. Attempting to analyze it during the experience makes it an experience of analysis, not an experience of greater selfhood.

As we face the vast expanse of "out there" through our expanding awareness, there is much to consider. As we face the depth of our own "in here," there are belief systems and life experiences that can easily confuse our exploration. From my own journey, I can only offer advice, not direction. I advise that what is real and meaningful for you must be determined by you. I also advise that your ego can be your enemy and your friend in such a process. This choice heightens our personal responsibility, as we cannot blame a god or the universe for the choices we make.

My experiences in nonordinary states have presented a profound sensation of union and interconnectedness of all things. I believe this is, at the most rudimentary level, common to all of the great spiritual and religious traditions. To me, the great teachings of each major religion mirror those of the others. I find common themes of unconditional love, compassion, and service to others.

Beyond these lies a vast realm open to the self-serving games of the ego and analytical mind. Surely, experience of divinity cannot be limited by language, yet there are fights over sacred texts that may simply be descriptions of individual experiences of bliss states. Most such disagreements are entirely ego-based. Yet attempting to be objective and fair when two people with great emotional investment are discussing such things usually upsets both sides because of the ego attachment to the outcome.

Sadly, many people use religious affiliation as a way of separating themselves from others. This is merely the ego creating an exclusionary filter to be "better than." Now, I do not seek to impugn the religious beliefs of anyone. Everyone is entitled to his or her own belief system, and I feel strongly about this issue. I would be remiss, however, if I did not note that many fundamentalists lack tolerance of those who do not share their faith. The idea that "my belief system is the only true one" may be a strong indicator of a level of belief of an individual, but it can clearly complicate discussions about broader spectrums of consciousness.

This type of ego-based activity stimulates significant damage to truth-seeking by bloating emotions and values that support a "false self" perspective in arrogant and self-defeating ways. To me, a person of faith shines as an example by not judging others because they do not follow the same faith.

Ego-based tactics are not limited to the realm of the religious fundamentalist. Many New Age followers externalize and separate themselves from the rest of us by saying that their path is the only true one or that their guru is the only one with the true spiritual answers. Some say that their inner guidance process or spirit world guides are superior to any that you might have.

The words "Spirit guides me" and "It's God's will" are the same at a rudimentary level of language. Both phrases reflect a level of separation and externalization. These people may have a clear connection with some level of guidance. Indeed, they may have a very good one. My concern is that their language and action appear to be based in an ego-stimulated "better than" approach. This type of language and action, to me, are more common among people who have read about the world of the nonphysical self rather than personally experienced it. Firsthand accounts from near-death research, experienced meditative adepts, and laboratory-documented psi performers all indicate increased humility, inner calm, and feelings that everything is interconnected.

I believe that it is perfectly all right to have divergent opinions and different belief systems. Arrogance about the superiority of your opinion or belief system, however, is another thing. Becoming aware of your emotional state is an excellent barometer of such arrogance. There is a mechanical nature to defensiveness, and getting your buttons pushed is a good sign of predictable ego-based responses.

When you find yourself becoming defensive, realize you are trying to defend against something that challenges the false self created by the ego. This manifests in many ways of "feeling better than" or even "not feeling as good as," which is the same thing from an ego perspective. It is wise to be suspicious of all who proclaim that their way or belief system is the true one. Such is an ego-based orientation, and one that is not open to challenge on any level of examination. Such a belief system may be the true way for them, but not for you.

Challenge everything, including yourself, in the pursuit of your own truth. It can certainly be a formidable task to experience physical reality, explore the totality of who and what you might be, and seek a balance in all that you do. This is what life is about.

As we seek, we must not predetermine what we might find. Because our egos and analytical minds play such a significant role in our actions and worldview, we must take special care to embrace them, yet not allow them to take us in directions that are not support-ive of our innermost core selves. Their job is to be in charge, and they must guard against the thought that they might be only a part of something much larger.

Perhaps the fear of full self-realization is a primary one for the ego-directed consciousness. Spirituality writer and lecturer Marianne Williamson eloquently notes this idea in her book *A Return to Love*. Since Nelson Mandela used the following words of hers in his presidential inauguration speech in 1994, these words are now widely quoted:

> Our deepest fear is not that we are inadequate. Our deepest fear is that we are powerful beyond measure. It is our Light, not our darkness, that most frightens us. We ask ourselves: Who am I to be brilliant, gorgeous, talented and fabulous? Actually, who are you NOT to be? You are a child of God. Your playing small doesn't serve the world. There's nothing enlightened about shrinking so that other people won't feel insecure around you. We were born to make manifest the Glory of God that is within us. It is not just in some of us; it is in everyone. And, as we let our own Light shine, we uncon-sciously give other people permission to do the same. As we are lib-erated from our fear, our presence automatically liberates others.[6]

> The clues are always there. The question is whether or not we are willing to pay attention.

—J. R. M.

without taking the time to walk with me through the intervening chapters, you may only partially understand the answers you find there. As the old axiom of computer software development says, "Take the time to do it right, because the time to fix it later will be much harder to find, and it will be a lot more expensive."

The expanded state of consciousness, whether gained through using TMI tapes, meditative techniques, chi gung exercises, religious ritual, or other prescribed protocols, allows expanded insight to occur from deeper levels of the self. From my perspective, each additional experience in an expanded state adds to a blurring of the boundaries of the mental/nonphysical and spiritual/nonphysical. Put another way, expanded states of consciousness enable the emergence of a multidimensional perspective that can become a doorway to the totality of self.

Armed with the expanded perspective of the whole-brain approach, I have come to understand the power of personal experience as a profound teacher. As I have said throughout the last few chapters, the analytical mind can limit our perception, whereas expanded states can empower additional perceptive abilities. It is challenging, however, to create a balance between expanded exploration and an appropriate degree of objective analytic skepticism. Seeking this balance requires a level of vulnerability that challenges the ego in its role of being in charge of our surroundings. An ego view of being in charge includes preventing threats to our belief systems.

Gaining personal experience in expanded states of consciousness opens doorways to developing such a balance. In my case, my time at TMI allowed brief but convincing experiences. Many other people have taken such explorations into the expansion of consciousness and specialized talents have resulted. Numerous books and a growing body of scientific research chronicle human capacities for remote viewing, intuitive medical diagnosis, touch healing, and even measurable psychokinetic (PK) phenomena (the ability to affect physical matter using only the power of the mind). The replication factor remains a question in the scientific capacity to study these events, but documented phenomenal cases exist in abundance in scientific literature. While the scientific method requires predictable repetition, documented events cannot be denied, and neither should they be avoided because of their anomalous nature.

More important, in the absence of a culturally acceptable explanation, public ridicule must not displace objective inquiry. Ridicule does not change the experience or event; it merely places a cultural prejudgment on it.

Following my immersion in the nonphysical at TMI, I was led, through a series of synchronistic events, to explore the impact of expanded states on our physical world. These experiences grew out of my being drawn to a totally unexpected field—the world of subtle energy healing. This is a world, like TMI, that I never knew existed. I learned of a network of healers who work quietly and in the background of our consensus culture. The work is significant and sometimes miraculous. Yet many in this network do not seek payment for their work; they consider it an honor and a service to humanity to perform the healing.

In the next section, I share these experiences and the research I did in attempting to understand them. I illustrate certain points that then serve as a background for addressing the problems of social stress and the need for direction in our lives.

Part V

Embracing the World of Vibration: The Many Levels of Awareness and Healing

The most beautiful thing we can experience is the mysterious. It is the source of all true art and all science. He to whom this emotion is a stranger, who can no longer pause to wonder and stand rapt in awe, is as good as dead: his eyes are closed.

—Albert Einstein

17

The Miraculous Becomes the Mundane: The Experience of Healing Touch

"Excuse me, Richard, may I ask you a question?"

The voice startles me. I have drifted into a distracted state as I take in the atmosphere of the room and survey the mix of people.

"Er, certainly," I stammer, as my focus shifts to the gentle feminine face now in front of mine. "What would you like to know?" I realize she has read my name from the tag pinned to my shirt.

"Are you a physician? A medical doctor?" She questions me with a tone to her voice that indicates she thinks I am a health professional. It takes a second to realize that she is one of the instructors. "We have two M.D.s in this class, and I thought you might be one of them."

"No, that's not me." A second later I begin to realize the impact of what has been said. "We have *doctors* in this class?" I ask this with curiosity and bewilderment.

"Oh, yes, and nurses, too," she says. "We have all kinds of people in this school." The pride in her voice is apparent as her attention drifts to other parts of the room. She is continuing her search for someone who has the appearance of a medical doctor.

This is going to be interesting. I feel that same excitement and uncertainty I felt during my first few hours at The Monroe Institute. I wonder what I have gotten myself into and am intensely curious about what this experience might entail. On one hand, I am sitting in a rented community center room in San Diego awaiting my first class in the School for Enlightenment and Healing, or SEH, as I am hearing it referred to around the room. On the other hand, I am not sure why I am here. It is a curious intertwining of events that has brought me here.

It began by meeting Quinton through a mutual friend. Quinton is a prominent attorney in my town. He handles big cases in his area of legal specialization, the kind that end up on the front page when huge settlements are awarded. Over lunch, we connect, and I discover that Quinton has a secret life that would shock his coworkers. He has studied "touch healing" at the Barbara Brennan School of Healing and is now in his senior year at the School for Enlightenment and Healing. Discussion of auras and healing touch is certainly not the type of conversation I expected from the knife-edged mind of a brilliant attorney.

Assuming you have never heard of Barbara Brennan, let's take a moment to outline her phenomenal story. As noted on her web page (www.barbarabrennan.com), she is an author, healer, teacher, and physicist who devoted more than 25 years to researching and exploring the human energy field. She holds a master's degree in atmospheric physics and worked as a research scientist at NASA's Goddard Space Flight Center. This former NASA research scientist claims she can "see" human energy fields or "auras" and can treat disease by correction of these "fields."

Quinton explained his background in the world of touch healing, and I shared my TMI experiences. We were intrigued and interested in each other's activities. Later we decided to experience what the other shared: I enrolled in SEH while Quinton set off for a week at TMI.

SEH was founded and is directed by Michael Mamas, former college honor student in physics and math, veterinarian, nine-year ashram dweller in India, and now schoolmaster.

My focus returns to the community center in San Diego as the room becomes quiet. Dr. Mamas has entered and is making his way to the chair on the raised platform at the front of the room. "Welcome to SEH," he says warmly. Then, with an impish grin, he pronounces, "In the next two minutes, I am going to tell you everything I know."

Dr. Mamas traditionally begins his first class with a lecture he touts as "everything he knows." Students are challenged to seek deeper meanings in a few simple and profound concepts. The first session introduces Dr. Mamas's approach to "the three realms of existence," which he dubs the "physical," the "psychoenergetic," and the "transcendental." Viewed superficially, these three realms reflect stages of movement across normal three-dimensional reality toward ever-deeper states of consciousness, the nonphysical, and eventually union with the divine. The intermediate stage of the psychoenergetic is the realm of subtle energies and a netherworld dance between physical matter and pure consciousness.

There are different philosophical models proposing that consciousness creates matter or vice versa. In Dr. Mamas's version of the universe, the psychoenergetic realm is the point of transformation from the transcendental to the physical. I find this an insightful construct and a stimulating one, as it provides a simple, understandable model for what I experienced at TMI. From this perspective, I had moved from the here and now of the normal physical world, through experiences of sensations of being outside my body, which related to Dr. Mamas's description of the psychoenergetic realm.

The descriptions of the transcendental certainly sound much like the profound and life-changing "oneness" I experienced in deep states at TMI. Dr. Mamas has written a book, *Angels, Einstein, and You: A Healer's Journey*, that contains an extensive overview of the constructs and implications of the three realms of existence.

The class continues with an overview of a reality construct that lays a basis for the healing of disease by beginning to apply nonphysical and nonlocal resources at the transcendental and psychoenergetic levels, which are then manifested in the physical as a repaired and properly functioning body. This key insight opens areas for new explorations for me. The idea of a broader sense of self and expanded states of consciousness being directly involved in affecting our physical world is illustrated through the healing of disease. This construct intensifies and stimulates the perspective I gained at TMI and adds to it an expanded concept of what is real and how it becomes real to us.

As the class progresses, I am able to learn a little more about my classmates. I find the class makeup to be as varied as at TMI. There are two physicians. One is a general practitioner who is there to learn how this approach might help her patients. The second, a pediatrician, has injured his back and is there both to learn more about how this approach might help his own injury and how he might find additional tools to assist his patients. There is a large contingent of nurses and massage therapists along with several emergency medical technicians (EMTs) and psychologists. There are also two airline pilots, a bank executive, several New Age workshop seekers, and several college students. Three of our classmates are from Japan and made the grueling 14-hour flight just the day before. Two of my close friends from TMI have joined the class on my recommendation, so I don't feel as alone as I initially did at TMI.

During the afternoon of that first class, we have our initial experience of touching others with our hands. I must stop here and comment that human touch in itself is an intimate and profound thing; however, I did not understand how profound until this afternoon.

My concept of intimacy is sexual in nature and grew from the normal explorations of adolescence, military service, and life as a young person in the 1960s. Now, after 30 years of blissful marriage, I think I have experienced the full range of intimacy related to touching someone. In our first practical exercise this afternoon, however, I discover not only new levels but also new concepts of intimacy that are neither sexual nor romantic in nature. This touch involves opening a new array of sensations associated with one human being uniting in touch with another at deep levels.

The first exercise has us assemble in pairs next to makeshift massage tables. A professional massage table, as I found later, is an expensive investment. Lacking sufficient "real" tables, class members have assisted in assembling the poor man's substitute for large-scale classroom use. This makeshift approach involves a one-inch piece of foam, a standard folding banquet table, and bedsheets from an industrial linen supply.

After we have 27 tables assembled in three rows of nine, we pair up and decide who will be on the table first. Most people gravitate to someone they have familiarity with even at this early stage of limited interaction within the group. Tina, one of my close friends from TMI, and I seek each other out. Being with someone you know makes you more comfortable and less nervous.

With Tina and the others on their respective tables, the lights dim and soft music fills the room with a soothing ambience. We are asked to still our minds. We began this post-lunch session with a 15-minute formal meditation, so we are already relaxed, if not in a slightly altered state. We are given instructions to explore very gently and with the softest of touch the back of our facedown partner, to explore the musculature, skin tone, and "feel" of the person. What can we learn from this person's reaction to our touch? What can our hands sense? Is this person active or passive physically? What about this person's emotional state? The type of life this person leads?

It is an understatement to say that exploring someone in this way is intimate. This type of touch goes far beyond a simple handshake, yet I later realized just how far a handshake accompanied with focus and intent can go in revealing someone. I already know some background about my partner, yet the exploration through physical touch reveals more. Gaps are filled in the same manner that experiencing a symphony is different from knowing only a melody from it.

I am beginning to merge with the impressions of this person I only thought I knew when an unexpected instruction jars me. We are told to release contact slowly and gently from this individual and move to the table to the right. This instruction is unwelcome. I am just getting comfortable with Tina, and now I suddenly am terrified of invading the "space" of a stranger by touching her back.

The others on the tables, sharing in a similar heightened sensitivity, are faced with not knowing who might touch them next. This is a class immersion experience. We are there to learn healing aspects of human touch and right there, right then, on the first day of class, we realize that we are going to spend some time touching classmates in the upcoming three-year course of study. At one minute per person, this becomes rapid-fire activity.

I can easily see and feel the muscle tone of people beneath my eyes and hands. I am also struck by the reaction to the contact of my hand. No matter how gentle my touch, some flinch as if I have struck them, while others rise to embrace the touch as if starved for contact. Others simply detach themselves and their bodies become a heap of sleeping meat, as they hide the energy of their vibrant self. Much is revealed about client and healer in this experience.

I am moved by the reaction of two Japanese classmates as I perform the one-minute exploration on their backs. Clearly, touch has cultural boundaries, and the boundaries differ around the world. This exercise is physically and emotionally painful for these two who have traveled halfway around the world for this class. My emotional identification with and reaction to their plight surprises me. I attempt to honor their obvious pain by placing my hands near but not actually on their backs.

We underestimate not only the power of touch, but also close human proximity. This exercise is simple—a one-minute explorative touch of ten classmates—yet I feel and identify deeper levels of pain, life experiences, and emotional trauma than I imagined possible.

The instructor tells us to switch places, and those who have been touching take a turn on the table. I find that an equal amount of exploration about the healer takes place from this point of view, even while lying on my stomach with my eyes toward the table. There are pleasant and unpleasant sensations in the touch of others. I wish some would maintain their touch much longer, while I desire others to finish quickly. The simplest touch can carry levels of meaning and feelings.

Just as at TMI, a debriefing and discussion follow the exercise. Deep feelings have been registered by all, filtered through our life experiences. Everyone agrees that we have a new viewpoint concerning the impact of human touch. We are also instructed that we should speak up immediately if we are uncomfortable with any person touching us in a future exercise. No ill feelings will ensue; we all need to be able to admit that sometimes touch is not comfortable. These exercises are about the exchange of subtle energies and any such effort must be done within the comfort zone of the individual. (During my time in the SEH program, I see this option exercised only once or twice.) Our class is bonding in an exploration of each other and ourselves. We know we are moving into a deeper understanding of who and what we are. Touching and being touched by others is clearly a path of self-exploration.

Two days later, we do another exercise that opens a new way of viewing the interaction of the mind and body. An unusual team of chiropractor and medical doctor lead this exercise. They are both senior students at SEH and have volunteered to help us explore human anatomy from a clinical and energetic perspective.

At the outset, we spend an hour reviewing a high school biology perspective of bone structure. We talk about the role of the skeletal system; we utilize anatomical charts and slices of cow bones to reacquaint ourselves with the makeup of bone. We examine the surrounding cartilage, periosteum sheath, the protective and strong construct of the compact bone, and the spongy bone surrounding the "blood factory" of the red marrow.

We pair up again. I join with the commercial airline pilot who came to SEH after discovering through martial arts practice the healing aspects of life energy. We have done several exercises together over the previous two days. He volunteers to play the role of healer and I the client. Our instructions are to close our eyes and quiet our minds. Again, the lights dim and soft music creates a background ambience. After several minutes of silence, we are again in a slight state of expanded consciousness and relaxed.

The instruction comes for the healer to place his hand on the client's thigh and to allow it to rest easily there. Healers are asked, eyes closed, to consider what they feel beneath their hands. After a moment, the suggestion is made that the cloth of the trousers or dress will be a good answer at this point. I hear a ripple of chuckles around the room. "Seriously," the chiropractor says, "feel the cloth, but explore it in a new way. Explore it as you did the person's back on the first day of class." He guides us through exploring the weave and the color of the garment by touch. Then he tells us to feel the skin through the cloth with our expanded senses.

I almost gasp as I imagine I feel the pilot's hand slip beneath the cloth of my blue jeans without any physical movement. Power of suggestion, I immediately think. Then the instruction comes to go deeper, to feel the fatty layer of tissue just below the skin. I feel a warmth grow under the pressure of my partner's hand on my thigh.

"Feel the large muscle groups that fill the area of the thigh," the instructor coaxes. I feel spreading warmth deepening into my mid-thigh area. This is an eerie but fascinating sensation.

"Go deeper and deeper until you can actually touch the periosteum sheath surrounding the femur bone itself. You may find it a bit sticky to the touch."

At this point, it begins to feel as if there is an invader deep in my musculature. It is not merely a warm sensation of touch. It feels as if his hand is moving deep into my thigh. I know that my partner's hand is still on top of my blue jeans, but the sensation of it being deep within the tissue of my leg is real.

"Go deeper and deeper until you can actually wrap your hand around the bone itself."

I don't know what my partner is feeling with his hand, but I am feeling something quite *physical* going on deep inside my leg.

The instructions take us through the layers of bone and into the marrow. After exploring the innermost bone structure, we do a reverse process of withdrawing the hand. This is done ever so slowly, tissue by tissue, taking almost as long as it took to insert it. We are then given a few minutes to relax and discuss the sensations from both the client and healer perspective. I am amazed to find that nearly 30 minutes have elapsed. We do not discuss the exercise as a class; we simply switch places, and it is my turn to explore the tissue structure of my partner's leg.

My experience is phenomenal. There is a different feeling and sensation to each tissue. At TMI, it was clear that perception defines artificial boundaries, because we limit ourselves to the boundaries of physical space and time. This new exercise is a practical one for moving beyond the physical and learning to sense, feel, and perceive using our ability to "feel" as a sense organ. This is a physical and nonphysical event.

At the outset, I feel the heavy cloth of my partner's trousers, a normal physical sensation. When the instruction comes to move to the level of the skin beneath the cloth, the sensation is dramatic. I do not just have a sense of where the cloth stops and the skin begins. I can *feel* it. It is so real that my hand recoils briefly and I open my eyes to make sure that my partner still has his pants on.

It feels as if my hand has penetrated the cloth and is touching his skin. It feels spongy. I distinguish the hairs on his leg and small droplets of perspiration that are forming under the warming influence of my hand. It has merely taken the appropriate shift in the focus of consciousness. Likewise for the thin layer of fatty tissue that supports the skin. The bundles of strong muscle have a sensation unique to them as well. I am amazed that I can feel the tackiness of the periosteum as my imaginary hand finally makes contact with the outer layers of the thighbone. Going deeper into the bone and into the cellular level of the marrow, I enter levels of perception that approach the "quantum sensations" of TMI expanded states.

Whether the sensations are real or suggested, the impact gives me a new respect for the intricacies of the body. One could spend a lifetime exploring the body in this fashion and never be bored. Never again will I touch or be touched by someone without the realization of the deep and intimate exchange of subtle energies. We are probably far too casual about our bodies as they come into contact with each other in packed elevators, get bumped on busy streets, or are jostled about in public transportation. We must begin to realize the impact our proximity can have on others.

As the exercise ends, we open a general class discussion. One of our classmates is in tears, yet wanting to share something of her experience. As her emotions subside, she begins her commentary.

"I am a nurse, and I have been in the operating room on a daily basis for the last 14 years. I have *never* had an experience like what just occurred here. I will never view the human body the same way again." She loses composure again briefly and the class supports her in her experience through silent respect. Then she continues. "I have always treated the body as being quite mechanical. I help work on the component parts. I now have a new appreciation for the pure life energy of the body and the sacred nature it represents. I just want to thank the instructors for providing me with such a profound and life-changing experience."

It is hard to follow such a deeply felt testimony, so we take a break and drift outside to consider our own experiences. The first four-day class session at SEH seems filled with exercises that challenge our notions of what is real and what imaginary. Dr. Mamas gives us several forays into aspects of the three realms of existence model, and every time it seems to be a new concept, even though it is the same information again and again. As he speaks, new ways of looking at the world emerge, as if the perspectives we use to view the world are merely aspects of light reflected off some magical jewel. Each ray of understanding represents a source reality, yet each of these insights seems to be only another perceived model of reality.

One of Dr. Mamas's favorite games is model-busting. He can weave a very logical version of what makes the universe work. We know that he is making absolute sense, that he has finally figured it all out. Then he breaks it apart as being only a model and not actually how things work. Dr. Mamas provides strong and practical lessons about the fact that our perception plays a large role in what we consider real. SEH students and TMI participants are provided the opportunity to realize the role that perception plays in their worldview and to understand that their ways of perceiving are habitual and that habits can be changed.

We spend several hours doing exercises to heighten our sensitivity to the energetic realm around us. We create fields and focused beams of subtle forms of energy just as one first practices notes and scales in learning to play a musical instrument. As these activities are experiential, it is difficult to describe them. Let me share a couple, however, which you can easily experience yourself.

One exercise involves pointing your finger. Find a spot on the wall across the room. Point at it. Well, that doesn't amount to much, does it? You are merely pointing your finger at a spot on the wall.

Now, close your eyes and imagine yourself feeling a great deal of hatred. Really get mad and focus on the feeling of how that emotion becomes physical in your body. Let it well up and build. When you have yourself worked up, open your eyes and point your finger at that same spot on the wall again. But this time focus all that pent-up energy you have built up in your body and shoot it out your finger, imagining it to be a beam of light blasting the targeted spot on the wall. (Don't allow anyone to be in or near your line of fire!)

Try this a few times and see the difference between simply pointing your finger at the wall and creating forms of energy that can be physically palpable. Repeat this exercise, except build within you the energy of appreciation and love and blast the wall with that. Really do this, and you will experience the opening of a doorway in your mind that can lead to many wonderful things. If nothing else, doing this exercise should impress upon you the implications and physical impact of our emotions on ourselves and our fellow humans. It is no wonder we become so uncomfortable as negative emotions heat up and lead to unpleasantness between people. And how much interaction of this type of energy is going on as we walk down a crowded street?

Another exercise to build and experience subtle energies requires a partner. Stand facing each other. Rub your own hands together briskly until you feel them heat up. Like children playing "patty-cake," place your palms about an inch away from the palms of your partner and become aware of the heat between your hands. Close your eyes and move into a state of deeper connection with your partner. Attempt to pull your hands slowly away from each other, but maintain your connection and sensation of the energy being formed between your palms. You will be amazed as you continue to feel your partner even after your hands are several feet apart. Play with this connection. Move your arms around in circles and see if you can stay connected to your partner.

With a little practice, you will be astonished to find that you can continue this "dance" in unison with your eyes closed. When I performed this exercise for the first time, my partner and I tried to push to our limits, moving 20 feet apart. We still maintained our connection as if we had practiced some intricate "dance" for many years.

We also followed an instruction to have someone walk between us while remaining energetically connected. I was shocked to be able physically to feel the person walking between my partner and me. It was as if a gentle breeze could be felt over a distance of several feet beyond my physical hand.

Using these and similar exercises, we built up in the class at SEH to our first attempt to move such energy through the human body as an element of the healing process. The concept of subtle energy is obviously an intricate one. Let us simply note here that if one is willing to suspend the disbelief that such things can happen, one can successfully move forward in exercises that assume such energy exists.

In class, with an extended practice session, we are ready for our first attempt at using these energies for hands-on healing. The makeshift tables are assembled, and we are instructed to find a partner with whom we feel comfortable. My partner is again Tina. Dr. Mamas demonstrates a protocol that is a standard procedure in much of the world of hands-on healing.

The process involves building on our subtle energy awareness exercises and placing our hands on particular points on the body, mostly in the area of the joints—areas of easy energetic access for infusing subtle energy into the body. As we lay our hands on the prescribed location, we are to increase our focus and intent to "run energy," just as we learned to do in the energy-building exercises moments before. My perspective is that this involves moving into a slightly altered state of consciousness.

After the demonstration, there is an air of nervous excitement as we move to the tables with our partners. Reading about subtle energy healing is one thing, anticipating a process of learning something about it is another, but moving to a table with a partner to try it is unreal. As I said, Tina had come to SEH on my suggestion, and now her trust and my curiosity are both about to be tested. She climbs up on the table with a slight air of not wanting to be the first one to experience the healer role. The lights dim and soft music begins. Dr. Mamas guides us step by step as the other instructors move from table to table to observe and assist if necessary.

Dr. Mamas instructs us to center ourselves. To me, this is an opportunity to focus on the task and to drift into an expanded state of consciousness, around the TMI Focus 12 level. The instruction comes to place our hands on particular points on the feet. As we all focus on getting our hands in just the right position, Dr. Mamas tells us to "run some energy." Much to my surprise, I feel tingling between my hand and Tina's feet.

I must say that "running energy" is a misnomer. To me it is more allowing energy to flow. At any rate, there is a tingle in my hand, and I feel that something, I am not sure what, is happening. Tina moves slightly as if she is feeling something, too. Finally, she says, "I *feel* it, I *really do* feel it running up my legs!"

I look around the room and see that there are a number of surprised folks who, like me, sense something is happening. There are also some performing the proper actions with their hands, but from the looks on their faces, they are not feeling much. I wonder what has caused this difference in experiences. We are encouraged to continue whether we feel anything or not. Enhanced perception will come with practice.

Dr. Mamas compliments our work. He instructs us that we need to go slowly and allow things to happen. We are to encourage the energy flow, but not be discouraged if we feel nothing—the energy is moving whether we feel it or not. We move through the various positions of our hands up the joints of the body. There is a protocol to this, even if at this point it is like learning to play scales on the piano. Instructors are on the constant move around the room giving encouragement and offering minor adjustments in posture or hand placement.

As we progress, it becomes clear that Tina has moved to a very relaxed, even altered, state of consciousness. As I look around the room, the calm and relaxation are palpable. Lying on a table surrounded by soft music and reduced lighting is certainly having an effect. I move into one of my dual states of consciousness that I first experienced at TMI. I can watch the process as an observer and participate in it at the same time. I focus on the placement of my hands and the ever-growing awareness of the sensation of some form of energy passing through them. Yet, at the same time, I seem to be standing alongside and just above the table, watching my performance and the effects on Tina.

As the process reaches the upper torso, the instruction comes to place my hand on the heart chakra, a focal point of energy in the mid-chest. My other hand remains in a light touch on Tina's abdominal area. Tina begins to cry. It starts with gentle tears, but quickly moves into intense sobs. She does not move about, or express any sort of pain, but it is clear that something has affected her deeply.

An instructor at my side says in a gentle voice, "You're doing fine, just stay with it."

I keep my hands as they are and feel surges of energy moving through them. Tina's weeping continues and moves to a deeper level of her being. I am not sure what is happening, but I know it is significant. I am caught between wanting to watch and attempting to understand, all the while not certain what to do next.

"You're doing fine, just keep doing exactly what you are doing right now." The instructor is still with me, but is apparently not going to step in and do anything. Whatever I am doing, it is proper and I should continue.

Tina erupts in a gut-wrenching wail. A second instructor appears and drapes a blanket over Tina's shaking body. Tina is attempting to mouth words, but cannot get anything intelligible out amidst her sobs. Something within her has found a way out; the only stimulus has apparently been my series of hand touches and the sensation of energetic exchange.

The instructor at my side kneels beside the table and speaks softly. "Tina, everything is all right. You are simply having a release."

"No shit, Dick Tracy," Tina shoots back, a tinge of anger in her voice.

She has touched some deeply held memory, and it is uncomfortable. Its release is greeted with tearful gratitude and frustration. Finding hidden parts of yourself reminds you that you may not be in as much control as you think. She rolls onto her side and sobs. Tina is glad, and Tina is also mad. The process is running its course, and it is familiar to her from previous work with energy healers. I am not familiar with this kind of situation at all. The episode has scared the hell out of me. Emotional release as an aspect of the healing process is new territory to me.

The instructor nudges me aside and whispers, "Let her be with herself a few moments. Just be here if she needs you." I am certainly not going to leave Tina alone in such a state. I kneel beside the table and take her hand. Her reddened eyes look into mine. She smiles and closes her eyes as she gently squeezes my hand.

Meanwhile, the exercise has continued with the class learning the proper hand placements to finish the process. As I again become aware of the rest of the room, I realize that there are at least two other tables with weeping occupants. I am not sure what has happened, but clearly something major is going on.

As this phase of the group activity comes to a close, we are given a short break to be followed by a debriefing. Afterward, we will return to the exercise, and it will be my turn on the table. A short walk is certainly in order, as I need some air and a little time to think. Tina is all right, but it is obvious that she needs a little time by herself also. We part as we exit the door and take in the clear San Diego air.

I am curious and apprehensive. What has just happened? The events roll over and over in my head. I have come to a healing school, but maybe I'm not sure what that means. My mind reruns the events. My experiences at TMI were significant and deeply felt, but they were, for the most part, within me, or at least within the expanding boundaries of my own mental experience even when others were involved. Today's experiences are more physical, with effects on others. I am stunned. I am also exceedingly curious. Just as I have experienced in my introduction to the expansion of consciousness at TMI, my initial contact with the world of touch healing is challenging my long-held beliefs.

What is the link between mind and body? How does it interact in the realm of subtle energies? How can a simple touch bring on such a powerful emotional release? The tingling of the energy in my hand was real, not imagined. Tina's emotional release had certainly been real! What was the tingling sensation and where did it come from? What role did it play in Tina's emotional release? What had Tina released and why?

The questions overlay each other, but the answers were not apparent. I had experienced a powerful physical event, just as I had powerful mental ones at TMI. With considerable study and research, I had become more comfortable and understood my experiences at TMI, but now a new set of questions was being asked.

With my return to the classroom and during the ensuing discussion, these questions still echo in my mind. I find it difficult to verbalize them. These are not the kinds of questions one can ask a teacher in a class. These are the questions that people can only answer for themselves.

My turn on the table is not nearly as dramatic as Tina's experience. I feel a wave of energy move through my body, however, and relaxation takes me into a deeper state of consciousness. Toward the end of the exercise, I have slight tremors in my abdominal muscles. Tissues seem to convulse slightly of their own accord. Tina has touched some trauma within my body, but I have no clue what. This causes frustration, as I feel that I will at least need to know what my trauma is in order to release it. I find out later that is not the case, but at this point, it is one more question added to the list. . . .

As I continued at SEH, powerful events of healing unfolded and continue to do so. Some I use as examples in this book. As for the basic questions there were no immediate answers. Years later, I found insight and solace in comments by Dr. Dolores Krieger, nurse, author, and originator of the popular healing protocol known as Therapeutic Touch. In a discussion of the processes involved in Therapeutic Touch, she writes of the demands made on the practitioner:

> It involves other ways of communicating within yourself and with others—ways that utilize poorly understood functions of the psyche. The point of entry for this healing system is the farther reaches of consciousness. This realm of the deep self is invoked by the irresistible upsurge of compassionate concern for the welfare of another. It is a concern of such depth of feeling that it impels you to exceed the usual grasp of things.[1]

Dr. Mamas repeatedly commented that hands-on healing is an exploration of yourself as much as an effort to assist a client. He constantly warned us to avoid the pitfall of taking credit for something happening with the client on the table. This, too, was familiar territory. It was merely another example of the wily ego stepping in to place itself in charge. Apparently the intrusion of the ego is very detrimental to success in the world of hands-on healing. One of Dr. Mamas's favorite phrases is: "You cannot heal anybody. All you can do is facilitate the self-correcting mechanisms within the client."

I felt that this was excellent advice, but also a difficult challenge when success over disease was actually achieved. As I was later to find out, when you are involved in a dramatic healing experience, it is only natural for the ego to want to step in and assure you that *you* had a great deal to do with the other person's recovery. This tendency is so intoxicating that Dr. Mamas speaks forcefully about it in his book *Angels, Einstein, and You.* He cautions the unwary about the showman and con artist who prey on the gullible who might be desperate for relief from pain and disease. While relief and healing can indeed be found through a talented and compassionate healer, Dr. Mamas warns against the hands-on healer who has moved into showmanship and ritual. This is a sign that the ego has gained an unhealthy influence on the process.

Dr. Mamas writes:

> The vast majority of what takes place today in hands-on healing is foolishness, a sideshow for the spiritually immature. The better the show, the better the performance, the more the performers become recognized and even self-justified to the point of believing themselves that antics are necessary. Such spiritual entertainment has become an epidemic. Though it may be a reasonable substitute for grade B television, it does a great deal to undermine the credibility of the hands-on healing profession in the eyes of the public at large.[2]

I did not enroll in healing school to seek glory from a successful healing practice. I was merely trying to understand what goes on as the mind and body interact in these events. I studied and practiced

18

The Interconnected Matrix: Realizing That What You Think and Feel Affects Others

What happened to Tina that day at SEH? I cannot say for certain. It may not be possible to explain the specifics of that event with conviction. Yet something of great significance did occur. Whether it was life-changing, psychologically important, or even physiologically measurable is a point of discussion from a number of perspectives. While the tools of science allow us to gather data, they sometimes do not serve us well in areas of self-exploration that, to date, have been better examined by artists and poets. A mixture of science and poetry may be the best approach to exploring mind-body and nonlocal relationships.

A majority of hands-on healing activity relates to feelings and expanded states of consciousness. These phenomena may or may not be measurable by scientific instrumentation, but they certainly affect our bodies and our approach to life. My life continues to change as a result of continued exploration in these areas.

I have had numerous experiences of healing others by placing my hands on people with the intent of providing positive energies. I have witnessed dramatic and immediate reduction in swollen tissue after inflammatory chemotherapy treatment. I have "seen" tumors that the clients didn't know were present, which were then clinically found and excised. I have followed along as clients have moved into deep states of consciousness that offered them profound insights into their relationships with parents and siblings, relationships that they later expressed were sources of stress that had resulted in physical pain. I have watched many emotional releases similar to Tina's, where the client was not able to identify the source of the pain. The release of unknown pain then resulted in a new outlook on life, a brighter disposition, or the beginning of a new level of confidence in these people.

In my experiences with Tina, I was deeply moved by the emotions she experienced. Was that release related to some childhood trauma stored in her body? Did the movements of my hands using energy protocols connect the "invisible dots" of some energetic pattern? Was my altered state of consciousness manifesting an interconnection with the nonlocal selves of Tina and me?

I do not know with certainty, and I doubt that she could say either. Did the emotional release change her in a positive way? Yes. She said it did. She experienced feelings of something negative lifted from her psyche and body. She reported later that this release marked the beginning of a several-year cycle of significant changes to do with where she lived, what she did for a living, and her lifestyle.

How much importance we place on emotional release versus other factors that may come into play is an interesting exercise in belief systems. This is where the processes of science and poetry intermix. Does it matter that we understand emotional release of physical tension or is it more important that we feel better? The scientist might say the understanding is the important element while the poet would focus on the deep and personal self-healing that has occurred. Either way, we should admit that something important is going on and learn more about it.

Frontier scientists continue in the pursuit of answers; however, there are often more effects documented than causes discovered. There are laboratory-supported findings in the transfer or influence of energy between people. Scientific research indicates that the field of the mind and the bioenergetic field of the body are significantly intertwined. Examples of this research are summarized in the following paragraphs.

In 1977, Dr. Valerie Hunt of the University of California at Los Angeles was researching the measurable energy aspects of Structural Integration or Rolfing techniques developed by Ida Rolf. Rolfing is a deep massage technique that involves the manipulation of the myofascial system to realign posture and movement for more efficient human performance, as well as relief from chronic stress and pain. Dr. Hunt's research is reported in the "A Study of Structural Integration from Neuromuscular, Energy Field, and Emotional Approaches," Project Report, Rolf Institute, 1972.

During the course of the study, Dr. Hunt employed the services of the Reverend Rosalyn Bruyere to report the traditional metaphysical view of the aura and its colors during deep tissue manipulation. The findings were astounding and tied together the metaphysical concept of auras (or human bioenergetic fields), the transfer of healing energies between people, and measurable electromagnetic (Hertz) frequencies. Very sensitive instrumentation attached to the client revealed that particular Hertz frequencies were identifiable during the Rolfing protocols. Further, the colors reported by Reverend Bruyere were correlated to the frequency signatures of visible light. Reverend Bruyere could consistently match her description of the color of the energy field around the client or coming from the practitioner's hands with the electromagnetic frequencies reported by the instrumentation.

More recently, intriguing research conducted at the Institute of HeartMath (IHM), a California-based organization that focuses on energy fields generated by the human heart, demonstrates that our proximity to others may have more measurable effects than we might have thought possible. In one research design, a situation was created that allowed the measurement of the effects of emotional and physiological coherence in one person in relation to the physiology of a nearby person.

The results of this experiment demonstrated that a person in the emotionally compassionate coherent state generated by HeartMath protocols can even have their heartbeat signal show up in the brain wave patterns of a nearby person. Further, this effect was shown to be intensified and amplified by actual touch between the two people. As noted by Dr. Rollin McCraty, director of research at IHM:

> My colleagues and I call this energetic information exchange *cardioelectromagnetic communication* and believe it to be an innate ability that heightens awareness and mediates important aspects of true empathy and sensitivity to others. Furthermore, we have observed that this energetic communication ability can be enhanced, resulting in a much deeper level of nonverbal communication, understanding, and connection between people. We also propose that this type of energetic communication between individuals may play a role in therapeutic interactions between clinicians and patients that has the potential to promote the healing process. [1]

While science continues to explore the interactions between our "bioelectric bodies," we have our own experiences with these forces. We instinctively know when we are too close to someone or they are too close to us. Even the words "too close" in this context are interesting. Implied in this phraseology is that we are aware we have some physical sensation of a boundary line in the immediate space that surrounds us. We are, in one sense, extending our concept of ourselves to that boundary so that someone crossing that boundary is felt as an intrusive sensation.

It is important to note that we seem to be able physically to feel, or sense, when that boundary has been crossed because we perceive a level of discomfort when it occurs. We somehow seem to know when someone is standing too close even when they are behind us and have not been seen. That feeling of discomfort is a very important clue. There is something palpable in our sensation of our immediate physical proximity. We have all had such feelings. We may not have taken the time, however, to consider that such a sensation implies there is an interconnection among our mind, our body, and the immediate space surrounding us.

Psychologically, it makes sense that our emotional state affects those around us. Scientific findings that demonstrate energetic activity between people show us, however, that we need to take responsibility for our actions on others and our physical selves. If our emotions are measurably reflected in our bioenergetic fields and these fields in turn affect those around us, then we must acknowledge our greater role in creating the environment in which we live. Whether knowingly or in ignorance, our emotional influence is setting up field activity that reflects our state of consciousness at the time. The implications are profound and have been a source of serious reflection by consciousness research pioneers.

In rumination on the implications of such thoughts, emotion, and mind activity, Bob Monroe wrote:

> The idea that every thought I may have that is tinged with emotion radiates uncontrolled outward to others is heavy with implication. It is even more uncomfortable to be the recipient of such thoughts that others may emanate. This realization would support the effort of those who make the unrealistic attempt to spread love and light in a predator world, or those who hold that we are part of a Universal One.[2]

Such a view is staggering to consider. If our activity as individuals affects other people and we, too, are impacted energetically by the emotional states of others, it follows that groups of people could affect each other. Consider the power of the combined emotional energy represented in an unstable mob of people. Otherwise upstanding individuals can be swept up in the group passion of a soccer riot, for example, and create damage to property and injure other people, only to express a short time later personal bewilderment as to why it happened.

Conversely, a group can experience positive energetic, physiological, and psychological sensations if emotional coherence is focused. Dramatic feelings of well-being easily occur during a compelling religious service or stirring speech by a charismatic political leader. Perhaps even a sociological concept such as peer pressure has significant energetic as well as psychological implications!

In exploring the science and reality of the human energy field, I am fascinated by its implications. In opening your thought processes to the broad range of possibilities, phrases such as "touch without feeling" or "sincerity in communication" take on new meaning. If we speculate on the concept of human subtle energy activity, we can easily conjecture that there might be Hertz frequencies involved that turn simple physical contact into touch with intimate feeling or a few simple words into a stirring emotional soliloquy. The implications for medicine and healing are also significant. Creating experimentation and instrumentation to find such frequencies may prove challenging; such a challenge, however, should be met with the full force of scientific curiosity.

We must recognize that massive amounts of vibrational energy are produced by technology in our culture. We are constantly assaulted with the sounds and vibrational energies of cars, airplanes, and machinery. Add to that the vibrations of loud music, crowd noise, and a constant barrage of media advertising, and there can logically be said to be a higher energetic influence that can result in increased levels of stress throughout our culture. If we are also now to add an actual measurable level of energetic pollutants being generated by the emotional state of those around us, then it is certainly appropriate to reflect on the nature of how we live.

It is a fact that the sounds and electromagnetic fields produced by our technologies are vibrational. The idea that people emit vibrational waves via their bioenergetic fields demands study. The possible relationship between consciousness and the vibrational energy of the human biofield moves the discussion into the nonlocal. As the realities of these nonlocal and field phenomena gain scientific interest, very interesting findings emerge.

Biochemist and natural scientist Dr. Rupert Sheldrake reported on a collection of scientific studies concerning the relationship of people and animals in his fascinating book *Dogs That Know When Their Masters Are Coming Home: And Other Unexplained Powers of Animals.* Dr. Sheldrake writes:

> The evidence I have been discussing in this book suggests that our own intentions, desires, and fears are not confined to our heads

or communicated only through words and behavior. We can influence animals and affect other people at a distance. We remain interconnected with animals and people we are close to, even when we are far away. We can even affect people and animals by the way we look at them, even if they do not know we are there. We can retain a connection with our homes, however geographically distant we are. And we can be influenced by things that are about to happen in ways that defy our normal notions of causality.[3]

We unknowingly and passively experience influence from subtle energy fields generated by a variety of consciousness and biofield interactions. Questions arise: What opportunities might be created by attempting to generate positive consciousness and energetic biofield environments? What sort of mischief might be possible through a focused and directed thought form?

Speculation on this is offered by one of the members of the ultra-secret Stargate remote viewing project funded by the CIA and the National Defense Agency. Third-generation army officer and highly decorated combat veteran Dr. David Morehouse, now retired from the military, writes:

> I believe that remote viewing for intelligence purposes remains now very fully funded, very hidden, and very protected—and now very deadly. . . . The word on the street is that remote influencing is all the rage in intelligence. I believe that the CIA is heavily involved in this insidious technique. If they could influence someone to kill from a distance of thousands of miles—and remote influencing has this potential—they would hold an extremely valuable weapon.[4]

Such a claim is extremely frightening and easily borders on the unbelievable. Yet this claim comes from someone who was involved in intelligence operations that also border on the unbelievable but are a matter of record. Whether we believe such things are possible or not does not alter the reality of their existence. We may only be limiting our potential by what we are capable of believing. I will, however, leave the world of espionage and malevolence to the conspiracy theorists and speculators on hidden government activity. My interest is in learning more about the potential of human consciousness.

As we experience and learn more of the dance of consciousness and the human energy field, I believe we learn more about the totality of who and what we are. While there may be malevolent uses of this field, I believe that our cumulative group consciousness can move to the highest levels of human potential if we will allow it. The words of Peter Russell are most insightful:

> The important point is that, in some way or other, one person's general state of consciousness appears to set off similar, though generally weaker, effects in other people. This implies that as more and more people in society start experiencing such states of consciousness, other people will gradually pick up the effect, making it easier and easier for them also to reach such states.[5]

Whether or not we can realize the power of our emotions and biofield energy is a challenge. Whether consensus society will allow these things to be accepted as true may determine the speed at which we can begin to solve many of the problems I discussed in the initial chapters of this book.

> Learning to believe what you are told to be true is based on faith; learning to allow the reality of what we experience is based on humility.

—J. R. M.

19

Medicine: A Battleground for Science and the Miraculous

As patients, we place a great deal of pressure on physicians. When we become ill, we go to our doctors in the same manner that we go to our car mechanics. "Fix it!" we demand, with a high expectation of immediate relief to enable our return to our fast-paced lives. Being sick is an inconvenience, and the illness must be dispatched with the least possible interruption to our schedules. We say, "I don't have time to be sick right now," as we gulp down pain-suppressing pills or powerful over-the-counter medications to suppress messages from our bodies that we need rest and recuperation.

What role consciousness has in the healing process is not our usual focus when we become ill. We want relief, and we want it fast. Sometimes we don't get better, and we have to go back to the doctor and get a different pill because the first one didn't work. This opens an interesting line of inquiry. Why didn't the first pill work?

There can be a lot of reasons: it wasn't strong enough; it wasn't the right medication to begin with (then why was it used—bad guess?); or it didn't suit our biochemistry or body type, or possibly there was an adverse reaction, and so on.

But most of the time, we get better eventually and forget about the whole thing. After all, as noted in previous chapters, our minds are already too occupied. We mustn't forget the bills, the kids' grades, war on the other side of the world, crime in the streets, the desire for a new car. We are much too occupied with these things to worry about the role the mind might play in healing.

What happens when the patient doesn't get better even after several medical interventions? At every step of the process, there is the option to get worse, and sometimes this occurs. Some patients in a doctor's practice have this "happen" to them in spite of accurate diagnosis and properly administered medications. We mustn't forget that the doctor is "practicing" medicine, which involves a lot of information gathering, analysis, and application of statistical norms to decide a treatment.

True, a misdiagnosis can occur, but on the whole, the physician is applying the odds of what is probably wrong and the odds of what medication should work under what conditions. When these odds and conditions are combined with the skills of practice and familiarity over time, the patient is cured—most of the time. But we mustn't forget that there is a game of odds and percentages being played here. Even in the testing that determined drug effectiveness to begin with, it may have been noted that the drug worked 99 percent of the time under certain circumstances. Notice that the drug did not work 1 percent of the time. Why?

There is also an interesting situation that sometimes occurs when a drug is given to two patients with similar body types and similar conditions. The drug somehow works successfully on one and not the other. These patients get lost in statistical models, but they are there. Medicine works within generalized and predictable sets of odds that enable the physician to work comfortably within a practice of medicine. But I wager that almost every doctor could give you an example of a strange case that puzzled her, a case that went against all the odds in a positive or negative direction. In other words, the patient was "miraculously" cured, or conversely, died when he "shouldn't have."

Could it be that the mind, or consciousness, plays a role in the living system of the body, adding a factor that, at this point, has been difficult to separate and investigate in medical research? It probably adds complexity to include the mind as one of the many variables in the process of the scientific method. Indeed, medicine separates out the role of the mind by giving it its own branches of study and practice, namely, psychiatry and psychology.

Consciousness may play tricks on us as an inherent part of the illness process. For example, research into the world of multiple personality disorder (MPD) indicates some interesting relationships between consciousness and activity in the body. There are numerous documented examples in which MPD-afflicted people have one personality with a disease, such as diabetes, while another personality in the same body does not exhibit diabetic symptoms. One personality may have to wear glasses, while another does not. Since it is the same body, this should not be possible. Surely, such an effect is attributable to the activity of consciousness. If it is, then we are facing significant challenges to basic beliefs about cause and effect in the physical world.

It is common in our society to treat the body as a mechanical device rather than as a complex and interrelated living system enmeshed within consciousness. A significant amount of time is spent during medical training taking apart dead things. Medical students dissect them to try to understand the component pieces, much as a mechanic learns the pieces of a carburetor by taking it apart and putting it back together. But the mechanic knows beforehand how a carburetor operates and the scientific principles behind the mixing of gases that occurs there. In other words, the mechanic is working from a good, although simple, model of the reality of the carburetor. He is aware of its function within the larger system of the automobile.

The major difference for the physician and medical researcher is that they are dealing with the reality of a complex *living* system. Remove life, or consciousness, from the body and we take away the fundamental element of what medical training is attempting to address.

In one sense, our approaches to medical treatment are built on a premise of knowing more about sickness than health. Indeed, we have a giant question mark when we are faced with the body healing itself through some process outside standard medical treatment. We call it spontaneous remission. While considered miraculous by many, spontaneous remission is not so rare that it is impossible to study. The Institute of Noetic Sciences, founded by former astronaut Edgar Mitchell, produced a volume that annotates more than 1,500 cases, just a portion of the published scientific articles documenting spontaneous remission in cancer and other diseases. The role of consciousness in the healing process is not yet fully understood. Further study of spontaneous remission, however, may hold keys to unlocking knowledge of the relationship between mind and body in healing.

It was not long ago that if you mentioned prayer, faith healing, or laying-on-of-hands as a potentially valid medical treatment, up would pop the "not one shred of evidence" response from the physician. The continuum of response among health care practitioners to alternative modalities, however, now includes, in addition to the negative emotional reaction, a full spectrum of acceptance levels. These may range from amused ambivalence and cautious experimentation, to actual embrace of alternative and complementary options that may encompass a role for consciousness in the healing process. Conventional doctors sometimes comment to patients seeking such alternatives: "Go ahead, if it makes you feel better." They may also be silently adding to the sentence: "But it won't make any real difference."

The "if it makes you feel better" comment is key. Why and how does "it" make you feel better? Let's look at an interesting situation: the placebo effect. The *Random House Unabridged Electronic Dictionary* defines a placebo as "a substance having no pharmacological effect but given merely to satisfy a patient who supposes it to be a medicine." It then continues to define the "placebo effect" as "a reaction to a placebo manifested by a lessening of symptoms or the production of anticipated side effects."

We could detour into the research about the placebo effect, but it may be easier for this discussion to quote the celebrated endocrinologist Deepak Chopra. In his book *Quantum Healing: Exploring the Frontiers of Mind/Body Medicine,* he writes:

Patients who are in pain can often be relieved by receiving a placebo, usually a coated sugar pill, which they are told is a powerful painkiller. Not everyone will respond to this but generally between 30 percent and 60 percent will report that their pain went away. This result is called the placebo effect, which has been noted for centuries, but it is highly unpredictable. The doctor cannot tell in advance which patients will benefit, or to what extent.[1]

This idea presents us with an area of medical anomaly worth exploring. When the role of consciousness is taken into consideration and questions are asked about the possibility of some sort of mind-body connection, we are moving into areas of beliefs, which can be sensitive and controversial. Before proceeding, here is Dr. Chopra:

Mind-body medicine makes many doctors extremely uneasy. They feel it is more a concept than a true field. Given a choice between a new idea and a familiar chemical, the doctor will trust the chemical—penicillin, digitalis, aspirin, and Valium do not need any new thinking on the patients' part to be effective. The problem comes in when the chemical is not effective.[2]

It is most interesting to me that much new research in the mind-body relationship is either centered in or related to diagnostic techniques utilizing intuition, prayer or some form of concentrated intention, and various forms of the laying-on-of-hands. All of these approaches are examples of nonlocal phenomena. In other words, something is involved that may be outside the laws of traditional physics and physical reality as we currently understand them. These are certainly areas of inquiry that fall far beyond the formative experience that we may have had during high school biology and physics classes.

One of the more dramatic demonstrations of the diagnostic remote viewing phenomenon is the documented performance of the skills and talents of the gifted medical intuitive Caroline Myss. Myss, now a successful author and lecturer, worked with and was studied extensively by C. Norman Shealy, M.D. The medical intuitive is a person who, by using a slightly altered state of consciousness, can psychically identify a disease or cause of a physical problem presented by a patient. This can be accomplished even without the intuitive seeing the subject, but merely being given the person's name and possibly a geographic location.

As with remote viewing, the accuracy is not one hundred percent, but we should note that no physician is one hundred percent accurate either. And physicians have the capacity to improve their statistical odds significantly by employing a battery of sophisticated laboratory tests as part of the diagnostic procedure.

The implications of the role of consciousness in activities such as medical intuitive diagnosis are staggering. As noted in the insightful book *The Creation of Health: The Emotional, Psychological, and Spiritual Responses That Promote Health and Healing*, coauthored by Myss and Shealy: "The results of this research show that intuitive diagnosis not only is possible, but can be highly successful. The real question is where it fits into the scheme of healing and medicine today."[3]

Myss is not the first to exhibit such talents. There are numerous examples of this technique, including probably the most famous intuitive in recent history, Edgar Cayce. The issue I raise here is how and why does such a thing work? As with remote viewing, medical intuitive diagnosis is considered a scientific anomaly. It should clearly be considered worthy of extensive study.

For a variety of reasons, practicing physicians and health care administrators often dismiss alternative approaches as not worthy of recognition or further exploration. This legacy is well illustrated in *Hands of Life* by Julie Motz. Motz worked as an energy healer in the operating room with Dr. Mehmet Oz of the Columbia Presbyterian Medical Center in Manhattan. They investigated the impact of complementary healing modalities on surgery patients as part of the research efforts of the Rosenthal Center for complementary and alternative medicine, based in Columbia University's College of Physicians and Surgeons. As part of her graduate research, Motz interviewed local health care administrators regarding their awareness of the work. She writes:

Among other things, the interviews gave me a much greater appreciation of the difficulty of Dr. Oz's position. Of the 22 people I talked to in positions of authority, half didn't even know that the Rosenthal Center existed, and only four knew the name of its director. Only one, the dean of the medical school, knew anything about its activities. No one knew the name of the director of the Office of Alternative Medicine at NIH [the National Institutes of Health, a federal government agency], or anything about what it was doing. Only three knew anything about what was happening with the cardiac surgery patients, and one of them, the director of the Heart Failure Center, told me that it was "nothing but a hustle to attract more patients."[4]

Pioneers like Dr. Oz, who are willing to explore nonlocal realms, are opening pathways that reveal the need for vast amounts of additional research. Following a curiosity about the mind-body relationship in the healing process, we find ourselves entering the controversial field of spiritual healing. Spiritual healing can encompass a wide range of techniques, modalities, and belief systems that may operate well beyond our current consensus-reality understanding of science and the physical world. Positive findings of clinical research involving spiritual healing move us into the realm of cultural beliefs, and may elicit even louder and quicker cries of "not a shred of evidence" from rigid skeptics.

Ironically, one aspect of research involves how the belief systems or emotional orientation of the researcher can affect the outcome of even rigidly controlled experiments. There is evidence that this is the case even in the double-blind study, the workhorse of the scientific method and medical research in general. Larry Dossey, M.D., discusses the implications of such skewed research results in his insightful book *Healing Words: The Power of Prayer and the Practice of Medicine:*

It appears that double blind studies can sometimes be steered in directions that correspond to the thoughts and attitudes of the experimenters. This might shed light on why skeptical experimenters appear unable to replicate the findings of believers, and why "true believers" seem more able to produce positive results. The validity of decades of experimental findings in medical research would need to be reevaluated if it is proved that the mind can "shove the data around."[5]

This is a profound and challenging premise if, indeed, it can be shown that the scientific method of research, as it utilizes standard protocols such as the double-blind study, is susceptible to nonlocal phenomena driven by the belief systems of the originating research designer. Not only would this idea challenge the reliability of the scientific method, it flies in the face of our basic understanding of the "reality" of physical reality itself! The scientific method is not something that will be discarded simply because of the initial findings of a few new though dramatic research studies. Clearly, these findings are worthy of additional research.

There is an embedded issue here, however, that confounds even the serious scientist. The replication of research findings is one of the basic tenets of moving from theory to acceptance in science. If nonlocal phenomena–based influence can affect the outcome of double-blind experimentation, then a basic underpinning of the scientific method may not be valid.

The research designed by the skeptics will rarely reveal a significant psi or nonlocal influence, while that designed by supporters will find positive correlation. Further, until the advent of frontier research designs, any sort of laying-on-of-hands, conscious intent, or intuitive diagnosis will be viewed as religious in nature, not medical. Another way of putting this is that anything that originates in the realm of the nonphysical is not viewed as science. The nonphysical realm is the world of beliefs, spirituality, or religion, *not* the world of science. Sadly, this long-held tradition complicates the honest and objective exploration of such phenomena.

There is a wide spectrum of perspectives represented between Dr. Dossey and many other practicing physicians. Dr. Dossey comments on the potential for affecting the outcome of medical research by the belief systems of the experimenters. This is at a time when many practicing physicians may still be echoing the "not a shred of evidence" emotional response to positive results achieved through alternative medicine. While many people will consider that beliefs can affect medical outcome, this idea may originate from a religious or faith-based approach, not a scientific one. While we might allow for the miraculous, it is not the common prescription we expect when we sit in the physician's waiting room. It appears highly probable that debates over the mind-body relationship will continue to be controversial for some time.

At this point, it is appropriate to return to the words of one of the leading researchers in nonlocal phenomena, Dr. Russell Targ, the physicist who played a major (and classified) role in the federal intelligence agency–funded study of remote viewing at the Stanford Research Institute. In *Miracles of Mind: Exploring Nonlocal Consciousness and Spiritual Healing,* he and coauthor Jane Katra write:

> Psychic functioning is a step in the direction of consciousness becoming aware of itself. Remote viewing is the nonlocal mind revealing itself. Likewise, a spiritual healer would say that the experience of healing is a manifestation of nonlocal mind unfolding in the physical world. A spiritual healer's surrender of separateness, and willingness to be used as an instrument of healing, affects the world of form that we reside in. The physiology of the body responds to the caring attitudes within the community of spirit of our nonlocal mind. We now have solid experimental support of this fact.[6]

It is not a surprise that there is a wide spectrum of reaction by physicians and scientists alike to the findings and the implications of research in realms that involve nonlocal phenomena.

There is significant research to lend credence to mind-body activity in healing. These studies note the need for new relationships between and new responsibilities for healer and client. The physician-healer must gain a broader perspective of the healing process and spend more time with the patient. Practicing physicians should be open to accepting a wider range of treatments than those learned in medical school. The patient must also begin taking a new level of responsibility in the healing process as well.

This is counter to our current "take a pill to make it better" approach. The mind-body connections are far more subtle than saying affirmations or willing yourself to get better. It appears that there are highly sophisticated interconnections between consciousness and health. Taking time to listen to the body and to explore at many levels may open one to a much broader perspective on the source of disease. This opening might also require consideration of a broader concept of the human as well. Altered states may help both the doctor and patient in this exploration. We need not only to understand the healing state better, but also to explore further the expanded states of consciousness from which it might arise.

Authors wiser than I and more experienced in the area of mind-body relationship have done excellent work in discussing this emerging field in medicine and healing. The interested reader should look at the works listed in the recommended reading at the end of this book. Of particular importance are the works of medical doctors Judith Orloff, Richard Gerber, Elisabeth Kübler-Ross, Larry Dossey, and Deepak Chopra. This is not a comprehensive list as this field has so captured the interest of the general population that new books appear daily on the shelves of our libraries and bookstores.

> The process of healing may be much more about what's going on within the patient than about the type of treatment that has been administered by the physician.
>
> —J. R. M.

20

Influential Consciousness: The Space between Thought and Physical Matter

Numerous studies have made it abundantly clear that anger and stress can negatively affect our physical health. But why is this so and what can we do about it?

In my own case, these questions became intertwined with my perspective on the mind-body relationship being developed and challenged by my experiences at TMI and the School for Enlightenment and Healing. What I had seen and experienced told me there is a much stronger connection between the mental and physical than acknowledged in the perspective of consensus society.

A major breakthrough in my understanding of mind-body interaction occurred unexpectedly. It came as I explored a program aimed at the relief of stress that was developed by the Institute of HeartMath, headquartered in Boulder Creek, California. HeartMath boasts an impressive list of clients including Fortune 500 companies as well as people from law enforcement and the U.S. Postal Service. HeartMath, like TMI, is a nonprofit research, development, and education organization. Their techniques for stress management are simple and easily learned. HeartMath techniques involve a meditation-like focus on emotional states of well-being that have been proven under strict scientific conditions.

The basic HeartMath process is known as the Freeze Frame technique. This protocol includes relaxing, concentrating on the area of the heart, and focusing on the physical sensation of positive emotional experiences. The effects demonstrate significant biophysical results and achieve a measurable reduction in stress. These research findings support a strong relationship between emotional states and a physiological impact.

Freeze Framing also assists one in achieving a slightly expanded state of consciousness. The result is a state of coherence in mind-body relationship demonstrated in HeartMath research to provide overall relaxation, immune system building, and promotion of enhanced mental and emotional capacities. HeartMath techniques are based on physiological research revealing that the heart has independent "decision-making" neurons that activate certain biological functions. In a sense, these heart functions may be thought of as a "second brain."

I traveled to Boulder Creek to join a group of 20 that had enrolled in the Inner Quality Management (IQM) course at HeartMath headquarters. The training process began with a thorough overview of stress and its impact on the body. I was fascinated by the description of the physiology of anger. It seems that when one becomes angry or is placed under stress, the classic flight-or-fight response is initiated. Signals are sent throughout the body to run away or to prepare for combat.

While this may have been an appropriate survival response during "caveman days," it is not physiologically beneficial at work or in a traffic jam. Unfortunately, our body cannot tell the difference, as the presence of stress sends an alarm signal that awakens bodily defensive actions. In other words, a missed deadline, a surly coworker, or a driver cutting you off in traffic may elicit the same physical response as being stalked by a saber-toothed tiger.

Your blood pressure rises, your breathing increases, and your muscles tighten in preparation for defending your life. While, intellectually, we may discern the difference between the threat of a tiger and the illusion of threat caused by a missed deadline, our bodies treat both situations the same. The resulting physiological stress produces significant long-term negative effects.

Most interesting is the description of the movement of electrical activity around the body. When stress or anger is present, the electrical activity is needed in the area of the heart to support additional beats to move blood around faster and with increased pressure. To concentrate it there requires the electrical activity to be shifted from its normal center in the head. That is, the electrical load is shifted from the brain to the heart. It does not take a genius to realize that if the electrical activity is leaving the brain, there is much less available to support the thinking processes. In other words, when you get angry, you literally get dumber. The HeartMath instructors made this very clear through illustration and example. This idea offers new insight into crimes of passion, road rage, and the lack of logic during highly charged emotional confrontations.

This instructional overview was followed by the actual Freeze Frame training and then an extended opportunity for practice. We were given the opportunity to be connected to a laboratory electrocardiograph instrument that monitors heart rate variability, or HRV. HeartMath researchers discovered that HRV monitoring provides an easy assessment of both ends of the coherence spectrum from stress to peak physiological functioning. The three-day experience was significant, and here I will talk about being monitored by their instrumentation.

Because of my extensive TMI experiences, I initially felt that the Freeze-Frame technique had little to offer me. It appeared to be a deep state of consciousness quickly achieved by breathing and concentration exercises. I assumed, with my TMI background, that I could easily achieve that state. Boy, was I wrong!

As I was wired to the EKG (electrocardiogram) monitor that reported HRV on a projected computer screen, I sensed I could show off a bit by performing this exercise well, and I would have machine-produced data to prove it. I would go to Focus Level 21 and my HRV graph would be quick and perfect in its instant shift to the desired sine wave that indicated stress reduction and movement into the coherent state. As the electrodes were attached to my rib cage, I closed my eyes and began my move to Focus 21. I quickly went into an expanded state of consciousness and felt the movement of my mind into that familiar territory. Focus 21 came easily, and I settled in to await the machine confirmation.

After a few minutes, the HeartMath instructor began to assist me by reminding me of the protocol to be followed. I opened my eyes and looked at the computer graph on the large projection screen. Much to my surprise, I was not only exhibiting a lack of coherent HRV, but I was actually stressed. This was very confusing. I was in a state of altered consciousness, and I thought I was also relaxed. Apparently, being relaxed in itself was not enough, as my HRV monitoring revealed that I had not achieved the coherent state as defined by HeartMath standards.

I wanted to explore this situation at length, but my turn on the machine was coming to a close and others in class awaited theirs. The electrodes were removed, and I returned to my seat, devastated at my lack of performance in an area that I thought I had learned a great deal about.

The sessions continued until dinner. Afterward, I sought out the trainer and asked if I could discuss my lack of performance and the Freeze Frame process. I explained my TMI approach and expressed my confusion as to what had happened. In the discussion that followed, the reality of the difference between the expanded states of TMI and the physiological changes inherent in HeartMath techniques became apparent.

TMI Focus Levels quickly took me to levels of expanded consciousness, but these were dissociated from the body. I was removing myself from feeling and sensation as I was focusing on expanding my state of consciousness. This consciousness expansion was being done at the expense of being connected to, or feeling, any sensations in my body. HeartMath techniques, on the other hand, focused on becoming so fully present *in the body* that one could *feel* the physiological effects of emotional states.

With instructor support, I was allowed to return to the training room and attempt the HRV monitor a second time. This time, I followed exactly all aspects of the recommended Freeze Frame protocol: relaxation, identification with the sensation of positive emotion, and the concentration on the heart area. It became apparent from the instrumentation that bodily feeling and sensation in the positive emotional state are indeed the key to the desired HRV monitor response.

Further, I felt a shift in my physiology as a state of expanded awareness moved through my body. It felt as if a wave of subtle energy appeared in and around my body as the coherent state manifested. Coherence of mind-body interaction involves much more than the mind; clearly, it involves the direct experience of the body.

With the support of the HRV instrumentation, I felt I had experienced scientific proof of "mind over matter." I prefer to call it "mind becoming aware of matter." The results of this activity demonstrated that diverse functional aspects of the body can be brought into a unified and coherent state through directed information flow. This experience pushed me into seeing the immense potential in the mind-body relationship.

How many more elements of physiological response might be subject to some directed mental activity or specialized protocol? Were there elements of enhanced mental performance that could be achieved through some unrealized, reversed, body-mind protocol? How might such activity be related to my experiences at TMI and with Tina at SEH in the hands-on-healing situation? One can quickly be carried away with speculation as to how unlimited the full human potential might be.

I spent time that night with the trainer and the HeartMath literature. I probed the implications of their research activity. The next day, I sought out Rollin McCraty, the director of research at HeartMath, and continued my efforts. HeartMath publications report breakthrough findings in subtle energy activity. Their research is far too extensive to summarize here. HeartMath information is available on their website (www.heartmath.com) or in their published materials.

By the time I returned home, my mind was exploding with possibilities as I began piecing together ideas from extensive reading, my visit to HeartMath, my TMI experiences, and my emerging activity in hands-on healing. My experiences at HeartMath highlighted the considerable potential for electromagnetic activity being generated as part of the powerful musculature and rhythmic pumping of the human heart. I later found that this idea raises even more issues of a philosophical nature.

If a biologically generated field extends beyond the physical boundary, then where are a person's boundaries? Is a person defined by the boundary of the body, or by the extension of the field that person generates? I found this question posed from a scholar's perspective by noted subtle energy researcher and author Dr. James Oschman:

> One of the academic questions created by the discovery of the heart's magnetic field is the location of the boundary between the organism and the environment. In the past, we could define an individual as that which lies within the skin; but it is a fact of physics that energy fields are unbounded. The biomagnetic field of the heart extends indefinitely into space. While its strength diminishes with distance, there is no point at which we can say the field ends. In practice, the field gets weaker and weaker until it becomes undetectable in the noise produced by other fields in the environment; but scientists are constantly developing tricks to make their instruments more sensitive and to separate signals from noise.[1]

My HeartMath experiences brought together the idea of emotional states affecting heart-brain coherence, and it would naturally follow that the magnetic field generated by the heart could also be amplified in this process. Could fieldlike phenomena be the missing link that ties consciousness and matter together? Could some aspect of our consciousness utilize subtle electromagnetic forces as a method of information transfer? While the concept may move the discussion into spiritual areas, could consciousness in some way be related to fieldlike phenomena?

The matrix of possibilities expanded, and I pursued information concerning fields, electromagnetics, and nonlocal phenomena. I found each of these areas to be fascinating in itself, but mind-boggling when considered together. The concept of fields is interesting, too. For one thing, I found it difficult to develop an easy understanding as to what a "field" actually is. It appears that a lot can be said about the "effects" caused by fields, but little about their true nature. This realization implies that the word "field" is a convenient term that may be used when we don't know what is the real cause behind certain effects.

We seem to be able to list and describe in great detail the particular effects that result from "field" activity, but can offer little about what causes fields to exist or how they operate. For example, I found gravity to be given many times as an example of a field. We can describe many effects of gravity, but we still have only theories about its nature. We can accurately measure what it does, but we don't yet know what it is, other than to label it a field and continue to study it.

If one begins to view the mind, or consciousness itself, as field-like, then the interplay of mind-body information transfer may involve fieldlike phenomena of some sort. I found authoritative support for the concept that body, mind, and nonlocal forces are inextricably linked. Physician, researcher, and author Dr. Richard Gerber has written extensively regarding the energetic interplay of mind, body, and spirit in physical health. His classic text, *Vibrational Medicine: New Choices for Healing Ourselves,* has now been followed by his newest work, *Vibrational Medicine for the 21st Century: The Complete Guide to Energy Healing and Spiritual Transformation.*

This newest work contains commentary on the theories of Dr. Larry Dossey concerning research on the healing effects of prayer. Dr. Gerber notes:

> This term "nonlocal" refers to various phenomena (remote viewing, distant clairvoyant observations, distant healing by prayer) that demonstrate that our minds can observe and even influence individuals, objects, and even events widely separated from the observer by distance and time. We need only refer back to the studies that have enlisted prayer, a form of focused consciousness, to produce significant healing effects in plants, animals, and even

241

people at great distances. Since our nonlocal minds may be able to affect healing changes in another human being at a distance through an act of prayer, they could also be the true mechanism behind the effects of laying-on-of-hands healing as well.[2]

While it might cause some concern in religious circles, the idea of replacing the concept of the Spirit with a perspective of the nonlocal might also create a bridge between science and spirituality. To me, it is plausible that fieldlike effects around the human body might explain certain phenomena that are now strictly the purview of spirituality.

What if the spontaneous remission of disease is in some way related to nonlocal effects being created by the deepest levels of consciousness? What if the incredible strength that magically appears to allow someone to lift a car at an accident scene is also related to some undiscovered information flow among fields that surround and interact with the body? Are fieldlike effects a possible explanation of my experience of "being barbecued" in an altered state in the TMI booth? Could we speculate that the apparition of a loved one immediately after the loved one's death might be some lingering effect of the human energetic fields interacting with an expanded level of consciousness?

When we ask such questions about the relationship between consciousness and matter we must be cautious about what we mean. I am *not* using consciousness here in terms of the ego and thinking mind, but in the broadest sense. This view of consciousness not only allows for nonlocal phenomena, but also offers potential solutions to many psi-type phenomena. I am *not* proposing that we turn our backs on the spiritual, but to interweave it in a more objective and physically based approach. These statements might sound contradictory, and in one sense they are. But in another sense, I am asking readers to explore these ideas themselves.

For myself, I find the best approach is to pursue such thoughts by allowing for all the perspectives to be true at the same time. While this might not satisfy the single-answer approach of the scientific method, I remind the reader that science currently views light as sometimes being a particle and sometimes a wave. It all depends on the perspective. I take the view that we may be very close to a major breakthrough in our perspective when a problem can only be solved if multiple conflicting answers are all true.

A multiple-answer approach to complex problems could be labeled an "either, neither, and both" approach to understanding. Faced with seeming contradictions in modern science, with some research finding prayer effective in healing and opposing research finding no effect, I wonder if both can be true depending on one's perspective. Further, the more I explore research in nonlocal fields and energetic healing, the more the following statements make sense.

First, Dr. Brian Weiss, a Yale-educated physician, psychiatrist, and author, writes:

> When physicists in their laboratories measure the energies that healers emit, whether they direct this energy toward patients, bacterial cultures, or elsewhere, I believe these energies are related to the energy of love (spiritual energy). Healing energy is a component of spiritual energy. With future research and improved technology, we will better understand this connection.[3]

And second, the Reverend Rosalyn Bruyere, a long-time participant in scientific research investigating the human electromagnetic field and its use in healing, notes:

> If we view the body as energy and consider everything that affects the body according to an energy model, we begin to understand the relationship between chemicals and the body, food and the body, light and the body, sound and the body, and the relationship between ourselves and others.[4]

> It may not be the individual atom or electron that is important, but the spaces in between that hold the secrets of the universe.

—J. R. M.

21

Human Bioenergy: The Dance of the Human Cell and Vast Unseen Forces

The single human cell is a marvel of simplicity and complexity. At the simplest level, it is the basic building block of our physical body and an elemental resource of life itself. At the most complex level, it is one of the most prolific producers of chemicals in existence. Relative to its size, the human cell can, by itself, or in concert with other cells, synthesize vast quantities and immense varieties of chemicals. Many scientists' lifetimes have been dedicated to the study of the mechanics of these microscopic factories, and there are libraries documenting cellular level functions and activities.

The ever-puzzling question that continues to confound us is how do these cells *know how* and *when* to do these things? What level of organizing intelligence exists that acts as the conductor of this symphony going on within the body?

The chemical processes of the human cell obey the normal laws of chemistry and physics in that they produce light, heat, and energy in the ordinary interactive manner. When you approach the exploration of the body as whole systems of cellular interactions, however, it becomes too complex to study easily. For this reason, since the introduction of the scientific method, scientists have attempted to break down each bodily or cellular function into smaller and smaller pieces until they can get the area to be studied small enough to wrap their minds and instrumentation around. While this has made it easier to study anatomy and biochemistry, it also means that more complex interactions involving areas of simultaneous interactions might be overlooked because the lens of study is focused too close. We need to stand farther back to get a good picture.

The scientific method has served us well, but its inherent reductionist approach carries with it severe limitations when trying to understand complex, intricate, and interrelated systems such as the energetic interplay in the human body. Dr. Oschman, an expert at pulling together complex insights from numerous disparate sources, notes:

> By its very nature, the reductionism approach assumes that it is virtually impossible to study phenomena at the level of the whole organism, simply because it is too complex. To make sense out of it, life must be taken apart and studied one piece at a time. The reassembly of the parts into a whole is a process that must be put off until some vague and distant future date, when we have come to understand all of the parts.[1]

Let us explore the implications of this issue with a brief review of research associated with one of the human energy systems, the bioelectric. While we are all familiar with the electrical activity of the specialized cells of the nervous system and the brain, we may not be as aware of cellular level electrical functions. The activity of every cell involves electricity in some form and at some level. Author and researcher Gregg Braden offers readers an insight into the capacity of human bioelectric activity. He notes the following:

> The path of internal technology remembers that each cell of our bodies is approximately 1.17 volts of electrical potential. Statistics indicate that the average body is composed of approximately one quadrillion cells. One quadrillion cells times 1.17 volts of potential

for each cell equals approximately 1.17 quadrillion volts of bioelectrical potential per person.[2]

The electrical potential in the human body is obviously large when viewed in this manner. It is also a simple fact of physics that electricity passing through a conducting medium (whether copper wire or human tissue) creates an associated magnetic field. So 1.17 quadrillion volts of electrical potential, by default, creates an immense opportunity for the creation of electromagnetic fields in and around the human body. This is indeed the case, and, now, due to the development of very sensitive instrumentation, biomagnetic fields can be investigated and explored scientifically.

With the invention of the SQUID (superconducting quantum interference device) magnetometer in the 1970s, the study of electromagnetic fields moved into new realms, including human bioenergy research. Extensive research now firmly documents the existence of such fields surrounding our body, and there is enormous opportunity for field-type interactions in human bodily processes.

Since electromagnetic energy is wavelike, or pulsing, in nature, an electromagnetic field has a rate of vibration associated with it. In scientific investigation, vibratory rates are measured in units related to the number of vibrations observed every second. The vibratory rate is commonly referred to as cycles per second, as in the measurement of ordinary household electrical current (i.e., a 115-volt current operates at 60 cycles per second). The scientific measurement is in terms of Hertz units, so household current operates at 115 volts and 60 Hertz.

Hertz (abbreviated Hz) is the officially accepted scientific notation now utilized to represent the number of cycles per second. A single Hz equals one cycle per second of any wave, pulse, or other vibration-based phenomena. A megahertz (mHz) represents one thousand cycles per second; a gigahertz (GHz) represents a million cycles per second, and so on. Named in honor of the nineteenth-century German physicist Heinrich Hertz, Hertz can express the frequencies of any phenomenon with regular periodic variations.

Today we often hear the nomenclature of Hertz because of the growing popularity of computer terminology. A gigahertz-capable computer chip can perform at least one million computer instructions per second. In addition to its popular use in "computer-speak," this terminology is used in connection with alternating electric currents, electromagnetic waves (light, radar, and so on), and sounds.

The implications of bioelectric research are fascinating. I highly recommend *The Body Electric: Electromagnetism and the Foundation of Life,* by medical doctor and pioneer electromedicine researcher Robert O. Becker and scientific writer and researcher Gary Selden. Their easy style of writing makes enjoyable reading, yet this classic work also incorporates an exhaustive review of the quality scientific research in electromedicine. They also include discussion of Dr. Becker's own research in electrostimulated regeneration of tissue. In this now famous experiment, Dr. Becker demonstrated that small voltages of direct currents of electricity could significantly benefit the regeneration of broken or amputated limbs in salamanders and frogs.

He discovered that the strength and frequency of specifically applied electromagnetic fields was a trigger mechanism in creating the differentiation of cell type and function as part of the growth process. This meant that an electromagnetic field somehow contained the *information* that directed each individual cell to become a bone cell, a cartilage cell, or a tissue cell. Dr. Becker was able to influence still-developing groups of cells under controlled conditions and direct their growth process toward becoming a targeted cell type depending on the electromagnetic field he applied.

Bioelectric research also reveals that bone, cartilage, and ligaments all exhibit the piezoelectric effect. The piezoelectric effect is the phenomenon of a small charge of electricity produced when pressure is applied. Most science class experiments show this effect by utilizing quartz crystals. A quartz crystal is placed under pressure and a small electrical charge can be measured as being created and discharged from within the crystal. Combining the discovery that bone and cartilage exhibit piezoelectricity with microelectrical stimulation has resulted in the demonstration, in certain cases, of speeded healing in broken bones by the application of small measured charges of direct current electricity.

One can envision bone, cartilage, and ligaments as "living crystal" due to their piezoelectric properties. In fact, recent research identifies crystalline properties and structures within these tissues. These ideas support the concept that *chi,* or life energy, is connected in some way with bioelectric and biomagnetic properties of human fascia and bone.

It does not take a large leap of imagination to envision Eastern exercise programs such as tai chi or chi gung as rooted in the creation of piezoelectric effects stimulated by the flexing of fascia during the body movements of the exercises. It is reasonable that exercises that stretch and bend fascial tissue (tai chi and chi gung) create small electrical charges in the body that then create positive fieldlike effects on the body system. It is certainly plausible that a stimulus for a general increase in electrical activity might trigger positive health effects.

In his second book, *Cross Currents: The Promise of Electromedicine, The Perils of Electropollution,* Dr. Becker recognizes the older wisdom traditions of the world and their cultural attention to the concept of an underlying energetic basis to life. He writes:

> We have seen how the latest scientific revolution has validated the ancient, preliterate concept of "life energy," not as some mystical, unknowable force but as measurable electromagnetic forces that act within the body as organized control systems. These electromagnetic forces appear capable of being accessed through some of the techniques of the shaman-healers as well as through modern, direct intervention with similar forces. These ideas have led to the development of the new medical paradigm, energy medicine, which is currently being slowly integrated into orthodox scientific medicine.[3]

The interconnected nature of electricity and electromagnetism playing a significant role in certain bodily processes leads me to reflect on how much we think we know about how the body works. While we seem to have intricate knowledge about structural and anatomical minutiae, how much do we know about the effects of electromagnetic fields dancing around our bodies?

Dr. Oschman proposes that such fields are the core of our internal information network:

> I am convinced that the various fields that spread through and over and around the body as a result of every heartbeat, and as a result of every other physiological process, did not evolve merely as artifacts for the convenience of the diagnostician. Instead, these fields convey essential biological information that tells every part of the body what every other part is doing.[4]

Pioneering efforts in this area of study are the focus of the International Society for the Study of Subtle Energy and Energy Medicine (ISSSEEM). ISSSEEM is an interdisciplinary organization of more than 1,300 members that offers peer-reviewed publication of research in its journal, *Subtle Energies and Energy Medicine.* Significant research and exploration of field-effect types of subtle energy anatomical activity is but one of the fascinating topics explored by ISSSEEM members and reported at annual conferences and through publications.

Another interest group is the Institute of Noetic Sciences (IONS) mentioned earlier. With more than 35,000 members, IONS is able to provide not only a reporting vehicle for subtle energy research, but also grant-based funding to underwrite research efforts in this area.

There are several views as to the source and implications of bioelectric or biomagnetic fields generated around the body. First, there is a Western materialist perspective, which holds that the human body is machinelike and the mind encased in the brain as a collection of neuronal impulses. In this view, any sort of measurable subtle energy is considered a simple by-product of cellular level electrochemical activity. In my opinion, this is a simplistic viewpoint, as it ignores mounds of quality scientific research to the contrary.

Second, there is the traditional approach of Eastern cultures, which, after thousands of years of practical experience, have institutionalized subtle energy constructs in the formal healing arts of acupuncture and related modalities. In this model, the flow of life energy, or *chi,* traverses structured paths called meridians so that a complete energy anatomy sits alongside the physical. Another Eastern construct offers the energy concentration areas known as chakras aligned along the spinal column; each chakra has an energetic role in the body and an emotional and mental influence as well.

There is a place in the Eastern approach for the influences of an expanded level of consciousness. Under the proper conditions, a nonlocal level of consciousness is able to interact with the subtle energy systems of the body. Adepts in chakra-based healing can, even under scientific scrutiny, perform successful healing interventions on diseased subjects. These approaches also contain energy-building and health-boosting exercises such as yoga, tai chi, and chi gung. In my opinion, these approaches offer, at minimum, a culturally accepted model of subtle energy systems.

Third, esoteric models use an energy-based construct of life. The human exists as energy first and is then encased in a physical body. That is, the spirit or energy form of the person exists so independently of the body that physical activity is akin to driving a car or animating a marionette. While this view is somewhat more spiritual than the other two models, it provides an understandable context to explore the role of psi in healing.

Clearly, these three models aid our visualization and comprehension of complex bioelectric, biomagnetic, and subtle energy interactions. There is no simple approach that explains how the mind-body relationship works. I believe that all three models may be correct. The differences are a matter of perspective as to what one is attempting to explain, in the same manner that physicists sometimes view light as a particle and sometimes as a wave in order to ensure that it fits into accepted models of understanding.

Perhaps the more philosophical approach of Dr. Michael Mamas in his comments on touch-based healing offers the best approach:

> If we want to understand hands-on healing, we have to move beyond creating elaborate models of the human energy system. There are more than enough models to memorize already. Our understanding has to be taken to a more sophisticated (far more

mature) level. The interconnectedness between the models is where the knowledge lives.[5]

Returning to the written material of Dr. Oschman, we find additional support for models that exist in the "interconnectedness between the models":

> The brain field, like the heart field, is not confined to the organ that produces it. We refer to "brain waves" as though they are confined to the brain, but they are not. The fields of all the organs spread throughout the body and into the space around it. One of the primary channels for the flow of electrical energy waves through the body is the circulatory system.[6]

Remembering that the blood is very salty in makeup adds another possibility. Because of its saline nature, blood and the circulatory system are an excellent conductor of electricity. This fact could account for a more direct interplay of electrical field activity than would be considered in a cursory view of human bioelectrical activity. Of course, consideration of the bloodstream as a carrier of electrical pulsation should remind one that the blood is already well recognized as a carrier of the mechanical waves of heartbeat and blood pressure.

As I pondered the various fieldlike interactions that might come into play all at once, I began to realize the difficulty in doing scientific research that is primarily based on controlling and isolating variables that could affect any process within the complexities of living organisms. In a discussion of various forms of alternative healing, Dr. Oschman notes that the information flow of such interactions might even be considered a basis of success in various therapeutic approaches. He writes:

> The dynamic rhythmic matrix has aspects that are mechanical, electrical, magnetic, gravitational, thermal, acoustic, and photonic. Different therapeutic approaches focus on one or another of these phenomena. Because of the complexity of the living matrix to

extract meaningful information contained in various kinds of energy fields, many approaches can be effective. Different individuals have different sensitivities and different skills that make it easier for them to take one route or another.[7]

Electromagnetic fields are generated by the brain, heart, and body itself. Focused brain wave activities are generated by hemispheric synchronization that results in expanded states of consciousness. What if a state of mind-body coherence could amplify both the state of consciousness and the electromagnetic fields present? Such a state of coherence might be achieved by an emotional state of love or compassion, but be destroyed by the physiological impacts of anger or hatred.

While this might not provide a comprehensive model for all disease, it surely merits investigation as a factor in the development of disease and in healing. We must be cautious, of course, that we do not jump to the conclusion that we have a total explanation with such a proposal. We have seen that there are many forces at work at both macro and micro levels of physiology and consciousness, and these are complex areas to explore.

Pursuing the interconnections of knowledge or looking in the gaps between known elements to seek the overall macro-interconnections of all elements of activity is a difficult approach and does not lend itself to the scientific method. Attempting to follow the subtle interactions of the nearly immeasurable is difficult in itself. Crossing the line between the activity of consciousness and the activity of cellular biochemical or bioelectric phenomena is seemingly impossible. There are those who have made this effort, however, and, in so doing, some brave pioneers have already opened doors of understanding.

The work of Charles Tart, Robert Becker, Dean Radin, Russell Targ, and Hal Putoff are good examples. While they may initially have been ostracized or ridiculed for their efforts, many now consider them the pioneers of this exciting new area of study. Even being able to pursue this study under the auspices of a major university has been a challenge in the past. Dr. Valerie Hunt notes with pride, however:

While numerous researchers have studied extremely low biological frequencies (ELF) and the magnetic current associated with healing, tissue health, and disease, the extremely high biological frequency (EHF) electrical currents associated with mind phenomena and human consciousness were first researched in my laboratory at U.C.L.A.[8]

Research that attempts to interrelate consciousness, emotions, cellular activity, and human energy fields has, in the past, been relegated to what many scientists consider the fringe elements of parapsychology. To me, the serious psi researcher should not only receive our respect and admiration, but we should encourage their work as much as possible. The value of insight in these areas is well summarized by pioneering researcher Dean Radin. He writes:

> After a century of slowly accumulating scientific evidence, we now know that some aspects of psychic phenomena are real. The importance of this discovery lies somewhere between an interesting oddity and an earth-shattering revolution. At a minimum, genuine psi suggest that what science presently knows about the nature of the universe is seriously incomplete, that the capabilities and limitations of human potential have been vastly underestimated, that beliefs about the strict separation of objective and subjective are almost certainly incorrect, and that some "miracles" previously attributed to religious sources may instead be caused by extraordinary capabilities of human consciousness.[9]

With new awareness of the potential impact of subtle energy and human bioenergetic fields in mind, I spent considerable time revisiting my experiences at TMI and SEH. An entirely new set of questions arose as to what possible interactions might be in play. As I face these issues, I try to have an open mind while keeping a healthy degree of skepticism. Yet I am also continuously drawn to the words of Bob Monroe: "The only limitations to human potential are belief systems."

22

Viewing Death as Merely a Short-Term Situation: Taking Consciousness beyond the Physical

Recent scientific research provides new information about the relationship of mind and body. Newly described "architectures" of field phenomena that surround the human body and mind challenge our most cherished beliefs about our relationship to our surroundings. There are major implications inherent in the idea that "mind fields" exist beyond the boundaries of our physical bodies. Faced with research supporting the quantum nature of consciousness, we must seriously consider the existence of "thought fields" that precede birth or linger after physical death.

We ordinarily avoid thoughts about the reality of our death because to consider them seriously would force our control-oriented ego and analytical mind to admit that there are some things beyond their manipulation. Avoiding thoughts of death does not delay its coming, but such avoidance may limit our pursuit of a broader context in which to consider our death and any sort of transition to something that might survive it.

Eminent psychologist and parapsychology researcher Dr. Charles Tart notes our skill at avoiding the issue of death:

It is all too easy to use the abstractions and intellectual cre-
ations of science as a means of distracting ourselves from the *fact*
of death. It confronts us all, and we all have a natural fear of anni-
hilation and of the unknown. Yet by avoiding the actuality of death,
taking ourselves away from the presence of mortality, we also shut
out an opportunity for a profound and valuable experience—an
experience that may transform the quality of our living.[1]

We live in a society so sanitized of the realities of death that
many in our culture have never witnessed anyone dying. We are
avoiding any contact with death in the hope that by ignoring it, it will
magically not happen to us.

In the journal article in which Dr. Tart's quote appears, he
speaks of time he spent with a friend who was dying and the insights
that experience provided. Of special interest are Dr. Tart's comments concerning speech patterns during the state of dementia that
a dying person enters. Dr. Tart realized these speech patterns contained experiences of altered and expanded states of consciousness
similar to those experienced by subjects in Dr. Tart's parapsychology
research. This implies that the dying process may also contain activities oriented toward the larger state of consciousness that will be
rejoined with the demise of the physical body.

Assuming that a state of consciousness exists before birth and
after death stimulates thoughts about the nature of physical life. Why
would an independent field of consciousness desire to become so
intimately integrated with a temporary physical vehicle in the first
place? There must be something intoxicating about experiencing
physical life that creates such a relationship between mind and body.
What possible combination of the quantum and the physical creates
such a symbiotic and seemingly single entity as is represented by a
human?

Such questions have been the subject of basic religious and spiritual inquiry for centuries. Dr. Tart comments:

The central question of many spiritual traditions is "Who am I?
What is my identity?" All my studies, and my researches of other

255

people's studies, have made me think that a *major* component of one's identity is the physical body. Our awareness is dominated for the most part by the physical representations of who we are. There is a constant pattern of sensations from our body that we are not even conscious of for the most part, but which nevertheless molds our consciousness, which in turn reinforces habits of thinking, perceiving and acting. Unfortunately, from a spiritual or psychology of liberation perspective, this is a problem.[2]

The contemplation of our death is not something that we are culturally or psychologically encouraged to do, unless our mortality becomes threatened by accident, disease, or advancing age, and then it is too late for an impartial investigation. As a consequence, when death appears imminent, we are ill-equipped to deal with it.

Such a restrictive cultural habit stimulated my interest in examining it. These questions are of the highest personal and spiritual consequence. As these questions became more important for me to answer in my life, I again turned to the resources of The Monroe Institute. Since my initial experiences there contained such a powerful separation from bodily sensations, I returned to TMI to explore these states of being at a deeper level.

TMI has a graduate program called Lifeline that offers more complex psychoacoustic support to approach the Monroe-defined Focus Levels of 22, 23, 25, and 27. These levels of expanded consciousness are purported to offer access to pre-birth and post-death levels of consciousness. Further, an aspect of the program involves the opportunity for contact with persons now known to be dead physically and provides a process for assisting those perceived to be having difficulties in their transitional process to rejoin their greater form of consciousness. This is a nontrivial claim and one that would logically require some evidence to support it. There is anecdotal evidence from Bob Monroe as well as verifiable information from TMI program participants in support of it.

Lifeline grew out of Monroe's experiences in which he (or others in his lab) came into contact with seemingly discarnate entities whose specific tales of their lifetimes offered an opportunity for research and speculation. During every TMI Gateway program, a tape recording of the "Patrick session" is played for participants. In this now legendary laboratory session, contact was made with an individual calling himself Patrick, who was alive more than a hundred years ago. Patrick was apparently killed in the boiler explosion of a small sailing vessel off the coast of the British Isles, but seemingly was unaware that he was dead.

In the role of laboratory session monitor, Monroe interacted with this discarnate intelligence speaking via the laboratory subject and assisted Patrick in moving to a place where help for the transition beyond death could be found. Although Patrick's lifetime could not be verified, the experience revealed significant issues for further research and inquiry. In ensuing years, contact with individuals whose lifetimes could be documented has been achieved at TMI.

Actual confirmation that a person lived and died under the circumstances related by a TMI lab subject in an altered state of consciousness yields interesting questions. Was such an experience an actual contact with the dead? Or is this an example of a fantastic capability of the brain to store casually obtained information and manifest it during these sessions?

Monroe hosted the initial Lifeline program at TMI in June 1991. During that session events occurred that support information originating from nonordinary sources. A participant in an expanded state of consciousness was shocked to be confronted by his discarnate grandmother. To his knowledge, his grandmother was indeed alive and well, but the impression was so strong that the participant telephoned after the session to check on her. All were amazed to find that she had passed away unexpectedly the day of the TMI session. It became a basic element of the Lifeline program to document such contact and to obtain verifiable data that could be used in further research.

My wife and I went to TMI and joined 14 others for the Lifeline program in November 1996. The initial experiences of the week offer participants reinforcement of their previous expanded consciousness training at the Focus 10, 12, 15, and 21 Levels; then there is the introduction of the higher levels of Focus experience. A gradual process unfolds in which the participants move through the experience of the new Focus Levels beyond 21 and finally of Focus 27.

Rather than spend a lot of time in reporting tape experiences at these levels, I will describe their characteristics so I can move on to a discussion of how such experiences may fit into a larger model of consciousness. The launch point for these deeper consciousness excursions is Focus 21, which offers a bridge to move beyond our three dimensions of time and space. Utilizing Hemi-Sync, the program participant is guided to move quickly through Focus 22, which contains the raw substance of dreams.

During my initial tapes at this level, I disregarded the caution in the instructions and spent time in this state. I found it to be an anesthetic type of experience, a void that could swallow one up. This was not unpleasant, but a kind of nonfeeling, a place that could lull one into a state in which no sensations, either positive or negative, are felt—a state of numbness. I have heard speculation that this type of numbness is the goal of the drug addict who seeks "nonfeeling" as a better sensation than the normal feeling of pain that is considered basic to being alive. I learned why this is a level that is to be moved through quickly, or better yet, jumped over. The potential for addiction to aspects of nonfeeling made me want to avoid it.

Returning to the program protocol, I followed the guidance to move to Focus 23. In this state, I encountered a world similar to ours, but its inhabitants were those who have died and cannot accept that fact. Monroe's final book, *Ultimate Journey*, contains passages about this type of experience, and I refer the reader to it for background. Moving beyond Focus 23, one encounters the worlds and scenarios created by the various afterlife beliefs of humankind.

We must be careful here about jumping to conclusions and we must use language carefully. Afterlife beliefs and religious constructs are personal and powerful. It is certainly not my intent to challenge or support any particular form of religious approach to the afterlife. My point is to emphasize that it is possible to experience these realms in expanded states of consciousness. I am not discounting any particular belief system. On the contrary, I believe my experience confirms the validity of them all.

In my experiences of the various traditional constructs of Heaven, they appear to have been created by the continuum of human thought from tribal cultures to the great religions of the world. It was as if each formation of a concept of Heaven was merely another doorway off a long hallway. Entering several, I encountered the great teachers of various religions and the scenarios they anticipated with death. Whatever your belief system of the afterlife may be, it turns out to be exactly what you find. I even found a doorway of nothingness that turned out to be the afterlife design of an atheist!

If you expect nothing when you die, that is exactly what you get. At some point, however, this will become boring, and you can continue your journey beyond the limitations of your earthly belief systems. The idea that one might have to stay within a cultural model of the afterlife for all eternity appears to me to be a construct of a linear mind. From these experiences, I understood that all the envisioned forms of Heaven appear to be experiences within higher levels of consciousness and that consciousness eventually moves beyond these limitations.

Utilizing the Lifeline protocols, I finally moved to Focus 27, the location of "the Park" of Monroe's experience. One could say that these states of consciousness represent Monroe's version of the "Summerland" model of the nineteenth-century Spiritualist movement. The Spiritualist leader Reverend Andrew Jackson Davis outlined an idyllic parklike setting he called Summerland in his writings of the mid-1800s. Summerland supposedly serves as the home base for the soul while the incarnation process occurs.

Similar in construct, Focus 27 contains life preparation schools and post-death processing centers. In Focus 27, each thought instantly manifests as reality. It is even possible in Lifeline to prepare yourself a living space for your immediate post-death experiences. The idea that you have prepared a familiar home base for your initial afterlife experience is psychologically powerful. (Bruce Moen has written extensively of his adventures in this realm, and I refer the reader to his Exploring the Afterlife series of books for additional information.)

Let me share one experience that offers a perspective on the transitional nature of death. This particular activity was not during a formal TMI Focus 27 tape session but is similar to many I had there. I include an account of it here to emphasize that TMI Focus Levels are not the only paths to such experiences. Shamanism and transcendental states achieved differently in different cultures can carry you to the same destination.

This event occurred spontaneously during a craniosacral therapy session with a massage therapist. It not only illustrates the dramatic levels of sensation, but also contains confirmation by another person that something challenging to normal belief systems was going on.

I settle comfortably on the massage table with soft music in the background. I have an agreement with the massage therapist, Barbara, that we will openly dialogue if there is something we feel needs sharing. The session begins slowly with a relaxation process. Together, we begin to explore. I easily drift to Focus 12 as relaxation overcomes my body. Barbara starts at my feet, but I feel sensations around my head. I feel pain and discomfort and tell Barbara. She asks if she should move to my head. I say yes.

She moves to my head and creates a tractionlike hold with her hands. Suddenly, I seem to be surrounded by the ocean. I am floating on the open sea. This is not merely visualization, but more of an immersion experience in another reality.

"I am sensing water," Barbara comments. I have said nothing at this point.

Finally, I comment, "Yes, I am near water." Then I say no more.

I focus on the scene. I am indeed on the ocean, on some very rough seas. Then the detail of the scene fully forms, and I find myself within it. I am a sailor on a raft in a storm at sea. There are others on the raft. We are apparently survivors of a shipwreck. The sailing masts of the ship are disappearing nearby. I am being cradled in the arms of one of the others who is carefully holding my head, but at an odd angle.

Intellectually, here and now, I sense that in this scene my neck has been broken and that I am either already dead or will die if my head is straightened. My raft companions are all very concerned that I (he) am going to die. There is great emotion and concern as apparently the dying man is their leader, and they are in dire straits.

I am aware that I am not this person now (I know I am on a massage table in another time and place)—he is in some other form, a part of me. I have no illusion that he and I are the same person. We are not. This dual form of consciousness is very interesting, however. I sense that in his mind he has started to realize he is dying and is attempting to deal with this.

I feel the need to assist him in some way. I speak aloud and ask Barbara to move my neck and realign it. While my neck is only very slightly off center, she slowly and gently moves it a few millimeters to align it. At that moment, the sailor dies, yet he is not willing to accept the reality of his death. He maintains a very strong "physical" presence. He doesn't want to be the source of the pain and suffering he feels he is causing others on the raft. So he keeps trying to "wake up." His mind is telling him that he is merely injured and has drifted off to sleep. With enough effort he can reawaken. He struggles to wake up.

After some effort in this mode, he starts to drift out of his body as a separated and luminous form. This is not acceptable to him, and he attempts to stuff himself back into the lifeless form. This effort produces no result except his growing frustration at its failure. At this point, he seems to become aware of my presence, and this adds to his confusion. His mind keeps telling him that he is dreaming or has become delirious. From his perspective, he is suspended above his body and looking down on it, yet he is alive. Meanwhile, on the raft, the other sailors are upset as their shipmate has died while the storm rages around them.

As the dead man floats above his body, two luminous orbs appear and begin to communicate with him. There is a clear thought-form communication coming from them attempting to get him to understand that he is dead and should go with them. This is fascinating and I am keenly focused on the two light bodies and the suspended luminous form of the newly dead sailor.

He resists. He knows that all he has to do is to get back into his body and awaken and all of this will just be a dream. He is not entertaining the idea that he is dead. After a bit of a struggle and not being able to get any closer to his body, he turns to address me. Apparently, in his perception, I represent somewhat more of a human form than the suspended "floating lights" trying to communicate with him. When he realizes that I understand his situation, he asks me about the "talking lights."

He keeps repeating that all he needs to do is get back into his body and "wake up" and everything will be all right. I explain to him that he is dead and that he needs to go with the "talking lights." After some time in this confused state, he repeatedly looks at his body, at me, the lights, and the implications of the real situation begin to sink in.

With this realization, we ascend slowly as a group. The sensation of floating upward stimulates his realization that he is, in truth, leaving life. He asks me if I can help him. I say I can try. He asks me if he is really dead. I say "yes," that he will have to go with the talking lights. He asks if it is possible to see his wife before he leaves. At this point, I seem to receive a direct thought-form from one of the luminous orbs in the affirmative. I tell him that we can do that.

There is a whooshing sound and we move instantly to England. He materializes at the foot of his wife's bed. His wife wakes up, sees him, and "knows" that he is dead. (Later I see his wife at his funeral. As he is buried, she thinks of the moment he appeared and how his doing that showed how much he loved her.) Time seems fluid in this state, and these events seem to occur simultaneously. With this process complete, there is another whooshing sound and we are back above the storm at sea, suspended above the raft.

Barbara mentions that she is feeling some sort of "sticky goo" on the back of my head. She says it feels and smells like blood, but there is nothing there. I tell her not to be concerned and that there is something going on in my mind that I will tell her about later.

The dead sailor is finally coming to grips with his fate. We are again moving upward, the sailor, two talking lights, and me. He asks again if he is dead. I say "yes." He peers at me, sighs, and says "thank you." As we move upward, I begin trying to emit the vibration of unconditional love. I figure that this will help the sailor separate from the Earth plane.

As we move further upward and above the clouds, he grows uncomfortable. He doesn't like this "talking lights" stuff. He seems much more comfortable being near me. He looks at me with fear and asks, "Will I see Jesus and the angels now?"

"Of course," I say, with no knowledge of what is going to happen next, "but right now you need to go with the 'talking lights.'" At that moment, a powerful thought form bombards me from the luminous orb indicating that I have said the proper thing.

Almost instantaneously, a firmament forms in the clouds and the two lights transform into the traditional form of angels with great wings. They embrace the sailor and he seems mightily relieved. As they move to carry him toward the forming space in the clouds, I detect the presence of religious and family figures ready to welcome the sailor to his Heaven.

I feel it is appropriate to separate from the angels and the sailor. I move down, or it seems I float in a downward direction. I have a large smile on my physical face and a strong sensation of his well-being, and I say aloud, "He will be all right."

"Excuse me?" Barbara says.

"Tell you later," I whisper.

There is another scene of a small girl dying, and Barbara, the massage therapist, is there as her mother. I do not comment. Then I perceive Barbara in light-body form and I see a small, darker energy behind her left shoulder. It is separate from her and the name "Francene" forms in my mind.

I again speak aloud to Barbara. "Do you know anyone named Francene?"

She tells me that is her sister's name. I perceive darkness in this energy. I ask if she is alive. Barbara responds affirmatively. Then I see a black veil between them, like a fine Spanish lace. Looking closely at the face, I don't see much of the veil. If I focus on the threads of the veil, I can see only the veil and not the face. I share this with Barbara.

It comes to me that this is the sort of relationship Barbara has with Francene. I tell her she should look at Francene and not the veil of her appearance. [After-session note: Barbara said that Francene is a very negative, angry person who sees no good in anyone and finds little reason for living. Barbara sees her sister as a person, however, rather than seeing all of the negativity.]

Barbara asks if there is more information about her sister. At this point, I realize my ego is taking some pride in the psychic "hit" of getting Barbara's sister's name, and I also realize such ego involvement is counterproductive. I cannot seem to undo the ego involvement, as I am excited by this verifiable form of psi.

At this point, I feel that the session should end. Barbara asks if I feel comfortable ending at that point, and I do. It is as if we both realize at the same moment that it is time to for this session to be over.

Did I travel back in time and "rescue" a stranded soul stuck in the process of dying? I have difficulty with the idea that a soul might be stuck somewhere and require rescue by another person. To me, that seems a bit arrogant and presumptuous. Post-death experiences must fall outside of time and space, so even the idea of being "stuck" may not have the same kind of meaning to a discarnate intelligence as to us. Further, I wonder whether we are dealing with the soul energy of the departed or merely an energetic "echo" of that person's personality.

I encourage the reader to stop avoiding consideration of what happens when you die. While the constructs I have presented may not match any religious design, and indeed may conflict with some, they are based on my experiences. How many of us have allowed ourselves to seek experiences in these levels of consciousness? Isn't the nature of death a question of such a fundamental nature that we should look into it?

Not only did these experiences provide me with calm in consideration of the dying process, but faced with deaths in my own family, I witnessed the efficacy of these ideas in action. Utilizing the gift of enhanced vision in an expanded state of consciousness, I witnessed the attendance of the departed at their own funerals and participated in the transition process with others. Did this occur, or was it my imagination? I guess I will not know that at the intellectual level until my own physical death. Whether real or imagined, the experience and the psychological comfort offered were most rewarding and emotionally rich compared to the normally accepted cultural and religious ritual of a funeral in Western society. Can such comfort be considered bad? I do not think so.

As I pointed out at the beginning of this chapter, we avoid thinking about our death in the hope of escaping it. Historically, our only support or guidance regarding the post-death experience was philosophical and religious in nature. Now we have new evidence of higher levels of consciousness that exist beyond the mind and body. We should examine our belief systems about death and the potential that exists for consciousness to exist outside of time and space. In my opinion, our Western materialist view has been far too limited in its outlook. While I do not propose that we shift our thinking completely toward traditional Eastern thought, I believe we are becoming well equipped to move beyond our traditional beliefs about Heaven, Hell, and the nature of the soul.

What we will accept as proof of something being true is an indicator of how open we are to change.

—J. R. M.

Collaborative Integration of the Physical, the Nonphysical, and the Spaces in Between

I have experienced challenges in writing about my thoughts, feelings, and experiences. I realize that the words will be frozen in time, and putting words on paper is very different from speaking them. In a conversation, one can get feedback on the understanding of the other person before going on to the next element of thought. If needed, additional information can be provided. Further, there are passion and emotion in one's voice that go with the words one says. In a book, each word must be chosen carefully because it cannot be changed once it is committed to print. While one can try to choose words that carry one's passion and emotion, whether they do or not is the experience of the reader.

I have shared things with you that might be subject to ridicule by some people. It is to be hoped that some of these things will strike a resonant chord with you. "Oh, yes, I have felt something like that" is a comment that would give me great joy. I thank you if this is the case. If not, I thank you for your time anyway.

I have shared my perspective on scientific research that, to me, demonstrates there is a great deal going on around us that we do not yet understand. Here, too, a comment of "Hmm, I never thought about that in that way, but maybe I should think about it a little more" would make my hours of struggle writing this book worth it. Time is a precious commodity, and you have spent a chunk of yours with me in reading this book. I appreciate that.

After many chapters of my comments and experiences, I must finally address in the next section, the original question from my niece Caroline: "Of what benefit is all of this to me?"

Part VI

Interactive Perception: How Can We Keep Score When We Are All on the Same Team?

What we see depends mainly on what we look for.

—John Lubbock

It's our choices, not our abilities that determine who we are.

—Albus Dumbledore, from *Harry Potter and the Chamber of Secrets*

23

Finding What You Are Looking for or Looking for What You Find? The Formation of Experience

Our minds seek certainty as we ask questions about who we are and why we are here. We are unwilling to accept merely *an* answer, as we demand *the* answer. Our logical intellects tell us that there can be only one true answer. Dualistic or conflicting explanations do not appear reasonable to our linear thought processes. Our belief systems are rooted in cause-and-effect relationships, and this approach carries over into our scientific and religious structures as well.

The background, meaning, and experience behind a religious rite are important. What were the experiences of the founders of the great religions of the world? Their source? Shortly after my experiences at The Monroe Institute, I visited several church services with friends and family. I was amazed to rediscover powerful words of light, love, and inner direction being said at each service, but I realized that these powerful messages were repeated ritualistically, seemingly without experiential insight by most participants in the service. Our separation from the feeling behind these passages has become so distinct that they have become words without meaning.

Our prayers have become part of a hollow ritual. Ritual can be a wonderful way to relive and rejuvenate the experience of the deeply profound. This can only occur, however, in an experiential activity, not an intellectual one.

Feeling a sense of universal interconnection, even with those one considers enemies, is a core element in the great spiritual teachings of the world. Sadly, some adherents of institutionalized religious teachings argue that their separate interpretations of these teachings are the only true version. The concept of separation was originated by the ego and intellect to lay the foundation for "better than" situations. The ego solidifies focus on "my way is better" by finding those who agree. By contrast, the core elements of the great spiritual teachings of the world are focused on inclusion, interconnection, and unconditional love rather than separation or superiority.

When we become aware of subtle and unseen influences, we will be able to shift our approach to life in a way that will put us in balance with the totality of who we are. This is not to say that we should abandon our intellects, but merely loosen the intellect's grip a little to allow a broader input from multiple levels of ourselves. In this sense, we will be looking for what we find, as we are following the path envisioned by our deepest levels of consciousness. We will be in tune with that portion of us that exists independent of time, space, and even this lifetime. By this logic, if we make decisions with the intellect alone, we are disregarding the larger portion of who we really are.

Issues of intellect versus higher consciousness parallel, however, the paradox between quantum physics and relativity as explanations of operational rules of the universe. Dr. Eric Pearl, a chiropractor turned energy healer, teacher, and author, explores these conundrums in his book *The Reconnection: Heal Others, Heal Yourself.* Dr. Pearl deftly summarizes the seeming impossibilities being faced by scientists:

> Quantum mechanics led to the development of the computer chip. Relativity gave cosmologists the tools to explain all kinds of strange activity out there in the vastness of the universe.
>
> The problem, they say, is if quantum physics is true, then relativity has to be false, and vice versa. When you try to apply the

rules that govern one realm to the rules that govern the other, they stop working.[1]

Claiming that I have the answers to such questions with any degree of certainty would be arrogant to say the least. What I do hope is that I have a mind open enough to the question to pursue it in earnest. Such pursuit involves both the robust forces of the intellect as well as access to whatever expanded levels of consciousness I may be able to achieve.

My approach to self-exploration has been one of reflection, study, and experience. I have also tried to pay attention to the growing body of research in nonlocal phenomena that clearly demonstrates that there is consciousness-related, psi-type activity that cannot be explained by ordinary physics. We must recognize the importance of quality scientific research that demonstrates that consciousness is more of a fieldlike phenomenon than a series of electrical interactions in the brain. Electrical activity of the brain certainly also plays a role, but it is clear that this is not the total experience. As we view the dance of electrical impulses in the brain interacting with the broader field of consciousness, we witness the dance of the physical and the quantum. One cannot exist without the other.

Models that interconnect the quantum and the physical give bold new meaning to the religious construct of "In the beginning was the Word . . ." if we view "the Word" as the vibrations of consciousness at nonlocal levels of the Total Self. In one sense, we may have touched divinity as we follow this endless loop of the creative spark. I have sought access to the Spirit, or quantum levels of selfhood, through expanded states of consciousness. I have suspended disbelief in order to enable my mind to open to information that could challenge my existing belief systems. I have allowed my mind to embrace the concept of nonlocal influences, that nonphysical realms possibly affect physical reality. I have attempted to become more aware of subtle messages in the feelings and sensations of my physiology.

My experiences at The Monroe Institute were so powerful and profound that I now consider them spiritual in nature. When I speak of spirituality, I believe that it includes elements of the divine inherent in humanity. It should not be confused with any sort of church-excused approaches to nationalism or global tribalism with built-in eye-for-an-eye retribution concepts. This inclusive approach to spirituality is not an exclusionary one that promotes being "better than" another approach.

The reality of a greater self has given me respect for the soul and how we might relate to it. It is challenging to seek an alignment of my conscious decision-making with a greater self that makes subtle guidance available. Inner guidance is assisted by expanded states of consciousness and reflected in greater awareness of bodily sensation. From my experiences, I now say that the body can be considered a barometer of the alignment of the mind and Total Self.

Our language reflects the subtlety of this process with phrases like "it just feels right" and "my senses tell me that this is wrong." The need to listen to body wisdom is noted by physician, neuropsychiatrist, and neuroscientist Dr. Mona Lisa Schulz. In *Awakening Intuition,* she writes:

> Our bodies speak to us every day in every way, through their own vocabulary of symptoms tied to emotions and memories from the past and the present. We can learn to read those symptoms in the same way we learn to read signals in relationships or other areas of our lives.[2]

Being able to listen to the wisdom of our bodies adds to the information needed to make decisions, and this will align mind and spirit with the body. I am not proposing an action-stopping set of rules that demand we go into a meditative state before we make any ordinary move in daily life. Such an approach would be preposterous. What is important is more time spent in formal attempts to contact and form a relationship with the totality of who we are. The more time we can spend unifying our bodies and our higher selves in peaceful inner exploration, the better equipped we will be to make wise choices.

The propositions that greater sensitivity to the messages from our tissues is beneficial and that the wisdom of our emotional responses should be heeded are not mine alone. Nor are these ideas new. Tying such concepts to recent scientific inquiry into the quantum and nonlocal gives them new prominence, however. Gary Zukav, best-selling author of the new physics masterpieces *The Seat of the Soul* and *The Dancing Wu Li Masters,* points to the capacity and sensitivity of the body to feel the content of an emotional response as a very powerful tool in learning to align the body, mind, and spirit. Using the body and emotional sensitivity in this manner is well stated in his book *The Heart of the Soul: Emotional Awareness,* coauthored by Linda Francis, a nurse, chiropractor, and teacher of multidimensional approaches.

They write:

> If you are not aware of what you are feeling in your body and what you are thinking, you are not aware of the present moment. You have no power. You are occupied with what is in front of you and only a small portion of that. You are unaware of what others are feeling and how they are behaving, except when their behaviors affect you. Most important, you are unaware of yourself. You have no memory of yourself as a soul, as an influence on others, of your contact with the Universe or the breadth and scope of your creative capacity. Becoming conscious of these things requires that you become aware of your emotions.[3]

This approach does not conflict with science or religion. Both are structured approaches for making sense of the world. By incorporating the quantum, intellect, and wisdom in our physical bodies, however, we can improve our effectiveness, even in scientific and religious pursuits.

For the scientist, it would represent a movement from studying individual components to the total system. Biology is a good example: We have spent centuries learning about ever smaller units of the body by isolating their functions. This is good background, but now we must step back and look at the interaction of larger organic systems such as bioenergetic fields.

> Finding Divinity is merely a matter of looking around. Finding your Self may call for a great deal more searching.
>
> —J. R. M.

24

Oh, Sure, It's All Connected, but to What? Embracing Multidimensional Possibilities

Modern lifestyles carry a sense of intellectual superiority that creates an expectation of a privileged existence. We may also carry religious dogma that gives us dominion over the Earth itself. With these beliefs, we face a world in which our future is ensured by either how smart or how holy we are. We expect easy and quick answers because of our intelligence that created the technological achievements of the modern world. We ignore things without utility. Theoretical constructs of nonphysical vibratory energy or inner guidance from a selfhood beyond the physical will be irrelevant unless they can be made a meaningful part of everyday life.

As our society faces ever more complex questions, we naturally demand ever simpler answers. Finding solutions with the aid of the full realm of consciousness requires, however, a new level of balance. We must somehow unify the findings of the esoteric inner explorer and the quantum physicist. A balanced approach requires that we move out of the comfort zones of easily understood black-and-white issues and straightforward cause-and-effect relationships.

The ultimate solution we seek will challenge things that we have long taken for granted.

We must admit to the existence of our greater and multidimensional Total Self. We must face the reality that our intellect is not in control of our Total Self, but merely occupies a seat at the council table of selfhood. We must align ourselves with the guidance and direction available from this Total Self. This is not a path of desperation or surrender, but empowerment. We *can* have access to the "instruction book of life" and use it to ease the difficulty of decision-making.

It is difficult, however, to make an understandable model of the Total Self. There are numerous paths and many belief systems that have attempted to create for us a relationship with all that we are. One model I find interesting can be found in the work of Jane Roberts. In her book *Adventures in Consciousness: An Introduction to Aspect Psychology,* Roberts, aided by the insightful drawings of her husband, Robert Butts, created a cosmology of consciousness and infrastructure for the findings of quantum physics and questions posed by mystical philosophers.

So who is Jane Roberts and how did she come to know these things? Initially, she was an ordinary person, but through a series of unplanned events, she unexpectedly became a trance medium. Roberts began research in 1966 for a book on psychic phenomena and personal experience. Playing with a Ouija board opened a communication pathway for her to a nonphysical intelligence who called "himself" Seth.

Roberts soon could easily shift into a trance state and Seth began to dictate books, line by line, chapter by chapter. Over the years, thousands of pages of text were created that now form more than 20 books known as the Seth Material. Whether you believe this was simply accessing deeper workings of her mind or represents contact with another intelligence is not the issue. The insights offered are the key.

Seth commented through Roberts in a trance on numerous subjects that she knew nothing about. Seth also carried on face-to-face and knowledgeable conversations with scientists, philosophers, and even Bob Monroe. The work of Jane Roberts, like that of Edgar Cayce, has become a classic among metaphysical students. Her experiences are a story itself, and a fascinating one, but the issue I want to discuss is her attempt to create a paradigm to encompass the nonphysical underpinnings of reality and the role of our consciousness in forming it.

By studying the material Seth dictated, Roberts created an explanatory overview of who and what we are at the Total Self level. Information emerged as to how we interact in the formation of our physical world and our experiences in it. I encourage you to study these views of the world. Before reading *Adventures in Consciousness,* however, I strongly recommend reading Seth's first two books: *Seth Speaks: The Eternal Validity of the Soul* and *The Nature of Personal Reality.* You will gain needed background terminology and concepts that are fundamental to the overall constructs presented in *Adventures in Consciousness.*

Roberts's version of the Total Self is proposed as a "source self" and the nonlocal site of our root consciousness. She writes:

> The unknown or source self can be thought of as an entity, a personified energy gestalt—energy that knows itself—that creates and then perceives itself through experience, as it constantly sends "waves" of itself into dimensional activity. These energy waves, striking our system, form the individual "particle" with its focus (of particle) personality. The energy waves bounce back and forth, to and from the source self, so that there is a constant interaction.[1]

According to Roberts, our experience of reality involves an interaction between physical and nonphysical realms. Source self is far beyond the limitations of time, space, and the human brain. Opening contact with this Total Self can activate new levels of inner guidance and self-direction. To me, this kind of contact is typified in my Focus 21 and Focus 27 experiences at TMI.

Self-guidance embraces the totality of who we are in physical and nonlocal realms. Assuming we can better align our ego/intellect with the Total Self, we can begin to align our intellectually driven actions with the designs set by the Total Self that operates on a much larger scale. While we have sought divine guidance from sources separate from ourselves for centuries, we have not felt worthy of finding the highest level of inspiration within. We limit the opening of access to our greater selfhood by creating a deity separate from us. It is as if guidance that originates from within us is somehow automatically suspect.

In Roberts's model, a multidimensional version of our selves includes our intellect and divinity. We react to this concept of a Total Self, however, by creating stumbling blocks to communication with it. Our ego becomes uncomfortable with the idea that our intellect is merely occupying a chair at a larger committee meeting of the Total Self. The ego demands that the intellect be seated in the chair at the head of the table. If inspiration and guidance come from the nonlocal portions of Total Self, however, they cannot be based solely in the intellect. A nonlocal source self must be free to create life plans for us without the "baggage" of the ego level.

Understanding the relationship of ego and Total Self is vital to appropriate use of the New Age phrase "You create your own reality." This powerful phrase is often misunderstood as implying that the intellect is in the driver's seat. Making this assumption sets up the consummate guilt trip, resulting in thoughts of "Why would I give myself cancer? I am obviously doing something wrong."

Creating reality is not an intellectual process but one based in the totality of consciousness. It is critical that we remember that our intellect is only one component of the Total Self. Finding balance between ego and inner guidance leads to a very different approach to life. This balance is critical to the effective use of expanded states of consciousness.

In one sense, positive performance in psi testing represents a form of "reality creation." This is a good example of the delicate dance between the physical and nonlocal. The psi testee wants to perform successfully, but must connect in some fashion to the larger Self from which physical reality is influenced. If he or she is successful, the laws of science are challenged; if he or she is unsuccessful, it may be because the ego/intellect interfered in the process.

Accomplished and highly tested remote viewer Joseph McMoneagle talks of his personal frustrations related to psi performance in his book *The Stargate Chronicles: Memoirs of a Psychic Spy.* When asked to perform a psychic demonstration for the curious, McMoneagle reports:

> I am constantly being placed between a rock and a hard place. If I do not acquiesce to the demands for proof through a live demonstration, I am accused of being a fraud, or worse, accused of having cheated on my previous work. If I do the demonstration and it fails (which it is apt to do a percentage of the time), then I'm also accused of "it must have been luck." If I succeed, in many cases the person walks away and refuses to talk to me again, as I must be doing the work of the devil, or it quite frankly scares the shit out of them and they are unable to cope with it.[2]

I believe that our capacity to connect consciously with our Total Self is a key to psi performance and nonlocal phenomena. Our connection to our greater being represents a challenge for each of us. If a successful connection can be made, we become empowered to become more than we ever dreamed.

The mere existence of a higher selfhood, however, raises questions of potential relationships in other realms. If there is a larger level of Self, is it not reasonable that there could be interactions with the selves of others as well? What are the implications of this? This issue is a focal point of a research project at Princeton University called the Global Consciousness Project (GCP).

The GCP builds on 35 years of successful scientific research at the Princeton Engineering Anomalies Research (PEAR) Laboratory. PEAR research has repeatedly demonstrated that focused human consciousness can significantly affect the mechanical function of random number generators (RNGs) and cause them to become momentarily nonrandom in their output. This is a hallmark illustration of psi.

Over the years, scientists have noted a statistically significant impact on RNGs during events of focused global interest. The death and funeral of Princess Diana, the trial of O. J. Simpson, and an opening ceremony at the Olympics were all events that rocked the mechanics of the supposedly "objective" RNGs. Today, Princeton scientists are joined by others in constantly monitoring activity of an international network of random number generators.

In the early days of the project, the idea of global consciousness was to be measured by a ElectroGaiaGram, or EGG. The EGG acronym has been carried forward by the participants and appears in the literature associated with this research. Utilizing Internet technology and complex computer analysis, scientists look for indications of concentrated human consciousness activity (random event generators, or REGs) that demonstrate measurable effects on the network. Many have been found, and I would like to use one as an illustration.

The world attention that focused on the September 11, 2001, terrorist attack in New York City significantly impacted the string of numbers generated by the RNG network. As noted on the GCP website:

> The terrible events of September 11 were a powerful magnet for our shared attention, and more than any event in the recent memory of the world they evoked the extraordinary emotions of horror and fear and commiseration and dismay.
>
> The EGG network reacted in a powerful and evocative way. While there certainly are sensible alternative explanations, this is not a mistake or a misreading. It can be interpreted as a clear, if indirect, confirmation of the hypothesis that the egg's behavior is affected by global events and our reactions to them. More important than any scientific question, however, is the question of meaning. What shall we learn, and what should we do in the face of compelling evidence that there may be such a thing as global consciousness?[3]

A machine being affected by consciousness is not a new idea. The PEAR Laboratory has demonstrated this effect for years. The idea of an awakening global consciousness formed from the interaction of multiple greater selves challenges our view of who we are and how we live. The idea that the "personified energy gestalt," as proposed by Jane Roberts, can interact with or influence what is going on in our physical reality highlights the need to establish a conscious relationship with our greater selves. Using expanded states of consciousness, we can perceive the order behind our physical reality. We must realize that all our thoughts and actions carry more impact on the world than we have imagined. We must admit to more responsibility in our daily affairs.

Another event relating to 9/11 adds credibility to the idea of physical influence from the interaction among greater levels of consciousness. On the first anniversary of September 11 in 2002, the New York "Pick 3" lotto game spit out the winning numbers 911. Thousands of New Yorkers had played these numbers on this anniversary day and there was incredible emotional intensity focused on those numbers that day. Was the lottery selection of these numbers a coincidence or nonlocal influence of collaborative greater selves?

To me, these events represent the clear and direct connections proving the interrelated nature of consciousness and physical reality. We can learn even more about this relationship by examining the tiniest level of what we consider physical matter—the atom.

When you look closely, the atom turns out to be a lot less "physical" than we thought. Atoms have a great deal of empty space in them. To get a picture of how empty an atom is, put it in the context of a football stadium. Place a softball in the center of the field at the 50-yard line to represent the nucleus of the atom. Scatter a bunch of peas around the stadium seats, and they will represent the size and spacing of the electrons that spin around the nucleus. It doesn't require much to wonder why a bunch of atoms with that much empty space can combine to appear as something solid. The more you think about all that emptiness within subatomic structure, the more the appearance of atoms as solid "building blocks" becomes hard to figure.

The nucleus of the atom is not a solid mass either. It is made up of oscillating bundles of protons and neutrons. If you get very close to an atomic nucleus, there is apparently a great deal of space there as well. As scientists get ever stronger instrumentation, they keep finding ever smaller building blocks of matter. They also find more empty space between the even smaller pieces. They have to keep making up names (like leptons and gluons) to describe these new almost infinitesimal components.

The thing that makes atoms appear solid is that all these little pieces are moving and spinning around so fast that there is an *illusion* of a solid object called an atom. This is in the same manner that we perceive spinning fan blades or airplane propellers to be "solid" things. If you slow down the action, you can see that you were focusing on the "blur" apparently created by smaller, rapidly moving objects. These small atomic components are simply moving very fast and appear as if they are a single unit.

There are two important points here. First, the spinning motion of electrons is vibration-type activity; second, the illusion of solid matter results from of our perception focused on the blur created by the vibration of discrete but high-speed component parts of the atom.

Saying that the atom, the basic building block of our physical world, conveys the illusion of being solid matter is challenging and immediately smacks of Eastern mystical thought and not modern science. What is proposed, however, is not that physical reality does not exist. Clearly, the physical world *does* exist as far as we are concerned because that is primarily what we experience. What we see, hear, smell, touch, and feel forms the bulk of what we must pay attention to as part of our daily lives.

The late Michael Talbot, author and researcher in the area of the intersection of science and the metaphysical, wrote about the unclear physical attributes of the electron:

> Electrons don't exist as objects exist. They only reveal "tendencies to exist" and even when we've taken a very accurate measurement of the position of an electron, it only means there is a high probability of finding the electron there. This is not a difficulty in measurement, but inherent in the nature of the electron. Because

electrons possess the properties of a particle and a wave packet, they cannot be said to have distinct geographic locations. An electron cannot be held like a leaf or a seashell. No physicist will ever "see" an electron or touch it, for the electron is a phenomenon which our concepts and our language cannot pin down. Not only is the universe queerer than we think, but it is queerer than we *can* think.[4]

Utilizing experimental protocols of quantum physics, it has become possible to explore deep realms of activity where physical and nonphysical realms begin to overlap. This type of research proposes that physical reality is an *effect* of greater unseen forces and does not exist independent of them. Fred Alan Wolf, author, consulting physicist, and former professor of physics at San Diego State University, refers to subatomic particles as "ghosts":

And now, according to quantum physics, there is a third reality. It has attributes of both the "in here" and "out there" realities. I think of this third reality as a bridge between the world of the mind and world of matter. Having attributes of both, it is a paradoxical and magical reality. In it, causality is strictly behaved. In other words, the laws of cause and effect manifest. The only problem is that it isn't objects that are following those laws (at least not the ordinary kinds of objects we usually refer to) but ghosts! And these ghosts are downright paradoxical, able to appear in two or more places, even an infinite number of places at the same time. When these ghosts are used to describe matter, they closely resemble waves. And that is why they were first called "matter waves." In modern usage, they are called "quantum wave functions" . . .[5]

Our consciousness thus can affect subatomic particles and our emotions can influence human biofields. There are multiple levels of influence going on around us all the time. In the past, when we faced influences we could not understand, we took one of two approaches. One approach emphasizes a deity of some sort; the other uses the tools of reductionist science to separate the multidimensional into small and unrelated discrete elements that can be studied in a controlled environment. Let's not do either.

Let's be willing to go beyond the need for either science or religion. Let's open the door to a broader level of responsibility in all of this. This is not proposing we cast out science or a concept of the divine. On the contrary, we will need the best minds and strongest frontier scientists on our side. Similarly, a multidimensional approach may mean we have a closer relationship to divinity than before. But it will take the form of interaction with nonlocal aspects of consciousness rather than with an anthropomorphic old man sitting on a cloud.

Our minds seek certainty and ease of understanding, and the dance between consciousness and physical matter is clearly not an easy concept to grasp. In one sense, we are attempting to understand reality blueprints that in simpler times we would have attributed to the gods. Our ever expanding intellect seeks to claim more credit for influencing the direction and creation of the world.

Thoughts are very high-pitched vibrations and may vibrate outside of physical reality, as difficult as that may be to understand. It is much easier to perceive and understand the vibrations that exist within the range of our five senses. Yet if we accept the idea that thoughts are vibratory aspects of consciousness and can interact with the vibratory nature of physical atomic structures, then we have moved to a new realization: Our physical reality is a continuum of vibrations emanating from consciousness.

Another view of the relationship of consciousness and physical reality is a holographic model. In this perspective, our experience of the world is somewhat similar to that of the character in the movie *The Matrix,* as we share a common *illusionary* experience. This holographic model was not born in Hollywood, however, but is a serious scientific proposal from eminent researchers. The late University of London physicist David Bohm collaborated with Einstein and then later postulated, in terms of a holographic model, quantum physics scenarios for the underpinnings of physical reality.

Michael Talbot, in his insightful work *The Holographic Universe,* masterfully interpreted the work of visionary scientists like Bohm and others who investigated these areas. I strongly encourage you to look at his book for a solid overview and a common sense approach to these concepts. Commenting on the importance of the holographic model of consciousness, Talbot wrote:

> But the most staggering thing about the holographic model is that it suddenly made sense of wide range of phenomena so elusive that they have been categorized outside the province of scientific understanding. These include telepathy, precognition, mystical feelings of oneness with the universe, and even psychokinesis, or the ability of the mind to move physical objects without anyone touching them.
>
> Indeed, it quickly became apparent to the ever growing number of scientists who came to embrace the holographic model, that it helped explain virtually all paranormal and mystical experiences, and in the last half dozen years or so it has continued to galvanize researchers and shed light on an increasing number of previously inexplicable phenomena.[6]

The holographic model proposes that at some point, deep within atomic structure, consciousness manifests as reality. This is where, in biblical terms, "the Word becomes flesh." This is difficult to grasp, but it is a concept that can begin to change the way you look at things. We are dealing with a fundamental point of creation, and that is certainly important to think about. What is the source of the blueprints for consciousness to become matter? What is the stimulus for such activity?

There appears to be a dance between science and mysticism here. A holographic model implies that although we perceive and experience the physical world as real, such a reality may exist only in our individual perceptions. Each of us creates our own physical version of the universe, and that is all that exists for us. What we perceive as the physical world is actually the intersection of our individually perceived worlds. When two people sit at a table, for example, both perceive it and can describe its reality. In truth, however, what is actually taking place is that the holographic universe of the consciousness of each is intersecting at the perceptual level.

What *actually* exists is the vibrational energy created by each individual consciousness at the nonphysical and quantum level.

Our mutual perception of the intersection of vibrational universes is what we view and participate in as the physical world. In that sense, there are about nine billion physical universes existing alongside each other right now. The experience of physical reality is an intersection of our various views. This viewpoint is reinforcing the idea that although the physical world is not actually real, our *experience* of it is. Our individual experience is so real, however, that we think it the same one shared by everyone else.

With statements like this, most of us tend to get lost. Thinking about the holographic model is similar, however, to the realization that we are on a planet spinning around and amongst various planets and galaxies also moving. Normally, we take for granted that our physical world is embedded within larger systems beyond normal perception. Yet the movements of the moon directly affect the gravity of the Earth and our ocean and tidal movements. The movement of the Earth around the sun affects our seasons and weather. Although we do not normally think about gravity or the moon, they affect our daily life.

Apparently Jane Roberts struggled deeply with issues of the quantum or unconscious levels of influence versus the reality of physical-based choices, and came to the following conclusion:

> I agree with Seth that we make our own reality, choosing from an infinite source of probable actions those we will experience as physical, and I've suggested a theoretical model of the universe which explains how probabilities become physical events.
>
> I see the conscious mind making such choices through its beliefs, though the actual mechanisms that bring about reality are unconscious. In this system at least, the nature of events and the nature of the psyche who experiences them go hand in hand. One cannot be considered without the other.[7]

Mixing the works of eminent scientists with material from trance medium Jane Roberts is an unlikely juxtaposition. They offer similar approaches to understanding the universe and the role of consciousness, however. It appears that consciousness influences physical reality from the micro to the macro level, and it is clear that consciousness plays a multidimensional role far beyond the mere level of the intellect.

Opportunities await as, in understanding that a holographic consciousness field underpins reality, we begin to relate with this consciousness that creates the world.

> If you even begin to think that you actually know the answers to the fundamental questions about the nature of the universe, it is probably a good indication that you are getting old and set in your ways.
>
> —J. R. M.

25

Assuming Your True Identity: Becoming Responsible versus Being in Control

This book began with a simple question from my niece about how she might benefit from pursuing the kind of inner exploration that has profoundly affected my life. I have shared with you my experiences that led up to her question. Now I address her question.

As noted in chapter 24, we are intertwined with everything in the universe in ways we never imagined and still do not understand. We *must* begin to act as if we are *aware* that our emotional states, biofields, and nonlocal features of our brain, mind, and consciousness create powerful effects in the world. The realization that we affect others with our thoughts and feelings raises issues of responsibility and control.

Responsibility versus control can easily become confusing. Our natural defense against feeling overwhelmed by the pressures of modern society is to attempt to exert more control over our surroundings. Being in control is a way to reinforce the survival of our self-identity. Becoming responsible for our actions involves a new level of decision-making. After all, being intimately connected to everything that exists is weighty, and taking responsibility opens us to vulnerability and blame. This makes us uncomfortable.

We lack experience in this type of responsibility for our actions. It is so much easier to place the blame outside us. It is challenging to live by inner-directed decision-making because we are well equipped with defense mechanisms developed through a lifetime of experience.

As I noted in the preface, many people refuse to share "special" experiences from their innermost selves. Taking responsibility means being willing to be so centered in who you are that ridicule is not an issue.

Denise Breton and Christopher Largent comment on being trapped between the need to follow the desires of our inner nature and the pressures created by society. In their fascinating book *The Paradigm Conspiracy,* they write:

> On one hand, if we accept current social systems as our life's context—as we must to survive in society—we risk being cut off from ourselves and what we consider meaningful, just, or right. Control-paradigm families, schools, churches, and jobs leave little room for soul values. In fact, they demand that we surrender our souls in order to do their bidding. We adapt to systems; they don't adapt to us.
>
> . . . On the other hand, if we make soul values our life's context, we don't fit into systems that require soul surrender as the condition for drawing a paycheck. We don't get the job, the grant, the contract, the promotion. We try to keep our souls intact, but it may mean, as it does for a friend of ours with professional training in community development, driving an oil truck for a living.[1]

The implication is that one may not be materially successful if one follows an inner-directed approach to decision-making. That may be a common, typical viewpoint. There is nothing that says that if you begin to make choices in terms of a broader concept of self, you will automatically end up poor or never get a new car. Being happy in the moment and over the long haul should be a basic goal in life. The key is the basic perspective from which decisions are made.

Taking responsibility means you must be in contact with your body and soul, as both have a lot of information you need to decide what is in your best interest. You will need to spend time becoming better acquainted with the rest of you beyond ego and intellect. Taking responsibility places you in a position of power amidst information overload and runaway schedules.

So, Caroline, to answer your question: You can benefit from inner exploration by gaining your total freedom and assuming your true identity.

Total freedom can take several forms—freedom from, freedom to, and freedom for.

- *Freedom from* is being able to work from a level of Total Self that breaks the bonds of enslavement to the pressures created by living through the definition of others. When you define yourself from within, no other can make a decision for you. You begin to make decisions from a perspective of what is best for you, and this creates new levels of independence. It also leads to decisions for which you must assume full responsibility, and will more than likely provide you with exactly the experience you need at that point in your life.

- *Freedom to* is being able to move and explore without limitations. Bob Monroe's comment about belief systems being the only limitation to human potential takes on new meaning within a total freedom to explore. Exploring in this way may take you down paths you never imagined possible. Moving via Self-directed decision-making leads to your destiny and life direction. Everyone has a special talent, and everyone has a unique gift to share with the world. When you move to explore with total freedom, you may finally discover your gift or talent, long hidden from you.

- *Freedom for* offers you the chance to be yourself. This is a foundation of happiness. I do not refer here to the type of happiness that briefly exists when you get a new car or have a good time at the beach, but the deep happiness that springs from the alignment of body, mind, and spirit with the divine. I speak here of the bliss that has been lyrically described by the great mystics and seers throughout the ages. I speak here of the realization that you have the support and unconditional love of the universe, and of the fact that you can become aware of this.

The need to realize the totality of who we are at subtle levels is fundamental to our evolution. The need to bring this awareness into the normal level of consciousness is a prerequisite for fuller utilization of technology and the mind (possibly together), which will enable the full potential of life on Earth to unfold.

As you move beyond the realization of how interconnected everything is and begin to live from within a version of selfhood open to unlimited potential, you will begin to experience the sacred nature of this approach. This concept is noted by professor of religious studies and author Dr. Christopher Bache:

> Once we have experienced the reality of Sacred Mind in nonordinary states, however, we cannot help but become more sensitive to its presence in everyday experience as well. Classically, this discovery is described as the awakening of the individual to the transcendental depths of experience. There is, however, a second dimension of this awakening, namely, the discovery of Sacred Mind alive with our everyday *collective experience.* Awakening inside Sacred Mind slowly sensitizes one to the fact that this Mind permeates every aspect of life. It is the medium within which we all exist, the mental field within which all minds meet. It is a living field with "sinews" and "fibers." It has "pockets" and "circles," "eddies" and "momentum." We must twist language to describe the undulations of the currents in which our lives are suspended.[2]

> Realizing our true inner being requires surrendering to something much larger than we normally imagine. Our egos view this type of surrender as death.
> Life begins for real when you realize that the inner place of power is not the end goal, but only a new beginning with unlimited potential.
> —J. R. M.

26

Transforming Human "Do-ings"
into Human "Be-ings":
A Direction for the Future

And so to my dear Caroline, looking inward provides you with the benefits of total freedom. But you also asked how working within expanded states of consciousness would give you an "advantage." We live in a competitive culture and we all try to be good at what we do. Because our experience of the world is complicated by time speeding up and information overload, we tend to seek our competitive advantages through mental and physical activity.

Seeking a balance of logic and intuition, however, moves us to a new perspective. Looking inward will help you find a relationship with the part of you that exists *beyond* any belief system. It is you and you alone that can discover what the totality of you *feels* like. Combining logic and intuition through balanced awareness links you to all that you are. This approach will demand that you release long-held beliefs.

You will have to realize you are not your body. You are also not your mind. You are not even some magical connection of your mind and body. You are a divine spark of infinite potential experiencing the opportunities of this reality and the uniqueness of this lifetime. When you experience a level of Total Self in which your reactions to things involve the boundaries of body and mind beginning to blur, you are on the brink of spirituality. Spirituality is about your realization of the interconnectedness of all things.

The advantage gained is realizing there are no real answers, only choices. This liberates you from the pressures of society, as you realize that you constantly define and redefine yourself through each choice. Knowing that your inspiration for making choices can come from your Total Self provides confidence. Your Total Self includes the parts of you that exist in the here and now, but your Total Self also includes nonlocal and quantum portions of your being. It exists beyond time and space. The wisdom of all that you are becomes available to you when you achieve a state of balance.

Taking responsibility for your thoughts and actions from a centered and aware state of *being* produces a very different perspective on the choices you make. Working from the deepest inner realms is not something that you *do*. It is part of your *being* fully in touch with the infinite self that you are. Choices made from this level may or may not be in line with the current trends of a consensus-based society.

I am not proposing anarchy. We live within a culture, a country, a civilization, and a world. You are entitled to structure, and the society in which you live provides that. How that model of social structure is organized is less important than how you approach your actions within it. Take responsibility for your personal approach to life within *any* social structure.

My response to Caroline carries the caveat that my answer is from *my perspective,* and that she can do with it what she may, just as you can. Ultimately, she will have to seek answers within herself. Another benefit of moving inward is you stop waiting for someone else to tell you what to do next and what *should* be important.

While I cannot and should not predict your experiences, I can offer you my observations as background. I offer these to you, the reader, in the same spirit that I offered them to Caroline. Take from them what you will. My only hope is that you will ask questions of yourself and the world at large regarding the nature of what is really going on in and around you every waking moment.

Listed below are a few indications from my experience that signal you are moving toward better alignment:

You take regular time to contact all that you are from a place of balance.

You are increasingly aware of messages and communications from your body.

You are focused on inner versus outer direction and decision-making.

You live in the conscious awareness of each moment.

You are able to release the need for predictability.

You feel a connection with everyone and everything instead of separation and isolation.

Many paths offer assistance in the move toward inner-directed behavior. The key is to identify the source of a belief system, thought process, emotional reaction, or habit. For example, if you are reading this section before you have read the introduction, go back and read that first part: it may help you discover the implications of some of your habits. But if you have read every page, I suggest that you too may want to reread the introduction before proceeding. How one reads a book can reveal a great deal about how one approaches life itself. Do you do things in a particular way simply because you have been told to, or do you approach each opportunity with an adventurous mind?

Your inner *feelings* about the things going on around you are a good mirror of the current state of alignment of your body, mind, and spirit. To the degree that you are in alignment with body, mind, and spirit, a level of recognition of a Total Self can emerge that is a much better guide for you than I or anyone else could ever be.

As Bob Monroe said: "Tomorrow is when, yesterday was then, there is only this moment and now. You can use it and be it in any way you so desire." So take note, my friend. As you put down this book, the next action you take can be a conscious one steeped in the totality of who and what you truly are. Your next action can also be a replay of repeating life scripts. The choice is yours.

Consider your next action well.

Enjoy

In Joy

> Alignment of body, mind, and spirit is not only a guidepost to reality creation; it is also a doorway to a working relationship with the Divine.
>
> —J. R. M.

Endnotes

Chapter 7

1. Michael Talbot, *The Holographic Universe* (New York: Harper Collins, 1991): 233.

2. Fritz Frederick Smith, *Inner Bridges: A Guide to Energy Movement and Body Structure* (Atlanta, Ga.: Humanics New Age, 1986): 69.

3. Charles T. Tart, ed., *Altered States of Consciousness* (San Francisco: Harper, 1990): 2.

4. Deepak Chopra, *Unconditional Life: Mastering the Forces That Shape Personal Reality* (New York: Bantam, 1991): 214.

5. Elisabeth Kübler-Ross, *The Wheel of Life: A Memoir of Living and Dying* (New York: Scribner, 1997): 220-221.

6. Robert A. Monroe, *Ultimate Journey* (New York: Doubleday, 1994): 230.

Chapter 8

1. Mitchell May, *Healing, Living, and Being*, audiotape, tape 2, side 1 (Carlsbad, Calif.: Hay House, 1998).

Chapter 9

1. Karen Nesbitt Shanor, *The Emerging Mind* (Los Angeles: Renaissance, 1999): xv.

2. Dawna Markova, *The Open Mind: Discovering the 6 Patterns of Natural Intelligence* (Berkeley: Conari Press, 1996): 154.

3. Peter Russell, *The Global Brain Awakens: Our Next Evolutionary Leap* (Palo Alto: Global Brain Inc., 1995): 250.

Chapter 10

1. Dean I. Radin, *The Conscious Universe: The Scientific Truth of Psychic Phenomena* (San Francisco: HarperEdge, 1997): 19.

2. Robert G. Jahn and Brenda J. Dunne, *Margins of Reality: The Role of Consciousness in the Physical World* (San Diego: Harcourt Brace Jovanovich, 1987): 4.

3. Nick Herbert, *Quantum Reality: Beyond the New Physics* (New York: Anchor, 1985): 16.

4. Beverly Rubik, *Life at the Edge of Science: An Anthology of Papers by Beverly Rubik* (Philadelphia: The Institute for Frontier Science, 1996): 7.

5. Candace B. Pert, *Molecules of Emotion: Why You Feel the Way You Feel* (New York: Scribner, 1997): 107.

6. Jane Katra and Russell Targ, *The Heart of the Mind: How to Experience God without Belief* (Novato, Calif.: New World Library, 1999): 48.

7. Ibid., p. 49.

Chapter 11

1. Radin, *The Conscious Universe*, p. 118.

2. Ibid., p.123.

3. His Holiness, the Dalai Lama, *Ethics for the New Millennium* (New York: Putnam, 1999): 36.

4. Charles T. Tart, *States of Consciousness* (New York: Dutton, 1975): 158.

5. Joseph McMoneagle, *Mind Trek: Exploring Consciousness, Time, and Space through Remote Viewing* (Charlottesville, Va.: Hampton Roads Publishing Co., 1997): 79.

Chapter 12

1. McMoneagle, *Mind Trek*, pp. 39-40.

2. Anna Wise, *The High Performance Mind: Mastering Brainwaves for Insight, Healing, and Creativity* (New York: Putnam, 1995): 165.

Chapter 13

1. Michael Newton, *Journey of Souls: Case Studies of Life between Lives* (St. Paul, Minn.: Llewellyn, 1996): 121.

Chapter 15

1. Valerie V. Hunt, *Infinite Mind: Science of Human Vibrations of Consciousness* (Malibu, Calif.: Malibu Publishing, 1996): 87.

2. Russell Targ and Jane Katra, *Miracles of Mind: Exploring Nonlocal Consciousness and Spiritual Healing* (Novato, Calif.: New World, 1998): 275.

3. Amit Goswami, with Richard E. Reed and Maggie Goswami, *The Self-Aware Universe: How Consciousness Creates the Material World* (New York: Tarcher/Putnam, 1993): 167.

4. Mona Lisa Schulz, *Awakening Intuition: Using Your Mind-Body Network for Insight and Healing* (New York: Harmony Books, 1998): 19.

5. Caroline M. Myss and C. Norman Shealy, *The Creation of Health: The Emotional, Psychological, and Spiritual Responses That Promote Health and Healing* (New York: Three Rivers Press, 1998): 369.

Chapter 16

1. Charles T. Tart, ed., *Transpersonal Psychologies: Perspectives on the Mind from Seven Great Spiritual Traditions,* Zen Buddhism, by Claire Myers Owens (San Francisco: Harper, 1992): 197.

2. Deepak Chopra, *How to Know God: The Soul's Journey into the Mystery of Mysteries* (New York: Harmony, 2000): 217.

3. Eckhart Tolle, *The Power of Now: A Guide to Spiritual Enlightenment* (Novato, California: New World, 1999): 18.

4. Stephen Cope, *Yoga and the Quest for the True Self* (New York: Bantam, 1999): 94.

5. Tolle, *The Power of Now,* p. 37.

6. Marianne Williamson, *A Return to Love: Reflections on the Principles of a Course in Miracles* (New York: Harper Collins, 1992): 165.

Chapter 17

1. Delores Krieger, *Accepting Your Power to Heal: The Personal Practice of Therapeutic Touch* (Santa Fe, N. M.: Bear & Co., 1993): 173.

2. Michael Mamas, *Angels, Einstein, and You: A Healer's Journey* (Willsonville, Ore.: BookPartners, 1999): 133.

Chapter 18

1. Rollin McCraty, *The Energetic Heart: Bioelectromagnetic Interactions within and between People* (Boulder Creek, Calif.: HeartMath Research Center, Institute of HeartMath, 2003): 9.

2. Monroe, *Ultimate Journey,* p. 189.

3. Rupert Sheldrake, *Dogs That Know When Their Owners Are Coming Home: And Other Unexplained Powers of Animals* (New York: Crown, 1999): 281.

4. David Morehouse, *Psychic Warrior: Inside the CIA's Stargate Program: The True Story of a Soldier's Espionage and Awakening* (New York: St. Martin's Press, 1996): 251.

5. Russell, *The Global Brain Awakens,* p. 265.

Chapter 19

1. Deepak Chopra, *Quantum Healing: Exploring the Frontiers of Mind/Body Medicine* (New York: Bantam, 1989): 62.

2. Ibid., p. 21.

3. Myss and Shealy, *The Creation of Health,* p. 65.

4. Julie Motz, *Hands of Life* (New York: Bantam, 1998): 113–114.

5. Larry Dossey, *Healing Words: The Power of Prayer and the Practice of Medicine* (San Francisco: Harper, 1993): 195.

6. Targ and Katra, *Miracles of Mind,* p. 64.

Chapter 20

1. James L. Oschman, *Energy Medicine: The Scientific Basis of Bioenergy Therapies* (New York: Churchill Livingstone, 2000): 29.

2. Richard Gerber, *Vibrational Medicine for the 21st Century: The Complete Guide to Energy Healing and Spiritual Transformation* (New York: Eagle Brook, 2000): 382–383.

3. Brian Weiss, *Messages from the Masters: Tapping into the Power of Love* (New York: Warner Books, 2000): 136.

4. Rosalyn L. Bruyere, *Wheels of Light: Chakras, Auras, and the Healing Energy of the Body* (New York: Fireside Book, 1994): 65.

Chapter 21

1. Oschman, *Energy Medicine,* p. 48.

2. Gregg Braden, *Walking between the Worlds: The Science of Compassion* (Bellevue, Wash.: Radio Bookstore Press, 1997): xiv.

3. Robert O. Becker, *Cross Currents: The Promise of Electromedicine, The Perils of Electropollution* (Los Angeles, JP Tarcher, 1990): 169–70.

4. James L. Oschman and Nora H. Oschman, *Readings on the Scientific Basis of Bodywork, Energetic, and Movement Therapies* (Dover, Md.: Nature's Own Research Association, 1997): C-5.

5. Mamas, *Angels, Einstein, and You,* p. 137.

6. Oschman, *Energy Medicine,* pp. 36–37.

7. Ibid., p. 241.

8. Hunt, *Infinite Mind,* pp. 21–22.

9. Radin, *The Conscious Universe,* p. 290.

Chapter 22

1. Charles T. Tart, "Compassion, Science, and Consciousness Survival," *Noetic Sciences Review* (Spring 1994): 9–15.

2. Ibid.

Chapter 23

1. Eric Pearl, *The Reconnection: Heal Others, Heal Yourself* (Carlsbad, Calif.: Hay House, 2001): 93.

2. Schulz, *Awakening Intuition,* p. 116.

3. Gary Zukav and Linda Francis, *The Heart of the Soul: Emotional Awareness* (New York: Simon and Schuster, 2001): 103.

Chapter 24

1. Jane Roberts, *Adventures in Consciousness: An Introduction to Aspect Psychology* (Needham, Mass.: Moment Point Press, 1999): 96.

2. Joseph McMoneagle, *The Stargate Chronicles: Memoirs of a Psychic Spy* (Charlottesville, Va.: Hampton Roads Publishing Co., 2002): 82.

3. Roger Nelson, "Interpretations of the September 11 Attacks," February 15, 2003, http://noosphere.princeton.edu.

4. Michael Talbot, *Mysticism and the New Physics* (New York: Arkana, 1993): 53.

5. Fred Alan Wolf, *Taking the Quantum Leap: The New Physics for Nonscientists* (San Francisco: Harper and Row, 1981): 184–186.

6. Talbot, *The Holographic Universe,* p. 2.

7. Roberts, *Adventures in Consciousness,* p. 197.

Chapter 25

1. Denise Breton and Christopher Largent, *The Paradigm Conspiracy: Why Our Social Systems Violate Human Potential—and How We Can Change Them* (Center City, Minn.: Hazelden, 1996): 111.

2. Christopher M. Bache, *Dark Night, Early Dawn: Steps to a Deep Ecology of Mind* (Albany: State University of New York Press, 2000): 183–184.

Recommended Reading
and Other Resources

I continuously seek out others with expertise and experience to learn more about the totality of who and what we are at all levels. I find information both in the laboratory research findings of "hard" science and in the philosophic musing of esoteric and "New Age" explorers. Our greatest challenge is to become aware of what we do not know. I have discovered that much that we take for granted is being challenged both by frontier scientists and by the personal experience of consciousness. Listed below is material that challenges much of what we learned in high school about how the universe supposedly operates.

Consciousness Beyond the Mind and Brain

Jahn, Robert G., and Brenda J. Dunne. *Margins of Reality: The Role of Consciousness in the Physical World.* San Diego: Harcourt Brace Jovanovich, 1987.

Radin, Dean I. *The Conscious Universe: The Scientific Truth of Psychic Phenomena.* New York: HarperEdge, 1997.

Russell, Peter. *The Global Brain Awakens: Our Next Evolutionary Leap.* Palo Alto, Calif.: Global Brain, 1995.

Targ, Russell, and Jane Katra. *Miracles of Mind: Exploring Nonlocal Consciousness and Spiritual Healing.* Novato, Calif.: New World Library, 1998.

Targ, Russell, and Harold E. Puthoff. *Mind Reach: Scientists Look at Psychic Abilities.* Charlottesville, Va.: Hampton Roads Publishing, 2005.

Visionary Scientists and Frontier Physicians

Braud, William. *Distant Mental Influence: Its Contributions to Science, Healing, and Human Interactions.* Charlottesville, Va.: Hampton Roads Publishing, 2003.

Chopra, Deepak. *Quantum Healing: Exploring the Frontiers of Mind/Body Medicine.* New York: Bantam, 1989.

Dossey, Larry. *Healing Words: The Power of Prayer and the Practice of Medicine.* San Francisco: Harper SanFrancisco, 1993.

Gerber, Richard. *Vibrational Medicine: New Choices for Healing Ourselves.* Santa Fe, N.M.: Bear & Co., 2001.

Hunt, Valerie V. *Infinite Mind: The Science of Human Vibrations.* Malibu, Calif.: Malibu Publishing, 1995.

Kübler-Ross, Elisabeth. *Wheel of Life: A Memoir of Living and Dying.* New York: Scribner, 1997.

Motz, Julie. *Hands of Life.* New York: Bantam, 1998.

Orloff, Judith. *Second Sight.* New York: Warner Books, 1996.

Oschman, James L. *Energy Medicine: The Scientific Basis of Bioenergy Therapies.* New York: Churchill Livingstone, 2000.

Pert, Candace. *Molecules of Emotion: Why You Feel the Way You Feel.* New York: Scribner, 1997.

Rubik, Beverly. *Life at the Edge of Science: An Anthology of Papers by Beverly Rubik.* Philadelphia, Pa.: Institute for Frontier Science, 1996.

Beyond Ordinary Physics

Bentov, Itzhak. *Stalking the Wild Pendulum: On the Mechanics of Consciousness.* Rochester, Vt.: Destiny Books, 1988.

Herbert, Nick. *Quantum Reality: Beyond the New Physics.* New York: Anchor Books/Random House, 1985.

Wolf, Fred Alan. *Mind into Matter: A New Alchemy of Science and Spirit.* Needham, Mass.: Moment Point Press, 2000.

Government Psi Activity

McMoneagle, Joseph. *Mind Trek: Exploring Consciousness, Time, and Space through Remote Viewing.* Charlottesville, Va.: Hampton Roads Publishing, 1997.

———. *The Stargate Chronicles: Memoirs of a Psychic Spy.* Charlottesville, Va.: Hampton Roads Publishing, 2002.

Schnabel, Jim. *Remote Viewers: The Secret History of America's Psychic Spies.* New York: Dell, 1997.

Smith, Paul H. *Reading the Enemy's Mind: Inside Stargate–America's Psychic Espionage Program.* New York: Forge Books, 2005.

Alternative Ways of Thinking about Things

Crichton, Michael. *Travels.* New York: Knopf, 1988.

Moen, Bruce. Exploring the Afterlife series. Charlottesville, Va.: Hampton Roads Publishing, 1997–2001.

Monroe, Robert A. *Ultimate Journey.* New York: Doubleday, 1994.

Roberts, Jane (channeler). *Seth Speaks: The Eternal Validity of the Soul.* Englewood Cliffs, N.J.: Prentice-Hall, 1972.

Roberts, Jane. *Adventures in Consciousness: An Introduction to Aspect Psychology.* Englewood Cliffs, N.J.: Prentice-Hall, 1975.

Seth (Spirit). *The Nature of Personal Reality,* notes by Robert F. Butts. Englewood Cliffs, N.J.: Prentice-Hall, 1974.

Talbot, Michael. *The Holographic Universe.* New York: Harper Collins, 1991.

Important Organizations

Global Consciousness Project (GCP), http://noosphere.princeton.edu

Institute of HeartMath, www.heartmath.com

Institute of Noetic Sciences, www.noetic.org

International Society for the Study of Subtle Energy and Energy Medicine (ISSSEEM), www.ISSSEEM.org

The Monroe Institute, www.monroeinstitute.org

Princeton Engineering Anomalies Research (PEAR), http://www.princeton.edu/~pear/

Acknowledgments

Sitting at the keyboard for more than 700 hours to write a book is a lonely task done in isolation. But talking to others clarifies what you are trying to do and helps the writing become better. Continued interaction with friends and acquaintances is always a good thing, but when you are writing a book it is even better. I want to formally thank the many people who have helped me complete this task and create the spark for the next book.

First of all, to Frank DeMarco, for the initial stimulus of saying that something important had happened to me and that I need to share it. And for the continued patience and encouragement that allowed me to move all the way through to a completed manuscript.

Special thanks to my wife and soul mate, Pamela, for reading countless drafts and continually encouraging me to discover the world of punctuation.

To Mary Ann for her initial editing efforts and to Suzy, Ed, Lisa, Ron, Nancy, Elaine, Susan, Helen, Carola, William, Suzanne, Victoria, Allen, and, of course, Caroline, for their reading of many drafts, feedback, and encouragement. To Tara, Ann, Carol, Penny, and Tom of Massage Therapy Associates for their invaluable assistance in bridging the realms of mind-body interaction.

To Richard Leviton, my editor, for helping me understand that sometimes I can say more with fewer words.

And finally, I want to thank Barbara Bowen, my agent, for providing the magic touch to make this actually happen.

This book includes events that happened to me over a period of four years with continuing profound physical and spiritual impacts. Sadly, however, others involved in these events may not yet be comfortable with openly acknowledging some of their experiences or their role in my experiences, and I respect their privacy. Therefore, some of the names of the people who shared or played a role in my experiences have been changed.

Thank you all.

Enjoy
In Joy!

—J. R. M.

About the Author

J. R. Madaus completed college at the University of New Orleans with the credentials to be a high school teacher in history and mathematics. However, following military service in Viet Nam, he returned to school and earned a Master's and Ph.D. from the University of Texas at Austin, and then worked as a university library director for over twenty years. For the last fifteen years he has headed a large-scale computer network providing statewide library automation services.

Following the experiences and insights outlined in his first book, *Think Logically, Live Intuitively: Seeking the Balance,* he continues to study and explore the nature of consciousness and its relationship to the world of subtle energies. He is working on his second book, *Active Serenity,* as he communes with his pet macaw and serves as "staff" to his housecat, while living in Tallahassee, Florida with his wife and soul mate of 33 years.

Hampton Roads Publishing Company

. . . for the evolving human spirit

HAMPTON ROADS PUBLISHING COMPANY publishes books on a variety of subjects, including metaphysics, spirituality, health, visionary fiction, and other related topics.

We also create on-line courses and sponsor an *Applied Learning Series* of author workshops. For a current list of what is available, go to www.hrpub.com, or request the ALS workshop catalog at our toll-free number.

For a copy of our latest trade catalog, call toll-free, 800-766-8009, or send your name and address to:

HAMPTON ROADS PUBLISHING COMPANY, INC.
1125 STONEY RIDGE ROAD • CHARLOTTESVILLE, VA 22902
e-mail: hrpc@hrpub.com • www.hrpub.com